Pavlo Kazarin

The Wild West of Eastern Europe
A Ukrainian Guide on Breaking Free from Empire

Translated from the Ukrainain edition by
Dominique Hoffman with Andriy Kononenko

UKRAINIAN VOICES

Collected by Andreas Umland

56 *Leonid Ushkalov*
Catching an Elusive Bird
The Life of Hryhorii Skovoroda
Translated from the Ukrainian by Natalia Komarova
ISBN 978-3-8382-1894-6

57 *Vakhtang Kipiani*
Ein Land weiblichen Geschlechts
Ukrainische Frauenschicksale im 20. und 21. Jahrhundert
Aus dem Ukrainischen übersetzt von Christian Weise
ISBN 978-3-8382-1891-5

58 *Petro Rychlo*
„Zerrissne Saiten einer überlauten Harfe ..."
Deutschjüdische Dichter der Bukowina
ISBN 978-3-8382-1893-9

59 *Volodymyr Paniotto*
Sociology in Jokes
An Entertaining Introduction
ISBN 978-3-8382-1857-1

60 *Josef Wallmannsberger (ed.)*
Executing Renaissances
The Poetological Nation of Ukraine
ISBN 978-3-8382-1741-3

The book series "Ukrainian Voices" publishes English- and German-language monographs, edited volumes, document collections, and anthologies of articles authored and composed by Ukrainian politicians, intellectuals, activists, officials, researchers, and diplomats. The series' aim is to introduce Western and other audiences to Ukrainian explorations, deliberations and interpretations of historic and current, domestic, and international affairs. The purpose of these books is to make non-Ukrainian readers familiar with how some prominent Ukrainians approach, view and assess their country's development and position in the world. The series was founded, and the volumes are collected by Andreas Umland, Dr. phil. (FU Berlin), Ph. D. (Cambridge), Associate Professor of Politics at the Kyiv-Mohyla Academy and an Analyst in the Stockholm Centre for Eastern European Studies at the Swedish Institute of International Affairs.

Pavlo Kazarin

THE WILD WEST OF EASTERN EUROPE

A Ukrainian Guide on Breaking Free from Empire

Translated from the Ukrainain edition by
Dominique Hoffman with Andriy Kononenko

Bibliografische Information der Deutschen Nationalbibliothek
Die Deutsche Nationalbibliothek verzeichnet diese Publikation in der Deutschen Nationalbibliografie; detaillierte bibliografische Daten sind im Internet über http://dnb.d-nb.de abrufbar.

Bibliographic information published by the Deutsche Nationalbibliothek
The Deutsche Nationalbibliothek lists this publication in the Deutsche Nationalbibliografie; detailed bibliographic data are available on the Internet at http://dnb.d-nb.de.

Translated from the Ukrainian edition Дикий Захід Східної Європи as published in 2022 by Vivat Publishing Ltd, Kharkiv, into English by Dominique Hoffman with Andriy Kononenko.

Cover design by Dmytro Podolianchuk

УКРАЇНСЬКИЙ ІНСТИТУТ //ІІІКНИГИ   This book has been published with the support of the Translate Ukraine Translation Program.

ISBN (Print): 978-3-8382-1842-7
ISBN (E-Book [PDF]): 978-3-8382-7842-1
© *ibidem*-Verlag, Hannover • Stuttgart 2024
Alle Rechte vorbehalten

Das Werk einschließlich aller seiner Teile ist urheberrechtlich geschützt. Jede Verwertung außerhalb der engen Grenzen des Urheberrechtsgesetzes ist ohne Zustimmung des Verlages unzulässig und strafbar. Dies gilt insbesondere für Vervielfältigungen, Übersetzungen, Mikroverfilmungen und elektronische Speicherformen sowie die Einspeicherung und Verarbeitung in elektronischen Systemen.

All rights reserved. No part of this publication may be reproduced, stored or introduced into a retrieval system, or transmitted, in any form, or by any means (electronic, mechanical, photocopying, recording or otherwise) without the prior written permission of the publisher. Any person who commits any unauthorized act in relation to this publication may be liable to criminal prosecution and civil claims for damages.

Printed in the EU

Content

Preface by Dominique Hoffmann 9
Introduction 13
1   Crimea 15
    Not Blood or Soil 15
    Strictly Personal 16
    The Nutjobs Were Right 19
    Pandora's Box 20
    The "Russian World" Has No Borders 22
    The Evolution of Lancelot 25
    Patriot Games 27
    Internal Deportation 29
    Three Myths – Just One Crimea 33
    The Silence of the Occupied 37
    Miscalculations 39
    Negative Selection 41
    If It Weren't for the War 42
    Requiem for Myself 45
2   Russia 49
    Rock Is Dead 49
    A One-way Ticket 50
    An Anthology of Cowardice 52
    More Hell 53
    Cold War Traumas 55
    Crooked Mirrors 58
    Putin vs Army, Language, and Faith 59
    A Pseudo-Federation 61
    Requiem for the Kosovorotka 63
    The Third Rome 65

The Heirs of October 67
Imperialist Russophobes 70
A New Novgorod 73
The Fight for Gogol 74
Ukrainian Lessons 76
Putin's Ugly Swans 79
A Look into the Abyss 81
The Kremlin's Horcruxes 83
Russia Down the Rabbit Hole 85
The Loneliness of Victory Day 87
People and World War II 91
Viral Diplomacy 93
Knockin' on Europe's Door 95
Resources for the Empire 97

3 War 101
Not Political 101
Not the War We Imagined 103
Territory is Secondary 105
The Price of Capitulation 108
Yugoslav Scenarios 110
A Different Point of View 112
The Nostalgia of Scumbags 114
A Made-up Soviet Union 115
The Rules of Propaganda 117
Censoring Common Sense 120
Memory Lessons 121
Pecunia olet 123
Ukrainian Barricades 124
Lost in Translation 126
In the Trenches 128

	The Belarusian Mirror	129
	Triumph of the Antimaidan	131
	The Pleasures of the Periphery	133
	On the Other Side of the Iron Curtain	134
	The Enemy of My Enemy	135
	The Grass is Always Greener	137
	Our Grandfathers Fought	140
4	The Media	143
	A Fake Future	143
	Get to Know the Country	146
	The ABCs of Manipulation	147
	Follow the Money	151
	Club Rules	153
	The Party of the Majority	154
	The Microphone	156
	Professional Standards	157
5	Changes	161
	The Impossible Becomes Possible	161
	The Lessons of August	163
	Peacetime Rules	164
	The Virtual Stepan Bandera	166
	Cultural Politics	168
	Our Children's Flags	170
	History Does Not Tolerate the Subjunctive Mood	172
	The Age of Experiment	175
	Symbolic Achievements	177
	Toxic Fantasies	178
	A Vaccine Against the Tsar	180
	The Anatomy of Corruption	182
	The Formula for Evil	184

  A Philosophy of Treason 185
  The Fight for the Indifferent.. 187
  L'État, c'est moi... 189
  A Land of Castes 191
  Survivorship Bias.. 193
  Growing Pains... 195
  After the Credits Roll 197
  The Burdens of Parenthood.. 199
6 The Future.. 203
  Ours to Lose... 203
  Not Everything is Moscow's Fault 205
  Something for Everyone 206
  Land of the Helpless... 208
  Subconscious Ukraine 210
  The Problem of "the Little Man" 216
  The Dangers of Stupidity... 218
  Fighting Against the Present... 220
  The Specter of Counter-revolution....................................... 222
  The Rainbow Bright Future... 225
  A Trap for the Far Right... 229
  The New Paganism... 230
  Serf Logic 232
  Facts and Cults 235
  God in a Test Tube.. 236
  Who Caused the Pandemic?.. 240
  Thanks to Quarantine... 242
  Trump, Vaccines, and the Antichrist 244
  Eastern Europe's Wild West.. 247
Epilogue 251
Postscript 255

Preface

At the start of 2022, Pavlo Kazarin was the host of a popular morning television show in the Ukrainian capital. His book *The Wild West of Eastern Europe* had come out a few months earlier and he had recently done the first presentation of the book in Mariupol. Throughout February, the capital was anxious. Russia was massing troops again along Ukraine's borders, Western intelligence services were warning of an imminent invasion, Russia mocked the idea, and Ukrainian politicians tried to be reassuring.

Then, on the morning of February 24, Kazarin was awakened not by his early morning alarm clock but by the sound of explosions outside Kyiv. He got up, put on a T-shirt that read *Ukrainians will resist*, and left for work. Kazarin writes, "I was scared, but I knew I couldn't transmit that fear to our viewers. Of course, none of the material our producers had prepared the previous day was relevant anymore. And so, for the first time in my life, I spent almost two straight hours speaking directly with the viewing audience. It was the longest live broadcast of my life. It was the most difficult live broadcast of my life." The following day, Kazarin enlisted in the Ukrainian armed forces where he continues to serve, defending his country from the Russian invasion.

The Wild West of Eastern Europe traces Ukraine's journey toward self-awareness from the perspective of one person who followed a similar trajectory. In the introduction, Kazarin writes, "This book is my attempt to make sense of the people and circumstances that have changed us."

The Ukraine of today is a nation that took shape on the Euromaidan of 2013–14, was strengthened through the trials of the Revolution of Dignity and hardened through 10 years of war against invading forces. Kazarin makes it clear that Russia invaded in order to stop Ukraine's developing sovereignty.

He devotes an entire chapter here to the media and Russian methods of hybrid warfare. As a journalist and a cultural observer, he is acutely aware of Russia's hybrid warfare. Increased military budgets will not solve this problem. Our naivety, our willingness to be manipulated, our apathy, and our longing for peace — all become weapons in the hands of the aggressor.

The alternative to this passivity is a sense of personal responsibility. A willingness to make difficult choices. He calls out infantilism, passivity, and both-sides ism. He emphasizes that passivity and empathy for the aggressor are not moral stances and that "neutrality" is a choice with consequences.

Commentators have written that one of the Kremlin's mistakes in February of 2022 was to imagine that they were invading the Ukraine of 2014. They were wrong. This book traces the developmental path that led to the fierce Ukrainian resistance that surprised both Western observers and the invaders.

Kazarin's book is addressed to Ukrainians. It is tempting to view the content as primarily topical — a window into some events in recent history in a distant country. Indeed, Kazarin writes in the epilogue that he looks forward to the day when the book will become irrelevant because Ukrainian independence and sovereignty are taken as a given.

That epilogue was written before the full-scale invasion. We are further than ever from the day Ukrainian independence can be taken for granted. In fact, is has only become more clear that the relevance of the book extends well beyond Ukraine's borders.

When I first read this book in 2022, the war had already been going on for some time. I felt that Kazarin had captured essential information about Ukrainian identity and also that he described it in a way that was important for Western readers to understand not just Ukraine, but ourselves and the moment in history we find ourselves in. Kazarin writes at one point in the book that his generation was fated to live at the center of history. The same reality is gradually dawning on many people outside Ukraine. I knew I wanted to translate this book to bring it to an English-language readership.

In 2014, many people outside Ukraine chose to look away from Russia's acts of war. They preferred to imagine that Russia's imperial ambitions would be satisfied with Crimea. And maybe the Donbas. And so we awakened in the world of 2022, with a nuclear-armed dictatorship determined to reassert control and return the world to an earlier time, when the only rule was to take what you could. A world in which spheres of influence drew the map of the world to suit the most powerful, a map in which individual lives held no relevance.

Russia's ambitions are not limited to Ukraine. Russian propaganda outlets have repeatedly made it clear that it does not stop with Ukraine. The airwaves have been filled with anti-US, anti-Europe, anti-Western propaganda for well over a decade now. Russia has been at war with us for a long time: we just chose not to notice. Will we notice now? Or continue to watch as the war plays out in Ukraine and Russia learns the lessons it will need for the next phase. Because there will be a next phase. In his infamous Munich speech in 2007, Vladimir Putin called the collapse of the Soviet Union the "greatest geopolitical catastrophe of the 20th century." Russia is now intent on correcting that mistake—and the effort will not be limited to Ukraine.

Ukraine's ferocious defense of its sovereignty has bought time for the West to prepare. Putin was clear already in 2007 that he rejected the current world order. In the years following, the Russian airwaves were flooded with anti-American and anti-European sentiments. Diagrams of Russian missiles striking American cities were broadcast on the popular weekly "news" program. Russian intelligence agents utilized radioactive agents against their enemies on foreign soil. Russian troll farms exacerbated conflict in communities across the planet to undermine political and social cohesion. Russian forces invaded a sovereign nation, annexing part of their territory, fomented armed conflict elsewhere, and even shot down a passenger jet with 298 people on board. Still, the democratic nations of the world thought the threat could be contained.

Even now, there is wishful thinking that calls for "peace" and "negotiations." Why do Ukrainians respond so negatively to calls for peace? As Nobel Prize laureate Oleksandra Matviichuk has reminded us, Ukrainians want peace more than anyone. But most of those calling for peace in the face of a brutal war of conquest accompanied by widespread war crimes, seem to be calling for capitulation. Stop arming Ukraine, they say. You're just prolonging the war. This is incorrect. Capitulation would only leave Russia with a larger, more experienced army and it's imperial appetites unquenched. When you feed imperial appetites, they only grow.

It is time that people outside Ukraine faced the reality of the current moment. We too must learn that passivity and wishful thinking are not an option. The divisions within our societies that make it difficult to take coordinated action were not invented by Russia, but they are definitely manipulated by external actors. Ukrainians have important knowledge for us in how to resist. The Ukrainians have been in the direct line of fire for Russian information warfare for a very long time. They understand how it works.

Ukrainians are living, thinking, writing, speaking and analyzing what is happening now. They understand the historical moment, at the global perspective, better than the rest of the world. It's time we listen more closely. Not only because, as the victims of a virulent aggressor they deserve that. But also because we need their hard-fought knowledge.

The next Great War has already started. Ukrainians just happened to get there first.

Introduction

I'm not claiming to be a saint. I drive too fast. I talk on the phone while driving. I park in the loading zone.

I could say I pay my taxes, but let's be real. My job pays them for me. I've never actually had to choose whether to give my hard-earned cash to the government or keep it for myself. My strong ethical stance comes for free—I wasn't given an opportunity to cheat.

Yes, I've refused to work for unethical employers. But I also don't have any sick relatives or major debts to pay off. I haven't had to make difficult choices with someone else dependent on me. So it wasn't all that hard to turn down big money.

I don't go to neighborhood meetings or join community organizations. I don't ask for receipts and I'm happy to pay cash when asked. I don't spend a lot of time volunteering: I spend my time as I see fit without excess effort.

I didn't join the army in 2014. For a long time, I hid behind my regional Crimean identity. I accepted the occupation documents and identity cards that allowed me to stay in Crimea after the annexation. My inner Crimean wasn't replaced by an inner Ukrainian right away.

Lots of my friends turned out to be more principled than me that year. While I tried to preserve my own little world, they went to the frontlines. While I tried to stay under the radar, they dedicated themselves to volunteering for the war effort. I have nothing to be proud of in 2014. My friends just bought me time—time I spent on reflection.

There's no way I'm going to blame my circumstances. I write my own story, that means the mistakes are mine, too. Of course, without those mistakes, that former Kazarin could hardly have become the current Kazarin. I'm not planning to touch up my biography retroactively.

It took me quite a long time to arrive at my current views. I don't always recognize myself when I read my older texts. I know people can change and I know that judging the past from the perspective of the present is pointless. We were different people in the past.

I try not to harbor illusions about myself. Or others. I also have no illusions about my life. I get what I deserve.

I don't believe in miracles and I don't like it when politicians pose as miracleworkers. I keep in mind my own limitations and I don't trust anyone who claims to have all the answers. I earn my own money and react badly when politicians make promises to spend my tax dollars to further their own ambitions.

I don't believe in the "wisdom of the people," because I'm one of "the people." And I have some pretty significant doubts about my own wisdom. I've made some poor choices and I'm not inclined to forget it. I've made incorrect predictions and my opponents have ample material to use against me. I've also been to a few soccer matches in my time and I know how easily a crowd can transform into a mob.

I don't like talk about the "simple folk" I prefer people who aren't so simple. People who know more than me, can do things I can't, and understand life better than me. I'm happy to take advice from people who are competent to give it and I can't stand dilettantes. I know their value because I'm a dilettante myself in plenty of things.

I don't like talk about prophets and messiahs. I don't think politicians have to be saints. I've accepted the fact that I'll often be marking my ballot for the lesser of two evils. That's because I know that in some situations I'm the lesser of two evils, and in others I may even be the greater of two.

I'm not inclined to complain about my fate. I've built my life out of the blocks I made the effort to gather. I don't intend to take anyone else's blocks, and I don't like it when someone starts eyeing mine.

I also don't like people looking at me with sad hound-dog eyes. My life is what I make of it through my own successes and errors, my own laziness and self-discipline. If I don't like something, I don't go looking for who to blame. That person is looking right back at me in the mirror every morning.

This book is my attempt to make sense of the people and circumstances that have changed us.

1   Crimea

Not Blood or Soil

It's easy to feel Ukrainian if your mom's from Lviv and your dad's from Poltava. If your lullabies were in Ukrainian, if you had hand-embroidered towels hanging in the kitchen and Shevchenko's *Kobzar* standing on the shelf. In that case, you've understood your own identity since childhood and you know exactly where you fit into your country.

That wasn't Crimea.

When I was growing up in Crimea, almost none of our parents were born there. We were a generation of immigrants. The Crimean peninsula's "Golden Age" was the Soviet 70s and 80s. The most popular Soviet resorts were in Crimea back when we were still living behind the Iron Curtain and under the command economy. After 1991, it lost that status and went on to suffer decades of nostalgia.

The nostalgia was omnipresent and the link between cause and effect was severed. Many of my neighbors failed to recognize the collapse of the Soviet system either as the logical result of losing the Cold War or as a natural consequence of ineffectual socialist economics. They saw independent Ukraine as the source of all their problems instead. Independent Ukraine, whose trident had come and tacked Crimea to the seafloor of society.

The fact that Crimea was Russian-speaking wasn't the problem. The bigger problem was the peninsula's preference for living in the past. People longed for the past. They idealized everything Soviet. It was hard to find yourself in those conditions. Nonetheless, some people did try to find common ground. Common ground that could link the peninsula with mainland Ukraine.

Then came the Maidan in 2013–14.

The Maidan was about values. On the Maidan, the individual choice of Ukrainian identity was more important than "blood and soil." The Ukrainian nation would no longer focus on ethnic categories.

For me, the Maidan was about the Ukrainian train trying to pull out of the post-Soviet station. Our Crimea should have been one of the wagons on that train. Crimea might have pulled the "stop chain" every so often but would have eventually arrived together with all the other wagons at the "West" station.

But then Russia arrived. Russia uncoupled my native wagon and hooked it up to a train headed straight for the past. A past that had no more real long-term prospects than a Spanish galleon: that is to say, none.

One difference between Crimeans and residents of the Donbas and Luhansk is that we left occupied territory for political reasons. We weren't forced out by shelling, we weren't fleeing actual war. When we meet another Crimean here in mainland Ukraine, we immediately know that person shares our beliefs — pro-Russian Crimeans don't come to Ukraine. The address on our ID doesn't suggest allegiance to Russia.

It's a cruel irony. The annexation of my home served as a defibrillator for Ukraine, forcing it to stumble out of its post-Soviet stupor. While the occupation of the peninsula stole our small homeland from Crimeans, it also gave us the gift of the greater homeland. The one in which what matters isn't "blood" or "soil," or the sound of your last name, or the language of your lullabies. Ukrainians aren't only born. They can also be made.

There's one thing I know for sure: the future can't be held hostage by the past. It took me thirty years to figure that out. It took me long enough.

Better late than never.

Strictly Personal

In February, Russia took over the Crimean peninsula by force. In March, they officially annexed the peninsula. I stayed until October, then I threw my things in the trunk and left for Kyiv.

Occupied Crimea was like the eye of a hurricane then. On the mainland, MH17 had been shot down, the battle for Ilovaisk had been fought, the first Minsk Accords were signed. On the peninsula, all was quiet.

From February to October 2014, I wrote about Crimea. The fact that I'd spent thirty years living in a remote province by the sea was no longer a problem. In early 2014, the peninsula was transformed into a global hotspot and everyone wanted to know more about it. The reserve of pro-Soviet sentiments I knew so well had suddenly become journalistic gold.

In February, Russia's "little green men" in unmarked uniforms invaded the peninsula. In March, they held a pseudo-referendum at gunpoint and suddenly the Russian flag was flying over Ukrainian Crimea.

By that October, the first shock had passed. The first tragedies had taken place. The first wave of immigrants were settling in on the mainland. But our cell phones still worked on both sides of the new border and the trains still reliably crossed the peninsula to the mainland.

Even the visual changes were few. The monopoly of Ukrainian goods was gradually diluted by items from Russia. Prices were still recalculated into Ukrainian hryvnia out of inertia. The remaining residents were divided into three groups. People getting ready to leave, people preparing for the internal exile of life under occupation, and the people who had finally stopped lying.

The latter frantically waved their new flags and filled social media with their ranting. Before long, their voices became the only ones to be heard from the peninsula. Everyone else either moved away or made their social media accounts anonymous. Even today, they rarely press "like" and almost never comment, but they read everything.

Expectations of a global war came to nothing. Russia stopped talking about "the Russian Spring," settling for a "Crimean" one instead. NATO didn't show up. There were fewer and fewer foreign reporters on the peninsula and more and more Russian accents.

My friends from the mainland called every day. I heard "How are things going over there?" less and less often. Now I was the one asking. Social media became our main source of information—that's where I heard the echoes of the battles from the constantly shifting front lines in the Donbas.

It's funny looking back. Before the war, someone who hit the limit of five thousand friends on Facebook was considered a top blogger. Then, after the war started, Ukraine suddenly had a lively blogosphere. Traditional media couldn't keep up with the demand for information and Zuckerberg's brainchild suddenly became our own CNN.

As I packed up, I thought about the fact that I didn't know a damned thing about my own country. My entire knowledge of the geography of the mainland was limited to the Maidan, a little bit more of Kyiv, and even less of Lviv. I was 30 years old and hardly knew my own country at all. The traditional isolation of Crimea showed. Our island mentality. Crimean identity.

After February 2014, that mentality began to lose its luster. The annexation forced each one of us to commit. We had to choose: which flag was ours? Which anthem?

Conversations with other Crimeans felt more and more like a minefield. One careless move could cause an explosion. More and more topics divided us. Fewer and fewer united us. And the minefield gradually developed into actual battle lines.

I had to leave.

I had no idea what awaited me. It wasn't a year for making plans. One thing was clear—my generation were now living inside history. The history that had been lacking in all those preceding years. There was no settling for cheap imitations.

I've been home to Crimea only twice since that day. Once at the end of 2014. Again in the summer of 2015. And then the FSB arrested my colleague who had stayed on and had written that the peninsula belonged to Ukraine. He was convicted on charges of calling for the violation of Russia's territorial integrity. Since then, I've only seen Crimea looking across the lagoon from the Arabat Spit.

I don't brag about my birthplace. I certainly don't want to become a "professional Crimean." I don't dream of the peninsula at night and I can't stand sympathy. I prefer to regard everything that has happened to me as experience rather than trauma.

And this experience showed me what I wanted. In October 2014, I hit the road with a clear view of the future I did not want. And I have no intention of packing up again.

Once was enough for me.

The Nutjobs Were Right

I remember flying to Crimea two days before the referendum.

The jetliner that had been reassigned to the Crimean route was packed to capacity. The cabin was full of Russian bureaucrats and journalists. There were French journalists in the rows ahead of me, Italians behind me, a Serb to my left and on my right a sailor from Sevastopol who'd heard about the invasion while at sea. He'd gone ashore in Curaçao and was making his way home in stages.

I spent the entire flight talking with the Serb. He was trying to work out some logical consistency and talked a while about the fact that he and his colleagues were in a no-win situation: "We support a strong Russia since Moscow is our ally, but how can we support the secession of Crimea from Ukraine? That would mean we also support the secession of Kosovo."

As our landing time in Simferopol approached, the Serb started talking about the centenary of World War I. He told me that it bothers Serbians that many Europeans blame them for the start of the First World War. He described conferences and symposiums in Serbia arguing that the war was caused by the accumulation of irreconcilable contradictions—not just because of Young Bosnia and Gavrilo Princip.

As I listened, I felt as though Crimeans would be making the same arguments in a hundred years.

In the movie *The Day After Tomorrow,* climate change results in a sudden environmental catastrophe all over the planet. In one scene, as the Vice President is being evacuated from the White House, his motorcade passes a local crank warning them to Repent, because Armageddon is nigh. The Vice President looks at him and sighs, forced to acknowledge that the nutjobs were right all along.

That's exactly how I felt in 2014. We used to dismiss the people warning us about "Russian tanks." We thought they were paranoid cranks. We were sure that they were stuck in the past: Russian tanks were impossible in the modern world. It turned out that they were the ones living in reality, while the rest of us soothed ourselves with comforting illusions.

After Crimea, the world woke to the era of conspiracy brought to life. Nothing was over the top.

Strangely enough, when the Soviet army entered Prague in 1968, the Czech army did not open fire. Not only because they didn't receive orders. Memories were still fresh of the Soviet liberation of Czechoslovakia. World War II had ended just 23 years earlier and many Czechs still viewed Soviet soldiers as part of a "brotherly nation," as "liberators." The events of the Prague Spring led to a dramatic change in national consciousness.

The same happened with Ukraine.

23 years also passed between the declaration of Ukrainian independence and Moscow's decision to annex the peninsula. And when the Russians invaded Crimea, the Ukrainian army did not open fire. Yes, there were no orders and the military doesn't act without receiving the go-ahead, but another key reason is that back then, in February 2014, many people did not see Russian soldiers as the enemy. That all changed after the occupation began. Any remaining reserves of "brotherly feeling" or sense of "one people" were used up that spring.

Pandora's Box

I couldn't quite believe that the events were irreversible. Everything that was happening violated my understanding of the postwar reality.

We were taught that World War II had settled everything. While new borders and new states might occasionally appear on the political map of the world, no one would ever again erase the existing borders by annexing foreign territories.

Moscow likes to draw parallels between Crimea and Kosovo. But Kosovo wasn't annexed to Albania. Kosovo was granted independence in 2008, whether you choose to recognize it or not. No one erased a pre-existing border from the political map of the world: they just added a new one. In terms of international law, this is a much smaller problem than what happened with Crimea.

The Kremlin didn't choose to declare Crimea an "independent state" in March 2014. They took us back to 1938 instead.

In October 1938, Germany annexed the Sudetenland of Czechoslovakia, where the population was 90% ethnic Germans. Konrad Henlein promoted their interests as head of the Sudeten German party.

The Sudeten German party pushed the idea that the German population of the region was suffering under the heavy hand of Czechoslovakia's Slavic majority. This rhetoric was used despite the fact that the Sudeten Germans had direct representation in the Czech National Assembly and attended German-speaking schools at state expense.

England and France acceded to Germany's demands in order to avoid war. When Chamberlain returned from signing the Munich Agreement which ratified the partition of Czechoslovakia, he declared that he had "brought peace for our time." Winston Churchill was said to have responded, "You were given the choice between war and dishonour. You chose dishonour, and you will have war." World War II began less than a year later.

The global slaughterhouse of the Second World War demanded new rules. Annexation was recognized as one of the most serious violations of international law. There have been very few violations in the last 60 years.

Some were related to the collapse of the colonial system. In December 1961, the Indian army took control of the Portuguese colony of Goa, declaring it a "union territory." The Portuguese government didn't recognize India's sovereignty over Goa until 1974. A year later, in 1975, the Indian army invaded the former British colony of Sikkim.

The next instance took place in the Portuguese colony of East Timor, following the collapse of the Caetano government in Portugal. East Timor declared independence on November 28, 1975. Nine days later, Indonesia invaded and then officially annexed

East Timor, declaring it an Indonesian province. Hundreds of thousands of Timorese died in the 27-year occupation. East Timor didn't gain its independence until 2002.

There have also been annexations that took place following wars. For example, Israel established control over the Golan Heights and East Jerusalem following the Six-Day War. The Knesset officially declared both regions Israeli territory fourteen years later.

In contrast, some wars were started as attempts at annexation. In 1982, Argentina attempted to regain the Falkland Islands by force. The British Navy was dispatched to recapture them.

Sometimes other countries come to the victim's assistance, as was the case following Iraq's occupation of Kuwait. Iraq invaded and occupied the emirate on August 2nd, 1990. On August 7th, the puppet government declared the independent "Republic of Kuwait" and requested annexation to Iraq. On August 28th, Iraq formally annexed the entire country of Kuwait. This story ended with the anti-Iraq coalition, "Desert Storm" and the liberation of the country.

But all of that felt very distant to us. We believed that Europe was immune to such things. We believed in treaties, common sense, and our own peace-loving nature. Then the spring of 2014 destroyed our preconceptions regarding what was "acceptable" and what was "forbidden."

And now just one simple question remains. Where does Russia end and where does Ukraine begin now?

The "Russian World" Has No Borders

In 2016, Vladimir Putin asked a nine-year-old boy where Russia ends. The boy said "the Bering Straight." And Putin responded, "nowhere."

You can't call that a joke. It's a core belief. An empire will continue trying to expand until it reaches the borders of another empire.

This is the Russian worldview. In 2014, most Russians didn't view the seizure of Crimea as the appropriation of someone else's space, but rather as taking back what's "ours." Like the division of property in a divorce. Within that framework, Ukraine isn't recognized as a separate sovereign state: it's more like a suitcase with various items. Some of those items are considered "ours," and some are "yours." As long the suitcase has any of "our" things, then we have rights to its contents.

The problem is that imperialists have trouble accepting any boundaries that limit what can be considered theirs. And it's impossible to guess when they will or won't respect the border lines.

Suppose Moscow does succeed in turning Ukraine into a buffer zone. Do you suppose they will then look at everything west of Uzhhorod as "not-ours." As territory where people hae the right to do as they please without asking for Russia's opinion? How much territory are we willing to give the Kremlin, in the hopes of soothing Russia's wounded imperialist vanity?

Some claim that for the imperialist, the category of what is considered "ours" only end where he meets armed resistance. They believe that a territory's ability and willingness to defend itself is what moves it to the category of "not-ours." But it is entirely possible that for the adherents of the empire, the Ukrainian soldiers defending their country are no more than a physical barrier to the return of "ours," — not a psychological one.

What about Poland, is it "not-ours"? Romania? How about the Baltic States? Finland — are the Finns just a bunch of reindeer herders or are they citizens of a sovereign state who have the right to live as they see fit?

"Not-ours." Does it begin where Russian isn't spoken? Or maybe it's where they don't pray to the Orthodox God? Perhaps it has to be land that the empire's soldiers have never trod. Does it end at the borders of the USSR? The Eastern Bloc? The Russian Empire? Europe? Or perhaps all the homelands of *Homo erectus*?

Revanche was probably inevitable for Russian society. After all, the empire appeared in Russia before they ever developed a national consciousness. The authoritarian vertical hierarchy of power always dominated. In the Soviet system, the state first eliminated anyone who asserted a right to their own opinion, then assimilated their children. Unlike their neighbors, Russians didn't gain independence from a foreign empire in 1991. Instead, they lost their own empire.

How could this not inspire demand for greatness? The collective "we" won out over any individual sense of "I." The Russian opposition assures us that Vladimir Putin has imposed his agenda on the country, that ordinary Russians just want prosperity and peace. At this point, that just sounds like self-deception.

Vladimir Putin didn't create the Russian demand for greatness. He simply satisfied it. Of course, high oil prices and the political zeitgeist also worked in his favor. "When the sun of culture is low, even dwarves will cast long shadows..." Indeed, Europe has shown itself to be a continent of political Lilliputians over the last decade—what else can you say when Gerhard Schröder goes from being German Chancellor to Rosneft bureaucrat and enjoys the seat of honor at Vladimir Putin's inauguration?

The trouble with imperial appetites is that they only grow. It's like a drug addiction—the dosage has to be constantly increased. The Munich Speech, the war against Georgia, the crackdown against the 2011 protests, the invasion of Ukraine, the war in Syria, election interference around the world—Moscow is constantly submitting the world order to a stress test. When they don't encounter resistance, the boundaries of the permissible and possible are expanded.

There's only one "but." Their efforts to restore the Soviet Union are threatened by unlearned lessons. The leaders in Moscow may discover that they've miscalculated their destination. They wanted to emerge in the '70s during détente and the Conference on Security and Cooperation in Europe. Instead, they've popped into the '80s: Afghanistan, a growing economic crisis, a renewed arms race and sanctions.

The Russian public keeps forgetting the words of philosopher Merab Mamardashvili. Mamardashvili wrote that Russia doesn't exist to serve Russians—Russians exist to serve the state. It feels good to view yourself as the foundation of an empire. But then it's even worse when you discover that you're just the raw materials.

Russians sometimes describe reality as a battle between the TV and the fridge. The TV proclaims your "greatness" by association, simply as a Russian, a citizen of a "great" nation. The refrigerator represents personal well-being—which may not be aligned with the greatness of the state. There is no end in sight for this battle between the television and the fridge in Russia. The greatness of the state is based on "we." But it's all the individual "I"s who will have to foot the bill.

It has fallen to Ukraine to test the ambitions of the imperial ego. But the Kremlin's appetite is not limited to the Crimean peninsula, or even to Ukraine itself. In 2014, the "Russian World" went to war. And, as we know, the "Russian World" has no borders. Only limitless horizons.

The Evolution of Lancelot

During the Second World War, Soviet author Evgeny Schwartz wrote a play titled *The Dragon*. In the play, a wandering knight named Lancelot arrives in a town controlled by a cruel Dragon. However, the townspeople urge him not to kill the Dragon. They assure him that they need the Dragon, who gives meaning to their lives and protects them from any other dragons. The play makes it clear that whoever defeats the Dragon runs the risk of becoming a dragon himself. Although the play is ostensibly about the Weimar Republic and Third Reich, it reads now as an allegory for the Soviet Union and modern Russia.

Yes, it's easy to say that all empires experience phantom pains. That a relapse in the hearts of its citizens was inevitable. That the jump in oil prices in the early 2000s funded the revival of the old system. That the Russian elite is motivated only by super-profits and super privileges. All this is completely true—and completely false.

Any historical pattern can be described as a collection of random circumstances. Dissect, distill, think of it as the sum of coincidences. In reality, the very existence of Russia is subject to a very simple law.

The Russian Federation, even after all the shrinkage and waste of the twentieth century, remains a country destined to live according to supranational laws. It has not become a nation-state, nor can it become one in its present form. The differences between its regions, the differences between the residents of Buryatia and Dagestan, between the Nenets and the Chechens, are simply too vast. It is inclusive by necessity, trying to convince the inhabitants of previously conquered territories that it is in their best interests to remain a part of a shared state.

That's why any elites who find themselves at the helm are forced to continually return to those "spiritual bonds" whose task is to bind the country together in its imperial armature. Hence all the talk about the multiethnic nature of the country and the appeals to World War Two as the chief signifier of brotherhood and unity.

Anyone who defeats the Dragon in Russia will find themselves face-to-face with an unresolved problem: the country is like a patchwork quilt. It is hostage to its own contradictions between "ethnic" regions and Russian ones, between regions that are givers vs those which are takers, between those who feed Moscow vs those on whom Moscow feeds. The situation if further complicated by the fact that, unlike in 1991, potential delineations of smaller states no longer exist on administrative maps. If the centrifugal forces gain strength, the outcome could be even more chaotic in terms of geography and consequences.

This is the reality facing any Russian politician who finds himself at the top of the food chain by dint of luck and government coup. His liberal past will be useless as he faces the fork in the road: either become a second Gorbachev, or a second Putin.

Reforms inevitably result in the appearance of new players who aren't embedded in the old systems. Any economic thaw leads to new political demands from business. Decentralization lays the groundwork for centrifugal dynamics. Neutralization of the security apparatus reduces its loyalty. Turning off the stream of propaganda opens the door to uncomfortable questions. Reduced opportunities for corruption destroys the elite consensus on which the country runs.

The uniqueness of the Russian system lies in the fact that it is impossible to reform. Any changes will inevitably set the system in motion, and there is no guarantee that the state will continue to exist in its current form. The other alternative is to preserve the existing order, embalming it with socio-political formaldehyde, erecting concrete monuments to unity.

In this sense, "vladimirputin" is not the architect of the system, but a function of the system. Anyone who replaces him will find himself facing the same choice. The problem isn't that Lancelot can't defeat the Dragon. The problem is that he then becomes the dragon's reincarnation.

Either that, or he can allow the country to fall apart, with everyone returning to their own corners.

Patriot Games

We are still juggling various forms of the subjunctive. The Ukrainian Army did not open fire in Crimea. What if it had? Would Kyiv have been able to hold the peninsula?

To answer those questions, we have to remember the Russia of February 2014. Oil was over a hundred dollars a barrel. Russia had just hosted and won the Olympics in Sochi. The Russian refrigerator had no intention of contradicting the television, and Russia held the chairmanship of the G8.

Moreover, the Kremlin viewed the entire Maidan as a special operation by the West against Russia. If you accept that logic, then the annexation of Crimea wasn't the first blow, the planners of the invasion were just fighting back.

Ukraine was attacked by a country whose president had not touched money in 15 years, who never goes to the store, and never uses public transportation. He doesn't use the internet, because he's convinced that it's a CIA project. He considers the collapse of the USSR "the greatest geopolitical catastrophe of the 20th century."

In February 2014, he decided to write himself into future Russian history textbooks alongside Catherine II. He claimed to be defending Russia from an attack on her "ancestral territories."

Why do we imagine that military resistance would have weakened his resolve?

Greater decisiveness from Kyiv might not have changed Moscow's plans at all. The Kremlin had entirely different elements at stake. Putin put himself to the Raskolnikov test in Crimea. And he was unlikely to settle for "trembling creature" when he'd already convinced himself that he "had the right."

Theoretically, return fire might have changed the outcome. Then again, it might have strengthened Russia's resolve to take things to their logical conclusion. Because a dictator's vanity is always worth more than the lives of his soldiers.

Of course, there's not much point in judging the past from the perspective of the future.

It's only in hindsight that the Maidan, annexation of Crimea, and invasion of the Donbas merge into a single, continuous stream of events. Today, we can see that Flight MH17 would never have been shot down if not for the shootings on the Maidan. Donetsk would never have been seized if not for the beatings of the students in November of 2013. All the tragic and heroic events of recent years are chapters of the same book. But at the time, when each of those events was happening, we had no idea of what was to come.

In the spring of 2014, it was easy to say "I knew the Maidan would win." But in 2013, the best we could do was hope: the history of the protest was being created on the ground in real time. It was only the stubbornness of the protestors who refused to leave the streets that freed the country from Viktor Yanukovich.

In the spring of 2015, it was easy to say that the Donbas was just a continuation of Crimea. But when Russian troops took control of the peninsula, we had no idea what bloody horror they would stir up in the east of the country just two months later.

In the spring of 2016, it was easy to condemn the Minsk Agreements. But in 2015, they gave us a chance to catch our breath and lower daily casualty figures that were in the double digits.

Time changes us and our perspectives. And this gradual transformation leaves us feeling as though we haven't changed at all. In reality, we don't actually remember ourselves, even from the recent past. If we met our 2013 self, or 2014, or even 2015, we would hardly find a common language.

During the annexation of Crimea, all of Ukraine was glued to their screens, watching as our military refused to lower their flags. Our army had been caught in a legal trap when Yanukovych abandoned his position. They did what little they could with the arsenal available: they refused to vow allegiance to the new authorities during that period of total chaos. We considered it heroism.

We'd forgotten that our country even had an army, so even passive resistance was perceived as a heroic act of bravery. Only later did we understand that we were at war—only after the battles of Ilovaisk and Debaltsevo, the Donetsk Airport and Savur-Mohyla. The active phase of the war taught us that an army doesn't just defend; they can also go on the offensive. They don't just have to just hold their ground with teeth gritted; they can also advance on the enemy. And then, for many people, those fierce battles seemed to cancel out the accomplishments of the "Crimean Siege." Like it wasn't enough.

People started to accuse the officers who left for the mainland of weakness and indecisiveness. Although in February 2014, the lion's share of those throwing stones said and wrote the opposite.

It's a psychological trick. Before the war, we were full of illusions and doubts, that we lost in the following years. But it's uncomfortable to judge yourself, so most of us prefer to judge others, to believe we've remained the same while everyone around us has changed.

Don't lie to yourself. We were quite different a few years ago. And in another few years we'll be different again. More often than not, the Inquisitor's cloak conceals a person who accuses others of his own mistakes.

Internal Deportation

When Russia arrived in Crimea, the Crimean Tatars were guaranteed to become targets. After all, their entire history contradicts the Kremlin's major "spiritual bonds." Consider the history of the "Great Patriotic War" for example.

May 9 and May 18 are just nine days apart. May 9th, "Victory Day," is a lavish and emotional affair with parades, fireworks, and the full glory of the state. The second date is mentioned only in passing, without fanfare. That's because it marks the Sürgünlik, the mass deportation of the Crimean Tatars.

Just nine days after the Red Army liberated the peninsula from the Wehrmacht in 1944, Crimea's indigenous people were rounded up and deported to Central Asia. They weren't allowed to come home for nearly fifty years. The USSR didn't just eliminate the Crimean Tatars from Soviet history. It also forced on them the role of outcasts, even after the demise of the empire. The Soviet government had declared the entire nation of Crimean Tatars traitors and collaborationists — despite the participation of Crimean Tatars in the Red Army.

After 1991, Crimea became a bastion of Soviet nostalgia. It only made sense given that transplants comprised the majority of the population. Soviet ethics and esthetics were maintained here in their pristine purity. People attended rallies with the flags of fallen empires and portraits of dead dictators, trying to convince themselves of the righteousness of their beliefs and actions. They lived in a land of rewritten toponymy and whitewashed history. They assured everyone that only they had the right to Crimea. They didn't want to think about the fact that their favorite dish of "Simferopol sausages" were just renamed Crimean Tatar kebabs. And "Belogorsk" was actually the old Karasubazar.

Soviet mythology was very convenient for them. It allowed them to erase Crimea's indigenous people from Crimea's history. They could call them traitors, and use that as just cause to deny them their home. Crimean Tatars were even denied the right to participate in the Soviet "religious communion" celebrated each year on May 9.

When people came to lay flowers at the Eternal Fire in Crimea cities, no one demanded that they acknowledge the reality of Russian collaborators. They weren't asked about Andrey Vlasov's Russian Liberation Army, the 15th Cossack Cavalry Corps of the

SS, or Kaminski's Waffen-Sturm-Brigade. In fact, Russian collaboration wasn't mentioned at all. There certainly weren't any articles in the paper describing the role of Russian collaborators in the war. But if the Crimean Tatars wanted to be part of the May 9th celebrations, they would need to publicly repent—at the very least.

In the Soviet Union, tradition held that all national groups were "victors" against the Germans, despite the fact that there were a few collaborators in their ranks. For the Crimean Tatars, this was reversed. They were declared collaborators, among whom were a few heroes.

There was a constant refrain that Crimean Tatars had the "highest percentage" of collaborators. However, those who compare the number of Russians to the number of Crimean Tatars fighting on either side forget one thing: collaboration is only possible in occupied territory. There were no German-appointed politsai in Tomsk or Vladivostok because there were no Germans. The local population didn't have to make that choice. So the people who are so eager to calculate the "treason rate" need to take a good look at the percentage of a given population who lived under occupation. They'll come up with some new numbers to consider.

Any attempt to discuss these facts triggered accusations of heresy. That shouldn't come as a surprise. Any discussion of the mass deportation undermined the chief "spiritual bond" of the Soviet empire—the myth of the Great Patriotic War.

The myth depicts everything that happened between 1941 and 1945 as a struggle between absolute Good and absolute Evil. But if deportation is a crime, it turns out that in 1944 "the good guys" committed a crime. Either they weren't all thatv "good," or the action wasn't a crime. For *Homo sovieticus*, the latter version was far more convenient and therefore accepted.

Then you would never have to apologize. Never have to question simple dogmatic logic. Never have to think about the decisions made by the chain of command and party leadership. You would never have to feel the ground shifting beneath your feet, the ground from which you looked at the past, present and future.

Crimean Tatars were a minority in Crimea. Just 15 percent, who provided a convenient target to unite against. The same 15 percent whom politicians in Kyiv would remember as Crimea's indigenous people whenelection season drew near and promptly forget immediately after. And so Crimea continued to be dominated by pro-Soviet parties right up until the annexation of the peninsula.

And then the Crimean Tatars were again placed outside the frame. Because after 2014, Russia itself sank into a raging pro-Soviet stance. They declared war on the whole world, demanding a re-do of 1991. Suddenly, Soviet ethics and aesthetics were hoisted on banners across the entire Russian Federation.

The Crimean Tatars were always the most un-Soviet people in overwhelmingly pro-Soviet Crimea. How could it have been otherwise? It was impossible to accept the ethics and aesthetics of the state that had deported their entire nation from their homeland and kept them out for a full forty years. So now the Crimean Tatars have been declared disturbers of the peace by Russia. Potential violators of territorial integrity. The main resistance in the land Moscow stole.

In the 23 years that preceded the war, the Crimean Tatars built up a solid structure of horizontal mutual aid called the mejlis that protected them from the abuses of the traditional power vertical. It was perhaps inevitable that the mejlis would be attacked by the Russian power structures: the Kremlin doesn't tolerate competition. The Crimean Tatar mejlis was banned as an "extremist organization" in 2016.

The government in Kyiv doesn't talk much about Crimea. It's like a zone of silence: while Donetsk and Luhansk are constantly discussed on air, while Simferopol and Sevastopol remain in a media ghetto. Why? Maybe because there just aren't that many refugees who've come from Crimea. So the question of Crimea issue doesn't offer additional voters to the person who chooses to draw it out of obscurity. But here's the thing: the problems faced by the Crimean Tatars aren't just a matter of politics. It's a matter of national ethics.

Some people view the Crimean Tatars as just one among many national diasporas present in Ukraine. This shows a lack of understanding. A diaspora has a mother state somewhere else. The Crimean Tatars have no motherland outside Crimea. That same Crimea that is part of Ukraine, but has been annexed by Russia.

But we're missing the main point behind a pile-up of tactical and situational information and the 24-hour news cycle. This war didn't start in the Donbas, it started in Crimea. This war with all its consequences and peripheral events. A war that has found its way into Europe. The Malaysian Boeing is part of it. So was the Skripal poisoning. Interference in the U.S. elections. An attempted coup in Montenegro. Troops in Syria. Russian mercenaries in Africa. Spy scandals all over the world.

The raising of the Russian flag in Crimea was the declaration of this war. And it won't end until the Ukrainian flag flies again over Crimea. We can't forget this. Nor can we forget all the people forced to live on the other side of the trenches all these years.

It's not just ethics. It's also logic.

Three Myths — Just One Crimea

Every country has its own mental map. The mental map is often more important than the official borders. This is especially true if you're talking about a recently collapsed empire whose residents can't get used to the new reality.

Mental maps trigger nostalgia, nostalgia creates political demand, demand results in political offerings. If the Russians had not viewed the peninsula as belonging to them for the 23 years following 1991, it wouldn't be any different from other Ukrainian regions. Now Ukraine needs to take the mental map test.

If the mental map is larger than the official political map, it creates a demand for invasion. The target is the region that found itself on the "wrong" side after the last drawing of borders. If the mental map is *smaller* than the political one, that means some portion of the country is viewed as outside the core—like a bonus. It lies outside the core identity and so there is no emotional connection.

We have to realize that Crimea's fate wasn't decided in February 2014. The Russian presence had continued unabated throughout the post-Soviet years. Moscow never entirely let go of Crimea, because Crimea was deeply embedded into Russia's collective myths.

Russia mythologizes Crimea as the baptism site of Rus and the two defenses of Sevastopol. It is the summer residence of Russian tsars and the Black Sea Riviera. It's the final refuge of the White Army before their final exodus to Bizerte and the site of Pushkin's "The Fountain of Bakhchisarai." The associations are firmly established and form an integral part of Russia's self-concept. Crimea holds emotional resonance and provokes nostalgia. Crimea is embedded in the imperial consciousness thanks to Tolstoy's Sevastopol stories, the Crimean War and the Black Sea Fleet. Crimea is the Yalta Conference and beautiful tsarist palaces along the coast.

Russia's Crimean myth is strong and stable. Like any myth, it cannot be defeated by facts. Go ahead and prove that the defenders of Sevastopol in the Crimean War were largely Ukrainians. It won't change anything. If the Crimean War is not integral to Ukraine's own story of itself, if Ukraine has not privatized this history, then it remains in Moscow's sole possession.

You can break a myth down to its constituent elements. Challenge the numbers. Refute the interpretation of events. But none of that poses any real threat to the myth. A myth lives in the minds of its adherents. Its irrationality ties it to the realm of faith. Both are accepted without proof. Thus, no amount of logical deconstruction can threaten the myth.

It's also worth acknowledging that Russia's myth of Crimea is actually more Soviet than Russian. The story we're familiar with was only invented after the deportation of the Crimean Tatars. Among other purposes, the myth removed the Crimean Tatars from the story, making it easier to justify their deportation.

Every empire lives on stolen land. Every empire lives at the expense of the indigenous people. Every conquest demands the "reinvention" of the territory. Often only the place names recall the original inhabitants. The Crimean Tatars were denied even that.

The deportation removed them from memory and from the map. The empire built a multi-level defense system to justify its crime. They needed a new myth to explain all the newcomers who arrived after the 1944 deportation.

The Crimean Tatar myth of the peninsula is the only real competitor to the Russian version. The story of a stolen homeland lies at its center. A crushed Muslim paradise. Centuries of independent statehood as the Crimean Khanate. The Crimean Tatar story of Crimea is a story of mass deportation of the native inhabitants, who were replaced by a massive influx of newcomers. The Crimean Tatars remember a pre-war, multiethnic Crimea in which the Crimean Tatar language was the language of trade and everyday communication.

The differences between the Crimean Tatar and Russian versions of history go deeper than the facts themselves. They also differ in their degree of universality. An imperial myth is inevitably inclusive: anyone can join and the cost is your own national identity. Your oath of loyalty to the empire means that you will accept the Russian version of history and the Kremlin's assessment of reality. In contrast, the Crimean Tatar vision is exclusive by definition. It is by its very nature a defensive concept designed to maintain the boundaries of the group, not to expand them.

This makes perfect sense. When they returned from deportation, the Crimean Tatars found they were a minority on the peninsula. Their task was to create themselves anew in their ancestral homelands and they tried to resist assimilation and dissolution. A clear vision defining "us" and "them" was central to the task. But there's the problem: it's hard to become part of that myth if you don't belong to that ethnic group. And that's why throughout the post-Soviet period the Crimean myth attracted as many detractors as supporters. Right up until 2014.

Then something important happened. The annexation of Crimea forced Ukraine to remember the peninsula. Ukraine added the peninsula to its mental map. The previous vision of the peninsula as mountains, sea and high prices, was replaced with a story of invasion and treachery. Ukraine had to learn to talk about the peninsula, to explain its importance to the world, and to ourselves. We needed a descriptive language that would weave the peninsula and the mainland into the shared space of who "we" are. It turned out that there was no Ukrainian myth of Crimea.

Crimea's 60 years as part of Ukraine were spent building the North Crimean Canal to deliver water to the peninsula, developing logistics, and strengthening infrastructure. This practical domestic narrative is inherently mundane, and therefore far less appealing than stories of military conquest or historico-religious narratives. Ukraine's Crimean story can hardly compete with either the drama of the "Russian Jerusalem" or the historical memory of an indigenous people. Recent attempts to expand the Ukrainian myth by recollecting specific battles such as the 1918 liberation of the peninsula from the Bolsheviks are unlikely to win hearts retroactively.

Ukraine needed a myth of Crimea with a broader worldview. Statutes may legalize power in terms of the law, but only mythology can make power feel legitimate. Legitimacy is not about laws, it's about people's consent to be governed. It's not entirely surprising that Ukraine eventually turned to the Crimean Tatar myth.

When the Ukrainian government talks about Crimea today, it speaks of the political prisoners, most of whom are Crimean Tatars. They talk about the specific human rights of the indigenous people, and about Russia's ban on the mejlis and discrimination. Kyiv sees Crimean Tatars and Ukrainians as having a shared history and a shared future. The traditional blue and gold Crimean Tatar flag is now broadly used in Ukraine, replacing the former Crimean tricolor adopted in 1992 and incorporated unchanged into Russian Federation heraldry in 2014.

In a sense, the Crimean Tatars have become the thread tying the peninsula to the mainland. Their fate animates discussions of returning the region to Ukraine. Their existence prevents Moscow from talking about Crimea as a zone of total unanimity.

In adopting the Crimean Tatar vision, Ukraine gains a strong ethical foothold. It takes on the role of defender of the weak from the strong. The role of a country that defends human rights and supports indigenous people. A country that values not only self-interest, but the needs of others.

But Ukraine has to stop limiting itself to words and take action. It's time for Kyiv to define its ethnic policy. Time to grant legal recognition to the mejlis and kurulai. Time to adopt the law on the status of the Crimean Tatar people. Take a clear stance regarding national-territorial autonomy for the Crimean Tatars. It is time for Kyiv to finally transform this "open relationship" into a "marriage contract."

Ukraine suddenly remembered it had Crimea at the very moment it lost it. However, it was this tragedy that led mainland Ukraine to discover the Crimean Tatars. The Crimean Tatars who brought food and other supplies to the besieged military bases. The Crimean Tatars who came to the Maidan in Kyiv and and poured into the streets in Crimea waving Ukrainian flags. The very Crimean Tatars who found themselves alone with an occupying power that wants to erase them from the history of Crimea.

If Ukraine wants to put Crimea on its mental map, it can't do without the Crimean Tatars.

The Silence of the Occupied

Any talk about attitudes in the occupied territory comes up against one stumbling block. We don't have any meaningful way to get that information.

And we're not going to. And it's not because Ukrainian pollsters can't conduct surveys there. Or because Russian surveys are unreliable. The problem is that it is impossible to carry out an accurate survey in occupied territory. When honesty is a punishable offense, many people either won't respond or won't give open answers.

We should keep the same thing in mind when we try to draw conclusions about attitudes in occupied territory based on social media.

The standard image of a commenter from Crimea or the Donbas is quite simple. He loves Russia and hates Ukraine. He longs to see Russian flags flying along Kyiv's Khreshchatyk. Moreover, he promises the imminent collapse of the EU, rejoices at America's problems, and is saddened by Elon Musk's success. He argues aggressively and tends to speak on behalf of the entire region.

Don't fall for it.

One simple factor dictates how radical a person is on social media. That factor is what fate awaits him when Ukrainian flags fly once again over his region. The people who've been living under occupation can be divided into two groups. One group has burned all of its bridges with Ukraine. The other hasn't.

People in the first group have taken up arms against the Ukrainian Army or served in the occupation administration. Maybe they openly looted in the Donbas or are building careers in Crimea's occupation government. People in the second group live their private lives. They steer clear of the government structures. They still have the ability to cross the demarcation line.

The former are well aware that when Ukraine returns, they will have to leave. The threat of criminal prosecution hangs over them. Ukrainian victory will mean a personal defeat for them. That's why they're so extreme on social media. They flaunt their intransigence and try to sound as radical as possible. The Russian occupation represents their only chance for a future.

The latter group is different. They haven't broken any Ukrainian laws. They haven't violated their military or civilian oaths of service. They aren't necessarily ardent Ukrainian patriots. What matters is that official Kyiv will not find criminal culpability in their actions.

And so, they are far less active on social media. A change in government in Crimea or the Donbas won't force them to flee to Russia. Some of them are awaiting the return of Ukraine. Some are just focused on daily survival. Either way, the reason we don't hear their voices is that they do not want to be heard. They have gone under the radar and all they have left are their anonymous accounts and private conversations in the kitchen.

That's why the only voices loudly representing the occupied regions and the people who've already burned their bridges. They don't have anywhere to retreat, so they furiously proclaim their support for the Kremlin. They have no other options left, so now they threaten Ukraine with reprisals. It would be a mistake to think they're all bots. They're just defending the only version of reality that has a place for them. If that reality changes, they've got nowhere to go.

It was just chance that allowed them to seize the megaphone. Everyone else fell silent by necessity. Pro-Ukrainian voices in the occupied territories are persecuted and so the pro-Russian chorus sounds united. It would be a mistake to imagine they represent popular opinion.

That's what makes the situation so unique. We do not know the attitudes in Crimea and the Donbas. We can't rely on polling to answer the question. Monitoring social media won't help either. All we can do is make prognostications and speculate, no more than that. That's why I find references to surveys or attitudes of the electorate laughable.

The word occupation suggests a lot of things. Honesty isn't one of them.

Miscalculations

Sometimes what we perceive as exceptional foresight is something else entirely. For instance, Russia could never have touched Crimea and would have kept all of Ukraine.

For the first decade and a half after the collapse of the Soviet Union, Russia never pushed Ukraine away. On the contrary, Russia used all the tools in its economic arsenal to tie Ukraine as closely as possible. All of the production might of Ukraine's east was focused on the Russian market, which explains why those regions remained a natural stronghold of pro-Soviet sentiment.

Ukraine was so tightly bound to Russia that the idea of any disruption was virtually unthinkable for the industrial and financial leaders. Economics dictated policy: Kyiv tried to manage an impossible balancing act. Moscow even successfully nullified the results of the first Maidan: by not driving Ukraine into a corner, they allowed Ukraine's elites to take the path of least resistance.

And they took it. There were more gas discounts for Ukraine, more cooperation, efficient supply chains. All this was followed by revanche and the success of Yanukovich's Party of Regions in the parliamentary elections. Public engagement declined. Just five years after the reformer Viktor Yuschenko was sworn in, Viktor Yanukovych won the next presidential election. Economics conquered and subjugated politics.

The Kremlin could have done the same thing in 2014. It seems impossible to us now, but that's the thing — it only seems that way. We have to remember that until the invasion of Crimea, Russia was not seen as an imminent threat. They were seen as a player who would use bribes to struggle for control of Ukraine. Who would pressure the West to take its interests into account. But not as a state that would undertake a direct military invasion.

That's the paradox. We thought Moscow showed a smart and calculated restraint in 2005. But the Kremlin saw their reaction to the first Ukrainian Maidan as an example of weakness and ineffectuality.

Where we saw a model of prudence, Russia's top political leadership saw only forced inaction. Russia didn't interfere solely because the army was in need of reform and they weren't confident in their capacities. If Moscow had been holding a different set of cards in 2005, we could have seen Russian flags flying over Crimea ten years sooner.

It's ironic. The Russians saw the very thing that allowed them to keep Ukraine in their orbit in 2004 as a disgraceful display of weakness. And the thing that actually did drive Kyiv away from Moscow and led it to break all of the bonds and strings uniting them, was seen by the Kremlin a measured and appropriate response to street protests in the Ukrainian capital.

Inaction from Russia would have been a much more effective response to the Maidan. Instead, the annexation of Crimea and the invasion of the Donbas rid Ukraine of its illusions. Russia's actions created demand from the public that Kyiv's government was forced to satisfy. Moscow gave Kyiv a military and diplomatic slap in the face and then had to watch as the former Soviet republic unexpectedly developed an effective army, an identity, and a politically conscious nation. They could, instead, have done nothing. And gotten almost everything.

People are not computers. They make mistakes. Sometimes historic ones.

Negative Selection

Moscow makes the same mistake again and again in the post-Soviet space.

It bets on the elites. It invests in big business, corrupts politicians, locks up the supply chains. Obviously, the Kremlin doesn't view regular people as having agency. The Russian elites don't believe that grassroots protest is possible. And so, rather than developing capable and committed allies, Moscow places its bet on corrupt allies of convenience.

Meanwhile, the West prefers to work with civil society. Western organizations invest in education, finance exchange programs, and organize seminars. This horizontal approach supports tomorrow's leaders of public opinion and people who will form the backbone of civil society. And the West doesn't even have to invent anything, it is enough to introduce young people to the logic and structures of Western societies. They are then inspired to implement those rules in their own countries.

As a consequence, street protests repeatedly develop along the same scenario. On the one side, we have a political establishment with dubious reputations. On the other, a society demanding a new set of rules.

Moscow is obsessed with "color revolutions." They keep talking about how similar scenarios play out in different countries. They conclude that everything is orchestrated from outside. They start looking like a gambler who always bets on the long shot and then claims the game is rigged when they lose.

Occasionally voices from within the Russian Federation try to convince the leaders that it's time to learn some lessons: start working with the grassroots. Stop supporting toxic politicians. Form a network of intelligent supporters with integrity. But that's the problem, the Kremlin can't do any of that.

Russia has no attractive vision of the future to offer. It has no image of tomorrow that is capable of engaging and mobilizing people. Unlike the collective West, Russia has no clear civilizational concept. Modern Russia offers discounts instead of values. It monetizes beliefs and principles. What can it offer to its neighbors?

Investment projects? Russian monopolies are the only beneficiaries. New technologies? Russia doesn't create any. Regional security? That idea is meaningless after Crimea.

Moscow bets again and again on the elites who share their values. And so the people they choose as partners simply plunder the resources of the occupied territories. Russia can't negotiate with anyone else: they won't trust anyone different from themselves.

Russia can buy allies, but can't create them. It can offer sex for money, but that has nothing to do with love. Its second-rate pop culture is no more than some duty-free matryoshkas and Soviet-style schmaltz.

"Men did not love Rome because she was great. She was great because they had loved her." Chesterton's formula doesn't apply to modern-day Russia. Russia will lose the battle for the future, because it has no vision of the future. It is losing the battle for hearts, because it is incapable of love.

But Moscow won't draw the right conclusions from their failures. The conclusions would be too depressing.

If It Weren't for the War

If it weren't for the annexation, things might have gone very differently.

We're certain now that the Maidan ensured our separation from the empire. That further relations with Moscow were impossible after the murders of the Heavenly Hundred. That the rupture was unavoidable, that Ukraine and Russia's paths were fated to diverge.

In reality, the Maidan didn't trigger Ukraine's divorce from Russia. Russia's invasion of Crimea and the Donbas did. If Russia had chosen a different path in February 2014, they could have achieved far more than they have with by force of arms.

If it weren't for the Russian invasion, today's Ukraine would look much more like the 2013 version. The overthrow of Yanukovych never guaranteed that Kyiv would immediately drift West. After all, the same people who elected Yanukovich in the first place were still part of the electoral map. Their nostalgia for the USSR hadn't gone anywhere.

Let's conduct a thought experiment. Let's imagine that immediately after the killings of the protesters, Moscow recognizes the new authorities. Condemns the Yanukovych regime. Offers an interest-free loan to the "fraternal country" of Ukraine. Calls for the formation of a "national salvation government" that would include supporters of Moscow along with representatives of the opposition.

In this thought experiment, humanitarian services are formally handed over to the Ukrainian right. Everything connected to real money then gets divided between the opposition and oligarchs from the country's south and east. The Ukrainian president flies to Moscow to negotiate gas prices and the Kremlin offers discounts on gas in exchange for control of key Ukrainian assets.

The following fall, a rebranded "Regionals" (Party of Regions) enters Parliament. Spooked by the Maidan, the Donbas and Crimea, voters turn out to the polls in high numbers. The Ukrainian elites who came in after Yanukovych see no point in severing economic ties with Russia. Their focus is "overcoming the crisis."

Moscow emphasizes the inviolability of borders. Russia's victories in the Olympics are the main topic of the year. The Kremlin and the EU discuss the terms of the Ukraine - EU Association Agreement. Voices in Europe call for the need to respect Moscow's interests. Iosif Kobzon performs in Kyiv's Olympic Stadium.

Crimea's summer season is in full swing. Local politicians continue to talk about the peninsula as a "bridge of friendship" between Ukraine and Russia. With great fanfare the Crimean Tatars are granted a few insignificant roles in the Crimean government.

Direct volunteer support to the military wanes. The army sits quietly rotting away in barracks. Its property has been auctioned off. Patriotic sentiments are gradually replaced with social concerns: falling incomes and the exchange rate are bigger concerns than dead protestors.

The price of oil is falling, but with Russia's low levels of national debt, it is perfectly happy to offer loans to the West. There are no sanctions. The Malaysian Boeing safely reaches its destination. The Donbas asks Kyiv for increased coal subsidies. Russia and other world powers discuss strategies to fight Ebola and ISIS.

Most Ukrainians have never heard of Sloviansk, Ilovaisk, or Debaltseve. Tourists flock to Odesa for the May Day celebrations. Igor Girkin attends a World War I reenactment event. The Kyiv Patriarchate is still dreaming of official recognition. The whereabouts of Viktor Yanukovych are unknown.

This scenario of our recent past would have been entirely possible if Moscow had reacted to the second Maidan as it did to the first. Inertia is a powerful force and the Ukrainian elites would have seized any opportunity to remain in their comfort zone.

It was Russia that forced them out of that comfort zone. It was over when the Kremlin decided that the Maidan was an EU-USA special operation that demanded a military invasion in response. If it weren't for Russian politics, today's Ukraine would be far more similar to the Ukraine of yesterday. And the people warning about a war would still be seen as extremists and alarmists.

In the winter of 2013, the Ukrainian protest was an uprising against the usurpation of power. It took the Russian invasion to move it to the category of a war for national liberation. If it weren't for the annexation of Crimea, who knows what Ukraine would be like today?

Requiem for Myself

I don't write much about Crimea anymore. I guess I've talked myself out after all these years. I've said all I have to say.

I remember one time in 2015, an interviewer asked me my favorite city. At first I started going through my mental photo album of beautiful places, but then I named Simferopol. No, I'm not crazy. I know my hometown perfectly well. I know it's small, jumbled and chaotic. But it's the city of my childhood memories. I could live out the rest of my days in Bruges, but my memories wouldn't go anywhere.

I clearly remember 2013, the last year before the war. On the eve of Maidan, Crimea felt like the outskirts of a former empire. Like a jar of grandma's pickles tucked in the back of the pantry, forgotten and unnecessary. Bizerte in 1930 might have been similar. The remnants of Wrangel's fleet still stood in the harbor. The French had already recognized the Soviet Union five years earlier, but the last battleship, the General Alekseev, had not yet been sent for scrap. The manners of the doormen still had a vaguely military flair, but the pianists with difficult Slavic names had learned to play new songs.

In 2013, Moscow was aflame with race riots in Biryulovo and arguments about illegal immigration and problems coming from the Caucasus. Meanwhile, Crimea just continued to live out its Soviet myths in their pristine purity. It rallied against NATO, denounced the 'Dulles Doctrine', yammered on about the 'friendship of nations'. There seemed to be very little left in common between Crimea, the last Soviet bastion, and modern-day Russia.

Then February 2014 happened. And it turned out that post-perestroika Russia was just a thin veneer over the same old empire. Crimea and Moscow were back in tune with one another, but not because Russia imposed its agenda on Crimea. No, Crimea absorbed Russia into its agenda.

I remember the local crazies. They would walk around carrying red or tricolor flags. They used Soviet words and thought in Soviet slogans. A few cartoonish monarchists even turned up with them. They were antisemitic, as expected. They worked at a local newspaper owned by some local guy with a Jewish name, but that didn't stop them from rambling on about "Zionists" and "conspiracies" in their free time.

These people lived in a cemetery. For them, the present day was no more than a staging area to return to yesterday. Being around them was dull and depressing. If they traveled abroad, they were always looking for signs of decline. They were stupid and uneducated philistines.

I lived in Crimea for thirty years. For ten years of those years I worked in journalism. That whole time we tried to stitch together the mainland and the peninsula. We looked for intersections. We searched for maps that offered non Soviet options. We wanted to move into tomorrow and they tried to pull us back into yesterday. We thought time was on our side. After all, we were young and they weren't. We were wrong.

In 2014, they suddenly became mainstream. It turned out that we'd overestimated Russia. We thought it was smarter, more modern, more progressive than it was. Russia turned out to be a perfect match for them. Orwell brought to life.

I lasted in Simferopol until fall of 2014. From February to October, I wrote about what Russia was doing to my home. It felt as though we were living in the novel *The Island of Crimea* in the chapter where the empire swallows up the entire peninsula. Everything I believed in was eliminated. Independent media, independent people, the right to disagree. By November, even the ripples on the water were gone. It was clearly over. It was time to leave.

Today my home lives under occupations under terms that contradict everything I believe. Although, I don't believe everything I used to.

I've shed a lot of illusions during these years. I no longer believe that grownups can always reach an agreement. If capitulation is offered as the only option, then dialogue is pointless. The power of the word only works if people want to listen. But if they want to come up with "crucified toddlers," then there's no point in talking with them. Anything you say will be used against you.

It turns out that things don't always work out eventually. That the flow of time doesn't always lead to tomorrow. In fact, it may well lead us all to yesterday. The generation of fathers pushes aside their children to steal their grandchildren's future.

Sometimes lies can prevail over facts. The person telling the truth is constrained by the truth, while the one telling lies is constrained by nothing. Being a grownup isn't a matter of age, it's a question of infantilism. If a person is an idiot, don't waste your pearls on him.

I no longer believe in that people will "sort it out" on their own. Once a region becomes a harbor of nostalgia, it has begun its descent to hell. People with their heads on backwards have no other option. Just ask Dante.

I don't know if I could reach agreement with the 2013 version of myself. I've shifted more to the right in recent years. Grown harsher. I've lost faith in the marketplace of ideas and in people's ability to make rational choices. It takes effort to move forward, while decline demands nothing of you. Sinking down into the past is the easiest thing in the world.

I've come to recognize that people's motivations are based on their perception of reality, not reality itself. I've learned that the battle for people's minds is how modern wars are won. Or started. Russian television offers living proof. I've mastered that lesson.

I've learned that it's worthwhile spreading democratic principles only to people who are ready to accept them. You should play by the rules only with people who won't change them after winning. "I have read and agree to the terms of the license agreement." That's how it works, right?

Occasionally my Crimea breaks through to me. It comes in flashes, like a half-forgotten dream. I can see them in old photos: the people who swore allegiance to new flags. The ones who went into internal emigration. The ones who left.

I still can't get used to snow. I'm still used to marking the seasons in the transition from Madeira to Cabernet. Every time I see mountains on the horizon it reminds me of home. My belongings are divided into the things I brought from there and the things I've acquired here. Over time, there are fewer and fewer in the former category. More and more from the latter.

I left behind three decades of my life in Crimea. And my illusions. I don't regret either one.

2 Russia

Rock Is Dead

I didn't bother taking my guitar when I left Crimea. After all, what would I sing after the annexation?

The music we called "Russian rock" was born of protest. There was the vast world of official propaganda, and then there was the musician who would step onto the stage and offer his diagnosis of the times. Their lyrics were anti-establishment, filled with rebellion, a refusal to "toe the line."

Then the 2000s arrived, and every Russian Sid Vicious was suddenly racing to become a Joseph Kobzon, crooning songs of love for the powers that be. They sold out. Putin took *Chaif* discs on vacation and Surkov wrote lyrics for *Agata Kristi* albums. Russian rock went from angst-filled protest to bourgeois comfort, replacing the demand for truth with lyrical longing. Rather than striking a raw nerve, they offered up precisely measured emotion mixed with a heavy dose of nostalgia as a soothing sedative for forty-year-old cubicle drones.

Russian rock went mainstream and turned itself into a business looking for a safe bet. While the musicians sang about their loneliness and being misunderstood, people showered them with love, offered them endless understanding and never rejected them. Listening to rock let people identify themselves with the intellectual minority. The period was an utterly louche and empty imitation of rock. Plenty of people failed to resist the temptation.

In 2014, this cozy world collapsed. In the new reality, each person had to choose which side of the barricades they would stand on. And that's not all: there were questions that required clear and unequivocal answers. The former rockers had to make a choice.

After all, true rock is always anti-establishment. If you're a rebel and a barricade appears, you need to be on the side against the powers that be. But when you're already pushing fifty, it's not so easy to crawl back into your 20-year-old persona. Plenty of musicians made the wrong choice.

In the battle for media support today, everyone claims to be the weaker and more oppressed party. We tend to sympathize with the person whose moral strength is in inverse proportion to their physical might. David vs Goliath, the Spartans vs the Persians, the Polish cavalry vs German tanks — we always root for the underdog. The struggle against a more powerful force represents a victory of the spirit over circumstance. So, Kyiv and Moscow compete for the right to carry that standard into the battle.

When Moscow says it is not a party to the war in the Donbas, that's not just geopolitics. It's a fight for ethical superiority, for the right to frame what's happening as a battle of the Ukrainian dragon against a little Donetsk-Luhansk Lancelot. Of course, if we say it like it is, we have to acknowledge that there is no Ukrainian Goliath fighting against a Donetsk-Luhansk David. In reality, we are three hundred Ukrainian Spartans defending Thermopylae against the armies of Xerxes flying the double-headed imperial eagle on their banners.

This is why Kremlin commentators never depict the war as giant Russia against little Ukraine. Instead, they see an epic battle of the "Russian World" against "the West," the heroic resistance of a besieged fortress under threat from the liberal tentacles of the world hegemon.

Russian performers had a simple choice to make: oppose the Russian Leviathan to express solidarity with the weaker group or declare Russia a valiant rebel opposing the powerful West. The ones who chose the latter path could still lay claim to be "rebels" as they took the stage to celebrate National Law Enforcement Day.

The musicians whose music I played before the war failed the test.

A One-way Ticket

There are no shades of gray in war. There is just one relevant question: who do you want to win? People who look for a compromise here keep in mind the aphorism that reserves the hottest places in hell for people who maintain neutrality in a period of moral crisis.

The problem is that hybrid war is experienced entirely differently by Russians and Ukrainians. Ukrainians experience it directly: six waves of mobilization, military funerals, daily memorials and obituaries in the media throughout the country. Meanwhile, Russians continue to live in a world free of war and can't comprehend why the country right next door categorically denies them any empathy.

For the first twenty-three years after the collapse of the Soviet Union, we tended to see Russia and Ukraine as largely the same. On both sides of the border, values stagnated. Identities were blurred and any convictions were entirely conditional. Everything everywhere was mimicry.

For Ukraine, that all ended the instant Russia annexed Crimea and invaded the Donbas. Kyiv had no other choice: we could feel the breath of the war in daily reports from the frontlines and the reality of one and a half million internally displaced persons.

Meanwhile, the war remains virtual for Russians. There are no official events related to it, no public accounting. People might see the war on their television screens, but it is presented as something largely unrelated to Russia. In Russia, there are no streets named or monuments erected in honor of the heroes of the Donbas. According to the official story, Russian soldiers and officers are only dying in training exercises.

The Ukraine war isn't woven into the fabric of Russian daily life—the ordinary Russian doesn't see the graves. They live as if there is no war. And so it plays no role in domestic politics.

Blood sacralizes a conflict. It leaves behind photographs swathed in black mourning, abandoned fishing poles on the balcony, rusting car parts in the garage. The initial causes of war take on secondary significance and death moves to center stage. The relevance of an obituary doesn't lie in the details, but in the fact of its existence.

Many children growing up in Ukraine today draw nothing but images of war.

At some point, all of Russia's talk about "Banderites" and a "junta" became a self-fulfilling prophecy. There's not much talk in Russia anymore about how Ukrainians "are just like us." No, that time is gone. Now Ukrainians are viewed as "other," as hostile and incomprehensible, incapable of empathy or compassion. This shouldn't come as a surprise. A country at peace reads the New Testament. A country at war turns to the Old.

Recent events have been woven into national myth in both Russia and Ukraine. On the one hand, Russia presents the "Crimean Spring" as the realization of its imperial ambitions and confirmation of its sovereignty, which includes the right to violate the law and human rights. On the other, Ukraine sees the Maidan as an archetypical national revolution and the fight in the Donbas as a war of independence. These stories are like unipolar magnets: they can't exist adjacent to each other, they can only repel.

The only way these stories can co-exist is through the invalidation of one of them. The people who talk about "reconciliation" have to decide which story they plan to eliminate.

An Anthology of Cowardice

I've met plenty of people who try to stay "above the fray."

Their logic boils down to this: Ukraine is hardly different from Russia. They say that it isn't only Russian artillery killing people, Ukrainian artillery is too. They say that Russia is fighting against the yellow and blue flag and Ukraine against the St. George ribbon. And then the refrain goes "a bad peace is better than a good war."

It's a very convenient logic. You get to wear the white hat and declare your support for peace and universal love. I have just one question for these people.

Did Russia invade Ukraine? Or was it the other way around?

The answer to that question clears matters up. War has its own cruel logic and you can't take part without getting your hands dirty. "Friendly fire" is a reality in every conflict, shells don't always hit their military targets, no army in the world is completely free of looters or bribes at checkpoints. The only clear ethical marker lies in the fact that one side decided to call their army out of barracks and send them into another country in armored vehicles.

You can criticize Kyiv's information politics all you want, but they don't compare to Moscow's. Say whatever you want about Ukraine's legal system, but there isn't a single law on the books which would allow Kyiv to send troops into the territory of a neighboring country. Meanwhile, both chambers of the Russian parliament have granted the Russian president that right.

The war started the day the Russian army entered the streets of Crimea. The peninsula's annexation makes clear who is the aggressor and who is the victim here.

Yes, it's very convenient to talk about a "atmosphere of mutual hatred" that needs to "brought to an end." There's no need to dig in the dictionary to find the meanings of words like reparations, restitution, or tribunal. Not when you can just throw up your hands and say "they're all bad." Sure, during peacetime, they may "all" be very "bad." But war is far too heavy a weight on the scales of morality to be balanced out with abstract discussions of "geopolitics."

If one country is the aggressor, that country is responsible for everything that happens going forward. And when a country is the aggressor, every citizen of that country bears collective moral responsibility. And there's no psychological bomb shelter that can protect you from that fact.

I understand the people who pour all their energy into the phrases "everyone's guilty" or "no one's guilty." They're frightened. It's scary to take responsibility, scary to make a choice, scary to speak the truth. But when did they decide cowardice was a political stance?

More Hell

We were saved by the "crucified finches."

I'm not kidding. Russian propaganda published endless stories describing the tragedy of finches being crucified in Ukraine because the Ukrainians view them as representatives of Russia.

This emotional story tugs on the heartstrings of Russians and replaces any sober thought or analysis. Of course, it's also blatantly false.

Russia's total lack of genuine expertise about Ukraine saved us. No one appeared capable of providing a sober analysis of our country. They had no actual specialists capable of evaluating the past, present and potential future.

It worked in our favor that Russia thought they already understood Ukraine. If you wanted to speak on television as a Ukraine expert, you didn't need any more than some relatives in Zhytomyr, memories of strolling down Kyiv's Khreshchatyk, or a vacation in Yalta.

Russia saw Ukraine through the prism of Soviet dichotomies. Half the country is just like us, there's nothing to discuss! Half the country is nothing like us, there's nothing to discuss! No one was interested in nuance. Slogans replaced analysis. Patriotism replaced expertise.

All of this benefited Ukraine.

Moscow was sure that Ukraine would collapse like a house of cards. The whole eastern half of the country would welcome the Russian tricolor. The eastern and southern regions would rush into battle to fight for the Russian World.

The Kremlin didn't anticipate the volunteer movement, or volunteer battalions, or the rise of Russian-speaking Ukrainian patriotism. It was caught off guard by the birth of a civic nation that wasn't interested in an ethnic definition of nationalism. Moscow was caught flat-footed by the grassroots mobilization that swept across Ukraine, encompassing regions that Russia viewed as its private fiefdom.

Russia couldn't have anticipated all this, because that would have required actually studying Ukraine. In-depth analysis. Research. Prognostications. Without idiotic ideology and baseless self-confidence. If you're getting all your information about Ukraine from Kremlin propagandists, then you're not getting information about Ukraine.

Of course, such distortions aren't limited to Ukraine. Not long after the war started, Nikolai Patrushev, Secretary of the Russian Security Council, claimed in an interview that Madeleine Albright had demanded that Russia give up Siberia and the Far East. Of course, Albright never demanded any such thing. That bit of fake news first appeared in 2006 when the state-funded newspaper "Rossiyskaya Gazeta" published an interview with Boris Ratnikov, a retired FSB general, who claimed that workers at the bureau had telepathically penetrated Madeleine Albright's subconscious to ferret out her plans and intentions. That's how they found out about Siberia, and the Far East, and the West's plans to annex them.

And then nine years later, we hear the Secretary of the Russian Security Council repeating this conspiratorial nonsense out loud. It turns out that the Kremlin leadership watches Russian television and now they're drinking their own KoolAid. There is no reason to imagine that these people are capable of sober analysis or logic behind closed doors. They honestly believe things we find laughable.

The longer this continues, the better. The further they diverge from reality, the more ineffective they become. Every new revelation about the "junta" or the "fascists" just helps Ukraine.

When the Kremlin spouts idiotic nonsense about Ukraine, that's not dangerous. It would be dangerous if they started making sense. Therefore, long live the crucified finches.

Cold War Traumas

Since 2014, any mention of negotiations between Russia and the West worries the average Ukrainian. They imagine conspiracies and betrayal. The fact is, those fears are unfounded.

Unfounded, but not groundless. Moscow would certainly like to reach an agreement with Washington and Brussels. The wish may even be mutual. But compromise between Russia and the West is not actually possible.

They're working from entirely different pictures of reality.

Many of the Russian elite don't believe Russia lost the Cold War. They don't believe that the Soviet Union collapsed due to its inability to compete with the West. No, they believe that the Kremlin voluntarily decided to join the club of Western players.

According to this version, Russia voluntarily decided to remove the looming threat of nuclear war. So Moscow didn't lose the confrontation—Moscow voluntarily agreed to compromise in the 1980s and was then betrayed.

Betrayed, because they weren't given a seat at the worlds "supreme council." Their "sphere of influence" was challenged. They were kept at arms length rather than being welcomed to the table with the key players.

Essentially, Russia acts as though the Soviet Union never collapsed. As if it was just reformatted, while the essential relationship between colonies and imperial center was unchanged. This is the Kremlin's vision. Once you understand that vision, their logic and their behavior make more sense.

But this all seems absurd from the perspective of the West, because the West has an entirely different perspective on what happened in 1991.

Europe and the United States see the collapse of the Soviet Union as a direct result of Moscow's defeat in the Cold War. In the competition between two systems, one dropped out of the race, no longer able to compete. And so the Kremlin lost its claim to be considered an alternative system and an equal.

The gap between these two world views leads to insurmountable contradictions.

Winners and losers have different rights. The loser gives up his standing, drops to the bottom of the rankings and starts to rebuild everything from the ground up. The winner retains his position and even strengthens it. The Russian elite believe they have a natural right to control their neighbors, a gift of history. To the rest of the world, that attitude is patently absurd. It's like a losing boxer demanding his title belt back.

When Barack Obama described Russia as a small power that doesn't "produce anything that anybody wants to buy," he wasn't trying to offend anyone. He was just expressing the Western consensus about Moscow. In the West, it's obvious that the Kremlin can't offer an alternative to Washington.

Moscow tries again and again to propose a new Yalta agreement to the West, because they see themselves as the Soviet Union. And the West shrugs their shoulders again and again in bewilderment, because all they see is a country that sells oil and gas and used the proceeds to buy everything they need.

The Kremlin is convinced that the West wants to dismember and destroy Russia because they see Russia as a civilizational alternative. The West views Russia as a source of raw materials and a large consumer market and genuinely can't imagine why they would want to destroy it.

For what? Conquest and dismemberment — why? And then have to deal with multiple new states with nuclear weapons on their territories? No one wants that kind of chaos next to their borders. A failed state that covers one seventh of the planet is terrifying and the West wants to avoid that scenario at all costs.

When Russia looks into the mirror, it sees the USSR. And so it thinks other people see the same thing. So Russia acts like the USSR and makes the same threats that the USSR made. But when the West looks at Russia, it just sees Russia. The West just wants to return to the pre-Crimea world order and keeps trying to understand where Moscow's red lines are so they can avoid crossing them.

Russia's phobias could be cured if it understood the truth. But that truth is too humiliating to accept, so Moscow remains hostage to its own paranoia.

As the line goes, "for Athos this is too much; for the Comte de la Fere it is too little." The West might have given the USSR what Russia is demanding. But Russia is not the USSR, despite their insistence to the contrary.

This will continue until the Kremlin achieves their goal. Or until the West finally sees that Russia actually is what it so insistently claims to be. Until the West understands that Moscow is feeling around for its new borders and will continue to do so indefinitely. And then the West will finally see what Russia sees in the mirror: the Soviet Union. At that point, the West will finally recognize the threat and weigh the risks. It may decide to go all in.

At which point, Russia may learn that it is no Soviet Union in terms of stability.

Crooked Mirrors

You know, the Luhansk and Donetsk "People's Republics" are just a projection. A projection of how Moscow sees Ukraine.

But how does Ukraine see these terrorist enclaves?

As occupied quasi-republics constructed by an external player. They appeared at a moment when the state was weak. Their sole purpose is to serve as a source of destabilization and the launching point for a future invasion. Of course, Russian nationalists see Ukraine itself as an artificial project constructed by the West when Russia was weak in order to thwart the revival of the empire and the Russian World.

From Kyiv's perspective, does the Luhansk People's Republic have any chance of survival? Of course not. It is entirely dependent on inputs from Moscow. The minute the Kremlin turns off the flow, they disappear.

Of course, Moscow's geopolitical "experts" would say the same about Kyiv. Kyiv exists only thanks to the West. Without that help, Ukraine collapses and then falls into the carefully placed hands of the Kremlin.

How does Ukraine view the population of the occupied territories? Most are hostages under enemy occupation; some are collaborators. The hostages must be freed. The collaborators must be neutralized.

Moscow uses the same logic. They believe the Ukrainians, who they call the "Little Russians," are groaning under the yoke of the Banderites who have usurped power. The "Little Russians" must be returned to the bosom of the "Russian World." Everyone else must be eliminated.

Ukraine knows that it is fighting Russia, not Donetsk and Luhansk.

Russia is convinced that it is fighting the West, not Ukraine..

It's called projection. Moscow accuses Ukraine of doing the very things they proceed to do in occupied Ukrainian territory.

All these pseudo-republics are a form of confession. Through them, Russia confesses how it sees Ukrainian independence and the Ukrainian state. Kyiv says, "Stop supporting separatists and return the territory to its rightful owner." Moscow then uses the same language in its negotiations with the EU and US.

The claims made by Russian propagandists about the "secret plans" of the West work the same way. Just listen to what they say. Listen to their revelations of their enemies' plans to destroy and dismantle Russia. They imagine that they are denouncing others. In reality, they're confessing. On live television. 24-7.

They are announcing what they hope to do to those who oppose them. They are describing what they will do given the opportunity. Their words outline their desired reality. And of course that justifies any retaliatory violence. Including "preemptive violence."

All their stories about "crucified toddlers" and "the atrocities of the junta" are just confessions. Russia lies on the therapist's couch and describes just how deep its rabbit hole actually is.

Psychological projection allows a person to distance himself from his unacceptable feelings, desires and motives and attribute them to someone else. Then he can deny responsibility. It's commonly seen in histrionic or paranoid disorders.

But who says entire states can't suffer from similar disorders?

Putin vs Army, Language, and Faith

We may all grow old with Putin still in power.

When the Russian Duma "reset" his term limits to zero, he gained the right to run twice more, which means his horizon now extends to 2036. He could outlast three more presidents of the United States. He'd outlast Zelensky by 12 years.

People who were born in the year he was first inaugurated will be turning 35. People who were 16 when he was selected will be past fifty.

The Ukrainian perspective doesn't accommodate those kinds of timeframes. We've had five different presidents since 2000. We take pride in our successful transfers of power and we're used to change. But if one thing remains stable, it's the threats we face.

Not so long ago we thought the threats were limited to our internal systemic problems: our archaic system of governance, oligarchic economy, corruption and legal nihilism. The lack of functional judicial and law enforcement systems.

In 2014, an external threat was added to the list. Vladimir Putin started this war and Putin plans to be in power until 2036. This means that the Kremlin's understanding of Ukraine is unlikely to change anytime soon. Putin never tires of sharing his version of reality in his interviews.

It's pretty simple: Ukraine was always just a border region of the Russian Empire. "Ukrainians" were invented by Austrian intelligence services in the 19th century just to undermine Russia. The Russian Orthodox Church belongs in Ukraine, but Crimea, the Black Sea region and the Donbas have no relationship to Ukraine. The Ukrainian language is just "Polonized" Russian and the "cooling of relations" between Moscow and Kyiv is the result of Western interference.

This person who started a war against Ukraine, who annexed one region and occupied another, is happy to discuss identity. His position is straight-forward and consistent: Ukrainians don't exist. They're actually Russians. The only differences between the two are the (invented) language and church. And of course the army, which allows them to maintain the boundary. If we remove these "artificial differences," everyone will understand they are "one people."

There are plenty of Ukrainians willing to agree that the Ukraine Orthodox Church's independence was an election ploy, promotion of the Ukrainian language is a nationalist agenda, and the army is a necessary, but hardly a critical issue. And yet, the Russian president doesn't consider them trivial. In fact, he considers them the only barriers to "unification."

Maybe Putin just says what he really thinks?

After all, there's nothing holding him back. There is no opposition in Russia, and no actual parliament, so the Russian president can affort to play the long game. His views have been consistent and his depiction of reality has not changed. Ukrainians may get tired of one reality and start seeking another one in their elections, but the person who launched the invasion in 2014 has no intention of changing.

Maybe army, language and faith matter more than some people are willing to believe. We forget that some walls are load-bearing. Even if you don't like the architect, that doesn't mean it's safe to tear them down. If you and Vladimir Putin are upset about the same things in Ukraine, then Putin's not the problem.

A Pseudo-Federation

In 2018, the Kremlin abolished the compulsory teaching of local languages throughout the Russian Federation.

Students in the Udmurt Republic, Tatarstan, Bashkiria and the other 18 republics now study their native languages to the extent of a foreign language. There may be the best demonstration of what the Russian Federation is not.

It is not a genuine federation. All references to its federative structure and dozens of republics are simply lies. They're Russia's legacy from the Soviet Union—a legacy they'd like to escape. Maybe not de jure, but certainly de facto. Russia is, instead, a unitary state in which all regional power is entirely subject to the power of the center.

The average Russian now freely discusses the perfidy of the Bolsheviks who "gave" Ukraine and the other republics their statehood. They complain that Vladimir Lenin created the internal borders along which the Soviet Union would fall apart 70 years later. Lenin in his mausoleum is routinely blamed for his nationality policies and held up as an example of short-sightedness.

In fact, the opposite is true.

When the Russian Empire collapsed, national consciousness developed in the outskirts due to the empire's discriminatory policies. For example, starting in 1889, a Muslim who obtained a law degree had to receive special dispensation from the Minister of Justine in order to practice law. In military units, the number of officers of Swedish, German, Finnish, Lithuanian, Estonian or Armenian descent could not exceed 20%.

Universities had quotas for Jewish students and Catholic churches in Belarus were forcibly Russified. It should come as no surprise that when the imperial gag weakened, previously suppressed voices rang out against oppression.

When the Bolsheviks started to rebuild the empire from the fragments, they encountered a new reality. They weren't fighting just a class war. It turned out that national identities also opposed the central government. People saw the collapse of the Russian Empire as an opportunity to form their own nation states.

Lenin was pretty rational. Bolshevik national policy was an attempt to knock the ground out from under the feet of the "nationalist separatists." The idea was simple: why seek national independence when the Soviet Union is prepared to give you everything you need, including your own language and culture?

The Bolsheviks did not actually create national republics. They just allowed them to appear on the map. This unavoidable compromise allowed them to hold onto the escaping territories. Thus the Soviet Empire successfully replaced the Russian one.

However, the Bolsheviks only managed to delay the logic of history, not to escape it. The events of 1991 reignited processes that had been put on pause by the repressions of the 1930s. The glue dried up and the country began coming apart at the seams. Purely "formal" borders became actual borders. Dormant identities began to awaken.

But Moscow had learned its lesson.

The Kremlin is now steadily removing any substance from the federative idea. The "national republics" of the Russian Federation have less and less room for national identity. Yes, the Udmurt constitution states that it is a "constituent state of the Russian Federation" and that the "Udmurt people exercise their right to sovereign power on their historical territory." None of that stops Moscow from draining all meaning from those phrases.

In 1926, the population of Udmurtia was 52% Udmurt and 43% Russian. And then a number of majority-Russian regions were transferred to Udmurtia. Add in the forces of migration and assimilation and you find that in 2010 the proportion was 28% Udmurt/62% Russian.

The abolition of compulsory study of the native languages in schools of the national republics offers a final solution to the nationalities question. The Kremlin will be entirely content to see all regional variety in the Federation reduced to folklore ensembles, festivals of traditional foods and isolated groups of national identity. Moscow sees this as a safeguard against any repetition of 1991. Without national identities, the demand for independent nations will disappear.

The Russian Federation's domestic policies offer a glimpse at its foreign policy goals. Their claims to protect the rights of Russian speakers in neighboring countries are just one more step toward absorbing their neighbors. Only Ukraine's sovereignty protects its from the fate of the Udmurts: its borders, army and national identity. Some people may feel that the battle for identity has already been won.

That doesn't stop Moscow from thinking otherwise.

Requiem for the Kosovorotka

Have you ever stopped to wonder why Russians don't wear their traditional national costume? On major holidays in Russia, you can certainly spot the blue and white striped military undershirt known as a *telnyashka*. What you won't see is the traditional belted peasant tunic called the *kosovorotka*.

This is particularly noticeable in contrast with Ukraine, where the traditional embroidered shirt called a *vyshyvanka* has long been a common sight on the street. The traditional patterns can be found on T-shirts and dresses, you can buy them in any regular clothing store and it is a normal part of the everyday wardrobe. This "success story" stands in stark contrast to the story of Russia's national shirt.

The kosovorotka is a reject. No one wears it for state events or traditional holidays. It's solely the domain of urban eccentrics obsessed with the "traditional" and the "handmade." This should come as no surprise, because the key word here is "national."

Russia has never been a nation state. It immediately emerged as an empire: beginning with the late Muscovite tsardom, the state apparatus always operated under some overarching idea and ideology. Initially, it rested on a religious foundation: the state as a barrier to the coming of the Antichrist. Accordingly, the state apparatus needed to unite the Orthodox and engage in missionary work.

Later the Muscovite tsardom grew into the Russian Empire, which became an Orthodox ideocratic state. The basis became more rational without losing its imperial foundation. Next came the Soviet Empire preaching the idea of spreading socialism throughout the world.

Nothing changed in the 1990s. Yes, the empire shrank a bit, but it didn't stop being an empire. As soon as oil prices made it possible, ideas of revanche rang out again in all their original purity. First Patriarch Kirill began talking about the "Russian World," and then the secular authorities chimed in with the project of a Eurasian Union.

The peculiarity of the Russian Empire lies in the fact that it stands in fundamental opposition to the idea of a nation state. It must find shared concepts to unite a broad variety of religious and ethnic groups. Moscow rejects ethnic national identity and is forced to find an answer to why the Chechen and Yakut should live under the same government and what could unite them enough for them to agree to it.

That's where all the talk of "spiritual bonds" comes in. They are trying to come up with enough arguments to tip the scales so that the centripetal forces outweigh centrifugal forces. The empire must create a national vision powerful enough to convince the colonies to live under a single roof.

All that searching for a new imperial idea in the 1990s and early 2000s, the conversations about "sovereign democracy," "a Eurasian superpower," and other geopolitical constructs can be traced back to those basic realities. But an empire doesn't just create its own lingo. It also creates its own aesthetics.

It's no coincidence that the telnyashka triumphed over the kosovorotka. The formation of an empire requires an army. This is what allows empires to devour "others" and defend its "own." The cult of militarism is inevitable for an empire—it's in the nature of the beast. Thus, military regalia becomes part of the "civilian everyday." In this context, the ubiquity of the military telnyashka during public holidays makes perfect sense.

In light of this logic, the kosovorotka comes across as a throwback to some "pre-imperial" time, a bridge to an idea of Russia as a simple nation. But that nation never existed and, in fact, its very possibility has been disputed for three hundred years of Russian history.

The kosovorotka is irrelevant because it suggests a Russia with entirely different borders. Russia's actual cultural baggage is entirely based on imperialism, and so the purely "ethnic" kosovorotka can't serve as the foundation for a national costume.

"Russian nationalist" is actually an oxymoron. "Nationalists" in Russia are actually imperialists. All they can do is call for the elimination of other peoples' identities, for the absorption and complete digestion of outsiders. The dissolution of nations and languages in service to the imperial idea. Their entire formulation of the "national" inevitably adds up to "we'll declare everyone Russian; whoever doesn't agree will be punished."

Contemporary Russia is a country with no national project. It cannot be articulated or fleshed out because it does not exist. The only logic that can trace the outlines of this territory is an imperial logic that continues its traditions of the absorption and dissolution of all other identities.

And that's why the telnyashka killed the kosovorotka. Now it's going after the vyshyvanka.

The Third Rome

It's a commonplace in Ukraine to compare modern Russia with 1930s Germany. However, for the sake of accuracy, we should acknowledge that Vladimir Putin is actually far more like Benito Mussolini than Hitler.

Il Duce was fond of vanity projects, just like Putin. Mussolini built the ocean liner SS Rex to win the "Blue Riband" (an award for the fastest transatlantic crossing). Italy's accomplishments also included the world fastest seaplane, the Macchi M.C. 72, and Italo Balbo's transatlantic flight. All were government-financed projects. No commercial entities were involved, just the greatness of the state.

There's nothing surprising in this. Like the current Russian leadership, the Italian leader wasn't interested in race theory. His focus was statism — the strengthening of the central government as the primary focus of domestic politics. Mussolini expressed the quintessence of his approach in a speech to the Chamber of Deputies in May 1927, "Everything in the State, nothing outside the State, nothing against the State."

By 1935, Mussolini had placed three-quarters of private businesses under government control. Banks and private individuals were required to forfeit all foreign stock or bond holdings in favor of Italian securities.

Today, Mussolini's Russian heirs also aim to bring all social and economic activity under government control. Empire is the highest value, power is sacralized, square kilometers are more important than quality of life. Government service is the only path to social mobility. A generation who dreamed of becoming businessmen has been replaced by a generation dreaming of secure positions in the government.

Putin is not an ethnic nationalist. He's an imperialist. It doesn't matter whether you have a Ukrainian last name, a German one, or Tuvan — you can still make a good career in the Russian Federation. As long as you profess the right values.

Mussolini eliminated the power of parliament — they lost the right to control his actions. Local elections were also eliminated: even mayors were replaced by appointed officials. The press, education system and movie industry all cooperated to present fascism as the sole acceptable alternative to liberalism. The opposition disappeared. The head of state controlled law enforcement, national defense, business, colonial administration and public works.

The Russian president has also successfully destroyed all institutions. The opposition is marginalized, elections are a farce, and there is no system of checks and balances.

Mussolini was building the "Italian World." He viewed the Mediterranean as his rightful sphere of influence. In 1923, he seized Corfu and established a puppet state in Albania. Italy's penultimate pre-war acquisition was Ethiopia. Its last one was Albania, which it conquered in five days in 1939, on the eve of the Second World War. All that time, Mussolini talked about the creation of an Italy which would be "great" and "respected," whose priorities Europe and the rest of the world would have to take into account.

Today's Russia unites around a vision of Russia "rising from its knees." The "Russian World" serves as justification for invading their neighbors. Talk of "traditional spheres of influence" are used as weapons against sovereign states. A Moscow that is dissatisfied with its status aims to submerge the world into turbulence so it can use the chaos to fight for its new place in the global orchestra. An "anti-Western" stance goes along with talk of national greatness.

We know the recipe for successful nation building. The conditions for the creation of an unsuccessful state are also pretty consistent. They include an emphasis on the "greatness" of the state and subjugation of business, propaganda and expansion, centralization and criticism of the West. And, for the cherry on top, vanity projects.

Spot 10 differences in this picture.

The Heirs of October

In October 1993, everything the Russians would later claim was happening in Ukraine, actually did happen in Moscow. There was a coup d'etat in which the legal authorities were overthrown and fired on. There was a constitutional crisis that ended with strengthening the victors. Then there was the civil war in Chechnya. It is also worth nothing that during that war, the government in Moscow followed a script very similar to the one they utilized in Ukraine. First they sent military "tourists" to help the the head of the Provisional Council of Chechnya, Umar Avturkhanov, take Grozny. When the "volunteers" failed, the regular Russian army was sent in.

For a long time, Russians were divided in how they understood those events. Some people saw 1993 as a victory of democracy over the forces of revanche. Others saw it as the victory of a future revanche over the forces of democracy. Today those arguments have lost their relevance. The annexation of Crimea and the invasion of the Donbas have now reconciled the camp who sat inside the Russian White House in 1993 with the people who ordered in the tanks.

The Russian mercenary who goes to the Donbas to fight the Ukrainian army is a direct descendant of the people who defended the Russian Parliament against Yeltsin's tanks. The Russian bureaucrat who provides logistics and legal cover to the mercenaries is a descendant of Yeltsin.

To understand the motives of the mercenaries, we have to understand where they came from. The defenders of Moscow's White House were a classic "lost generation." At least, if you can say that about people who had successfully completed every link in the chain of Soviet institutions growing up. They were forged in Soviet kindergartens, schools, and armies, but then the Union collapsed and they were ejected from the new social order. In October of 1993, some of them dreamed of a just social order without the rich. Some dreamed of revanche and the restoration of the empire. They were all trying to make sense of the new reality, but in 1993 they failed.

Then came 2014. All those builders of a future-that-never-came and soldiers of a no-longer-existing-country finally saw their chance. They believed that the annexation of Crimea and invasion of the Donbas would force Russia to change. That international isolation and sanctions would leave Russia with no choice and a new way of being would replace the old. They believed that the Kremlin would have to rebuild the country along new principles in order to survive. They dreamed of a reincarnation of the empire and were convinced that this new version would be spared the flaws of the old one. No more neo-feudalism, oligarchs, or social inequality.

What stunning naiveté.

In fact, everything went completely the other way. The Kremlin mobilized them for the war in Ukraine to solve their own problems. All these operetta "Cossacks," militias, re-enactors, members of marginal parties and perpetual protesters were once rivals of the Russian authorities in the battle for the future. But in 2014, they stepped into the role of armed puppets in Moscow's hands. In the early 1990s, they had fought for revolution. Following the events on the Maidan, they were sent to tame the Ukrainian revolution.

The Kremlin promised them a testing ground for social experiments, a space for historical re-enactments under the name "Novorossiya," or "New Russia." In essence, Moscow tricked its long-time opponents. While they went out to murder for some invented "other" Russia, the Kremlin was actually using them to preserve the status quo. Moscow wasn't interested in a paradigm shift. What they needed was a noose that they could tighten at any time. A locus of controlled instability. And as soon as the Russian mercenaries had fulfilled their task, they began to mysteriously disappear.

The Russian volunteers who went to fight the Ukrainian army identified with the Cuban revolutionaries. They saw themselves as freedom fighters in the mold of Che Guevara "exporting the revolution" and building "international solidarity." The only difference was that Cuban fighters went to the Congo and Bolivia; Russian fighters went to Donetsk and Luhansk. The thing is, the similarities were entirely false. The Kremlin had no intention of reincarnating Castro. Their only goal was counterrevolutionary. Rather than creating something new, they were only interested in preserving their own power. The heirs to the defeat in 1993 were granted space on prime time only as long as their script advanced the Kremlin's goals. And when it no longer did, they disappeared from the airwaves.

The Kremlin defeated its rivals twice. First in 1993, by shooting at them from tanks. Again in 2014, by sending them to die in the trenches of the Donbas.

Sometimes empires close accounts in bizarre ways.

Imperialist Russophobes

The more Moscow fights for the "Russian World," the worse things go for them.

In the fall of 2019, Putin condemned what he called efforts "to reduce absolutely unceremoniously the space of the Russian language in the world." He blamed "inveterate Russophobes" and the policies of specific countries. For once, I'll have to agree with the Russian president regarding the policies of specific countries. Kremlin policies really have damaged the status of the Russian language.

Moscow has deprived the Russian language of a key attribute: neutrality. Contrast this to English: studying English has no impact on identity. A Lithuanian studying English is still Lithuanian, a Kazakh studying English is still Kazakh. The Kremlin sells Russian as a package deal. Language study is served with a side of loyalty to the empire and support for Russia's version of history.

Moscow has gone to great lengths to turn Russian schools abroad into factories producing "Russian people." These "Russian people" are expected to undermine their own governments, and to reject the local history and language. And then the Kremlin will use them as leverage to interfere in local affairs. The worse these Russians live, the more Moscow has a right to scream in protest.

As a result, the neighboring countries have no choice but to defend themselves not so much from the language itself, as from the other elements of the "package deal." In the former Soviet republics, that "package" serves as a pretext for invasion. Native speakers now belong to Russia and Moscow has an "obligation" to defend them. That's exactly what we saw in the spring of 2014 in Crimea.

And the people who hope to remain "above the fray" are just dancing to the Kremlin's tune. They try to straddle the fence time and time again. They prefer a convenient half-truth to an inconvenient truth. They're the ones claiming we need a "fair referendum" in Crimea. They've chosen a side that equates language with national identity. Such statements confirm that wherever Moscow sees "Russians," they will feel justified to invade, annex and occupy. And although even Russian opposition leaders are convinced that they're "protecting" people there, the opposite is true.

In reality, Moscow is sending a clear signal to its neighbors. As long as there are people in your country who considers themselves "Russian," even in the basic ethnic sense of the word, your borders are at risk. Be on guard. And so, Russia's neighbors hear the warning and take action, absorbing and "de-Russifying" their Russian-speaking populations.

"Compatriots," "Russian-language schools," "compromise history textbooks." These terms have become bombs planted by the Kremlin under their neighbors' sovereignty. Crimea is a blatant warning. Do you want to avoid being invaded? Strive for internal conformity. Linguistic uniformity. Affirmative action. A cohesive perspective on your country's history and independence.

Otherwise, you may wake up one day to find the Russian flag flying over parts of your country. And both the Kremlin and the "opposition" will claim in harmony that since Russian trains are not being derailed in the occupied territories, everyone should just accept the new status quo.

For years now, the Kremlin has been trying to enlist the Russian literary classics as their footsoldiers. They've transformed the moral authorities of the past into traveling salesmen offering imperial banners.

They're not exactly subtle about it. For instance, Pushkin's "To the Slanderers of Russia," written in 1831 in response to the Polish Uprising. Russia's current leaders equated Poland's fight for independence with the Ukrainian Maidan, and then sent Pushkin's classic poem out to "fight for the Donetsk People's Republic." They freely set 19th-century writers as moral guideposts to the 21st century.

All of this is deeply concerning. A human being belongs only to the epoch in which he lived. Otherwise, we would have to deal with the fact that Pushkin owned serfs, Dostoevsky was xenophobic, poet Afanasy Fet was anti-Semitic. The only reason we don't do that is because we believe in leaving the past in the past. We can appreciate the aesthetics from previous centuries and leave behind the ethics.

You want to understand which side Pushkin would be on today? Okay, let's say he was born in 1970. He graduates high school under Gorbachev. He gets drafted in one country and comes home to a different one. He'll see "Swan Lake" on his screen in the summer of 1991 and make his choice in 1993. He'll see the sinking of the Kursk and the tragedy of Beslan, the cancellation of elections, and loss of freedom. Try putting the classics through the meat grinder of modern everyday life and then figure out which flags they'll fight under.

Instead, Moscow has assigned culture to serve as the locomotive for their political agenda. If you want to honor Chekhov and Tolstoy, you'll celebrate the invasions of Crimea and the Donbas. If you want to take pride in Gagarin and Dostoevsky, be sure you stop to pray to the Bolshevik leaders buried in the Kremlin walls. Russia has consistently strengthened its legacy with "spiritual bonds" and has branded dissenters as a "fifth column." Is it any wonder that the neighboring countries avoid this prix fixe menu?

It's entirely possible that the Kremlin will accomplish the opposite of what they intended. Use of the Russian language will decline. Russia's neighbors will no longer be reading Russian classics in Russian—instead they'll read them in translation as "world literature." Each country will arm itself with its own, national, version of World War II. There just won't be any space left for Russian spiritual bonds.

Moscow wanted to fight for the "Russian World"? They should be congratulated. They lost.

A New Novgorod

The warrior tales known as byliny are generally divided into several cycles. The cycle full of brave bogatyrs and feats of arms is known as the "Kyiv Cycle." The "Novgorod Cycle" describes daily life, merchants, and wealth. And if even the fearless warrior Ilya Muromets dies on the Kalka River, then the Novgorod merchant Sadko doesn't stand a chance against Moscow.

The Novgorod Republic existed from the 12th to the 15th centuries. It stretched from the White Sea to the Volga, from the Baltic Sea to the Urals. It survived the Mongol invasion. Novgorod was the site of the veche, which was a genuine medieval democracy in which all key posts were elected rather than appointed.

Capital formed the basis of the state, not the other way around. For a while that led to the rise of proto-oligarchs, who lobbied to place their subordinates in key posts. Nonetheless, Novgorod had none of the signature markings of absolutism: government was organized along a complex system of checks and balances between an elected monarch, archbishop, military and civil officials. The veche decided all questions of war and peace, approved laws, set taxes and selected the prince.

Novgorod was a true commercial "window on Europe" long before the appearance of Peter I. It isn't difficult to picture the emergence of a fourth East Slavic identity alongside modern-day Ukraine, Belarus and Russia. If not for Moscow.

In the 15th century, the Novgorod veche turned to Kyiv rather than Muscovy for confirmation of their new archbishop. Ivan III then accused the Novgorodians of treachery, defeated their troops in the Battle of Shelon in 1471 and seized control of the city.

Over the next seven years, Muscovy destroyed Novgorod's independence. The conquerors took over all judicial functions and parts of Novgorod's lands were transferred to Muscovy. In 1478, part of Novgorod's elite declared Ivan III as lord of the city, thus providing the pretext for a new invasion. In that year, independent Novgorod fell.

The veche bell, the symbol of Novgorod's freedom, was taken to Muscovy. The veche was disbanded. Supporters of Novgorodian independence were exiled, sent to monasteries or murdered. The city was enfolded into the Muscovite kingdom. 90 years later, in 1570, Ivan the Terrible's suspicions of "pro-Polish" sentiments in the city served as the pretext for yet another attack on Novgorod. The massacre of Novgorod lasted for six weeks.

In Russian history texts, this is called "unification."

Novgorod disappeared. Today the city is a small regional center with no greater ambitions. No identity. Of its former greatness, only the ancient city walls remain.

Historical parallels are limited, but striking. An empire's appetites always grow. Any border area is at risk. Any change of alignment or orbit is perceived as a threat. Any claim of independence is a pretext for invasion. Closed systems can exploit the weaknesses of open ones. Some wars are lost forever.

Does any of this sound familiar?

The Fight for Gogol

The annexation of Crimea set in motion the emancipation of Ukraine.

The first stage of emancipation was purely political. Then came economics and mutual trade. Up next were questions of our shared history and symbology. And then, it came to the moral authorities: Russian citizens who considered their moral authority universal suddenly learned that it was limited by their citizenship.

But the dispute over Gogol's legacy remains unresolved.

The thing that distinguishes Gogol from other Ukrainian writers is his target audience. Gogol wrote primarily for the imperial reader. In particular, readers from the "titular nation" — Russians. And he wrote not just for them but, and this is even more relevant, about them.

There is a rule in comedy about who's allowed to tell a joke. Only a Jew can tell jokes about Jews. Only an Armenian can mock Armenians. Break this rule and you risk being accused of bias and your joke becomes offensive.

In the years after the Soviet collapse, this rule was scrupulously followed. There was a popular comedy competition aired on television called KVN or Club of the Merry and Quick-Witted. On KVN, only the team from the Caucasus could tell jokes about people from the Caucasus. Only Khazaks and Uzbeks could tell jokes about Central Asian migrants. Each team would try to expand the range of their "geographical humor" by recruiting representatives of various national minorities to join the team. That way they could avoid accusations of bias.

And this fact explains why Russia will hold onto Gogol until the bitter end.

It's not only because he is a widely-recognized literary classic. Not only because he discussed the Russian aspects of his identity in his private letters. Not only because he is the token migrant who made his way into imperial literature. Gogol is important not just because of his friendships with Pushkin and Zhukovsky, or his choice to reside in the imperial capital or his literary fame. His tone also matters.

Gogol's *Inspector General* and *Dead Souls* are not so much realist works as satire. And the satire is scathing. It mocks and scolds. Gogol may love his characters, but he is merciless toward them. This should come as no surprise if we consider the fact that he saw literature as a way to change the world and the people in it.

The silent pause at the end of *Inspector General*, which Gogol intended to last for several minutes on the stage, is an attempt to place a mirror before the theater audience in which they were to recognize themselves in the character and then, horrified, change themselves. He envisioned *Dead Souls* as a trilogy in which the main characters would pass through a series of purifying trials, which would lead to their rebirth. But the reader refused to change in synchrony with the literary characters, so the second novel in the series went into the oven.

Gogol is a brutal satirist and his Petersburg works harshly ridicule Russian reality.

And so how could Russians acknowledge him as a Ukrainian writer? How could they even read his works in Russia?

Calling him a Ukrainian writer would destroy the legitimacy of his mockery. It turns out that he wasn't a Russian author calling out the failures of his own country, but the representative of another, now hostile, culture, who was mocking them. If you give Gogol to Ukraine, it turns out that Russia has been reading a merciless satire of its culture written by an outside observer for the last 150 years. It turns out that a foreigner has been telling jokes about Russia, to Russians, this whole time.

And that is entirely unacceptable.

Ukrainian Lessons

Ukraine followed the Russian protest movement much more closely in 2011 than they do today.

When Yanukovich was reigning in Kyiv and the Party of Regions had locked Ukraine up into itself, then the large-scale protests in Moscow in 2011 seemed like something new and exciting. Today the Ukrainian media pays far less attention to Russian protest activity. This should come as no surprise.

It's hard to believe in the possibility of a Russian Maidan. The Kremlin has spent way too much time constructing its power vertical to allow anyone to challenge its monopoly on power. Moscow doesn't have to consider the opinion of the West, so they have no need to limit their use of force. Putin feels like a king — the king Yanukovych longed to be but couldn't manage.

On Kyiv's Maidan, each side steadily raised the stakes. When the government utilized violence, the street responded with even greater mobilization. Moreover, Yanukovych was a surprisingly successful irritant. He managed to unite all levels of Ukrainian society against him: people of different ages, different professions, different regions. The Maidan was motley, multilingual, and multiregional. That was its strength and led it to victory.

The Russian situation is fundamentally different.

The usurpation of power in Russia is a product of the social contract: freedom for sausage. This contract dates back to the early 2000s, when Putin was just starting to build his regime under the pretext of restoring order. It wasn't difficult. Rising oil prices gave Moscow the resources to replace abstract benefits with more tangible ones.

A lot has changed in the last 20 years. Oil is cheaper. Sanctions are stronger. And now Russia's citizens themselves have become the oil of the state. But you can't eliminate inertia: Russian propaganda has managed to convince its citizens that the regime and the state are the same thing. They've successfully convinced the majority of the country that a collapse of the Putin regime would mean a collapse of the state. And so, the protestors in the capital are isolated.

Their protest was first and foremost a battle for complexity. Their demonstrations are a fight for the right to be heard. But if they ever want to go beyond their narrow frame, the Russian protest movement is going to have to reach the masses. Those same masses who are focused on "security" and "survival." Without them, protest will remain a niche activity for the elite.

Do you remember Maslow's hierarchy? The American psychologist divided human needs into five levels. The base level is physical survival. After that comes safety. Then social needs. The fourth level is self-esteem and respect and the top of the pyramid represents the need for self-actualization and self-expression. The concept is more than 70 years old, but it hasn't lost its relevance.

Consider for instance, why protest in Russia remains limited to a sliver of urban elites. Hint: because protest belongs to the fourth level of the pyramid. The people who take to the streets are demanding that the government respect their opinions. In this way, they are no different from the 2011 protests. But after 2011, after getting a black eye in the capital, the authorities turned to the sticks for their base of support. They have turned to those who have no choice but to base their lives on the values of security and survival due to the structure of Russian reality.

The Kremlin has convinced people that only the current regime can provide security. They've convinced them that anyone who protests the regime is a threat to their safety and survival. And so the Russian masses remain uninterested in the agenda of the urban rebels, who seem so alien to them both aesthetically and ethically.

Of course, plenty of other variables could be added to this simplified equation. For example, the effectiveness of Russian state propaganda. The loyalty of the security apparatus. The unanimity of the State Duma. And, of course, the fact that the Russian opposition doesn't offer any vision of a better future.

In Ukraine, the protest movement did have that vision. The Maidan had a civilizational dimension which counterposed pro-Soviet discourse with pro-European attitudes. In contrast, the Russian liberal doesn't offer either a vision of the glorious past or a clear image of the bright future. They can hardly offer up nostalgia for the '90s: that definitely won't appeal to hearts and minds. And in any conversation about the future, the Russian liberal is doomed to come up against the question of "whose is Crimea?"

It is difficult for people in the Russian "hinterland" to find common ground with the Russian elites in the capitals. They live in different realities. They have different emotional responses. The demands of the capitalist protesting in Moscow will inevitably sound like trivial luxuries to his countrymen who are fighting for survival, living at the bottom of Maslow's hierarchy.

Ukrainians can certainly understand that division. You can find the same thing in our country.

Opinion polls occasionally reveal the abyss between our values. One person will prioritize national sovereignty, the struggle for identity and moving away from the "Russian World." Another is more concerned with survival, the contents of the refrigerator, and the figures in the utility bills. The people in the first group are discussing complex categories at the upper levels of the pyramid of values. People in the second group have no choice but to focus on problems of daily life and stare in bewilderment at the person calling for "national dignity."

Those two groups met on the Maidan. Yanukovych's regime didn't collapse solely because they traded away national interests, served the Kremlin and usurped power. It also collapsed because it could no longer offer a convincing guarantee that tomorrow would be better than yesterday for the regular person. They could no longer offer security and stability as part of their base package. Even in the southern and eastern parts of the country, Yanukovych's support had grown shaky and few people were ready to rise to his defense. He had managed to destroy his legitimacy in the eyes of a broad cross-section of the country, which is why he lost power.

The Russian protestors may be flattered by comparisons to the 19th century Decembrist uprising, but it programs them for failure. They will only win when the protests include people from more than one social class. When, in the triangle between the capital cities, the hinterlands and the regime, it is the regime which becomes the third wheel. Yanukovych never did grasp that.

But you can be sure the Kremlin learned from his mistakes.

Putin's Ugly Swans

It's no coincidence that the Russian protest movement has started to break down along generational lines.

The "generation of children" is taking to the streets. They were born during Putin's rule. They grew up during the period of "rising from our knees." The authorities are outraged, threaten to limit social media, see conspiracies everywhere and hint at consequences. No surprise there. When children reject what their parents have built, it feels like a slap in the face.

The Russian authorities successfully made a deal with the generation of parents back in the 00s, when they offered them the social contract. The parents agreed to give up their rights and freedoms in exchange for stability and rising incomes. If anyone seemed hesitant, the Kremlin could hold up the specter of the 1990s as a warning of what to expect from democracy and glasnost.

That comparison doesn't work well with today's adolescents. They were born in the 90s. It's hard to scare someone with a word that doesn't hold any associations for them. What they see is a country steadily tightening the screws. The Russian government is aging along with its president, each year becoming less flexible and able to adapt. It is also becoming more and more anti-youth.

These young people have spent their entire conscious lives in a post-Crimea reality. The ruble has lost value. Athletes have been caught doping. A moribund patriotism pours from their screens.

Their teachers helped falsify elections. Their parents hypocritically held their tongues.

All those years their country was caught in one crime after another. Hypocrisy was the norm. The social pact their parents had agreed to now caught up with the youth in the form of state propaganda and denunciations, censorship and a lack of social mobility. The regime might be confident that they were holding up their end of the deal, but a different generation agreed to it.

And now the official mouthpieces assure the public that someone else is pulling the strings and "using" the children. This is an idiotic reaction. For young people, going out onto the streets is a way of demonstrating their independence, a declaration of their right to be heard. Denial of that independence ("you're not independent, you're being used") just pour gas on the fire.

The only thing the Kremlin has to offer the new generation is an image of the past. An image of "greatness" from old Soviet caches, modeled on imperialist templates or an image of the "wild '90s" as the antithesis of stability. The Russian government has no image of the future, because it's not a relevant category for them. They are trying to revive an imperial corpse and can't understand why the young aren't thrilled.

This generation grew up in a stratified society of clear haves and have-nots. The social heights were reserved for the fortunate few, who reveled in the ostentatious luxury of those who had found a place in the sun. Demands for justice would not be satisfied, including for social justice.

They recently learned that Putin could stay in office until 2036. By that time, people born the year he took office will be pushing 40. A beautiful, walled-in reality, where time itself works against you.

Now the Russian authorities are trying to find evidence of Western intrigue in the protest movement. Of course. Their attempt to murder Navalny with chemical weapons shows how their attitude toward him has changed. He is no longer "our rebel." Now he's an "agent of influence" and a "traitor." The Kremlin now interprets any protest rally under his banner not as evidence of home-grown outrage, but as imported instability. It's has gone from a police matter to a military one.

And the generation of "parents" are the most pathetic. They exchanged their freedom for a full refrigerator twenty years ago. It turns out, it wasn't just their freedom, but the freedom of the next generation as well. And now they are diligently looking for the people who forced their children to protest. Well, I have good news for them.

They can just look in the mirror.

A Look into the Abyss

A regime will always probe the limits of what's possible.

Especially hybrid regimes. They evolve, traveling the full path from unstable democracy to consolidated authoritarianism. Each new twist in the path tests the boundaries between the "acceptable" and "impermissible."

We can see this with Russia. For twenty years now, Russia has been rolling back the outcomes of its own Thaw in the 1990s. The regime intermittently probes its surroundings for strength and durability. It invades. Redraws borders. Kills its political opponents. Eliminates any stirrings of dissent.

This evolution is applauded by people who can't recognize any power but authoritarian power. The people who aren't prepared to deal with the reincarnation of the Soviet Union can emigrate. Most amusing, though, are the people who make every possible effort to justify and explain what is happening. They can't bring themselves to call things by their proper names. Like the frog in a pot of boiling water, they justify the rising temperature claiming, "it's the same everywhere."

They live in a deviant state with islands of normalcy. Yet they try to convince themselves and everyone else that Russia is a normal state with islands of deviancy.

It's probably a defense mechanism. An attempt to convince themselves that the reality around them is just another imperfect variant of "normal." It's easy to understand them: if they take off their blinders, they'll have to acknowledge what they don't want to see.

They would have to say it all out loud: Russia starts wars. Commits war crimes. Shoots down passenger jets. They would have to admit that their homeland is a terrorist state. A state that uses chemical weapons. A state that physically eliminates inconvenient people who criticize the regime.

That's not going to appeal to the average person. He would have admit that his country isn't a successor to the winners of World War II, but to the losers. And so, he desperately tries to convince himself that the annexation of Crimea and the war in the Donbas are just insignificant historical twists that are insignificant on a global scale, and will be resolved sooner or later.

But there's the rub: this isn't an insignificant twist. And it's not going away by itself—someone will have to make it go away. Because, as I said at the start, a regime is always probing the limits of the possible. If it doesn't encounter resistance, it goes further. Like a corkscrew, screwing in deeper and deeper with each new iteration.

Even total acquiescence to the regime's excesses won't ensure that you don't fall into disfavor. Alexei Navalny accepted the annexation of Crimea as a fait accompli and compared Crimea to a sandwich which can't be passed back and forth. He supported the war in Georgia. He fed the imperialist revanche. But in the end, in the next twist of its evolution, the regime decided to test the new limits of the possible on Alexei Navaly himself.

Most likely, the average Russian is just worried about the domino theory. First you say the regime has usurped power. After that, you acknowledge the reality of political reprisals. And then you start to notice the military invasions and interventions. Next you find yourself saying that Crimea is not Russia. And then finally you will have to admit that Russia is a huge, largely uninhabited country, that will start to fall apart as soon as the central authority begins to weaken.

You would have to admit that the Russian economy is a simulacrum existing only so long as oil and gas prices prop up government budgets. That when the situation changes, the economy will evaporate. Because in this system, everything that isn't oil is still fed by the pipelines.

You would have to say it out loud: the Russian state doesn't exist for its citizens. That it's highest value is not the citizen, but state greatness. That freedom is possibly only within the sharply limited outlines defined by the leadership.

None of this matches the average Russian's accustomed view of reality. And so, she'll keep trying not to see reality. She'll continue to declare that "everyone does it." Continue calling deviations normal. And she'll justify herself by saying that if you gaze for long into an abyss, the abyss gazes also into you.

The only problem is that the abyss is going to start peering into her sooner or later in any case. No matter how hard she tries not to look.

The Kremlin's Horcruxes

J.K. Rowling has given the world new words. "Horcruxes," for instance, are magic objects that grant immortality to users of the dark arts. In the world of Harry Potter, each horcrux contains a part of its creator's soul. So long as the horcruxes remain intact, their creator is invulnerable.

Good literature is characterized by the fact that its images take on a life of their own. Any politician dreaming of political immortality constructs his own horcruxes.

Putin has several.

His first Horcrux was the victory over the separatism that characterized the 1990s. The Second Chechen War became a de facto election campaign, in the absence of an actual one. The "strong hand" began to string the country along "the vertical of power."

At the start of Putin's rule, pacification of the rebellious republic was followed by the complete elimination of gubernatorial elections, the expulsion of regional powerbrokers from the Federation Council and finally the elimination of the "Federation" itself in favor of a hyper-centralized system. The fight against centrifugal forces served to legitimize Putin's first term as president. It was the prime answer for "why him?"

The second Horcrux was improved living standards. Petrodollars created the foundation for a new social contract. Rights and freedoms were exchanged for higher salaries and mortgages, car loans and beach vacations to Egypt. For the first time in decades, Russian citizens plunged into consumerism, living a lifestyle they'd only seen on TV.

Consumerism made people apolitical. The price of oil increased and its splatters flew around the country. For the first time in a long time, the Russian government was associated with full refrigerators and closets. Consumerism gave birth to loyalty, tomorrow looked more promising and planning for the future came back into the fashion. Putin's legitimacy in his second term was built on this fact. The second Horcrux was created.

And that led to the "castling" move where Dmitry Medvedev and Putin swapped places temporarily. Medvedev's rule wasn't based on his merits, but on support from the central figure, i.e. Putin. For the next four years, people argued about where Medvedev ended and Putin began. In 2012, those arguments were shelved — Putin returned to the presidency.

The Olympics could have been the third Horcrux. Singlehandedly held and won in Russia. Russia was chairing the G8 and selling oil at $100 a barrel. Russia created the Customs Union and mastered European business. None of it was enough for the Kremlin. Putin decided that Crimea would be his new Horcrux.

Appealing phrases such as "Holy Korsun," the "Russian Mecca," "polite people" and "the glory of Russian arms" served as an attractive facade to coverover the ugliness of the war in the Donbas and the battle against diversity of opinion, both of which the average Russian preferred not to notice. The imperialist dream was too powerful a narcotic. Paranoid imagery again became dominant: the besieged fortress, close ranks, the enemy is at the gates.

Each of these Horcruxes serves as a guarantee of survival for its creator. This is why the Kremlin won't risk calling out Ramzan Kadyrov, who does whatever he wants in Chechnya and beyond.

This is why Moscow locks up anyone who states that Crimea is Ukraine. This is why the president blames low salaries on purely local mismanagement. Each of these three instances carries of risk of destroying those points of legitimacy that keep Vladimir Putin in power.

And the destruction of the Horcruxes would mean death for their creator.

Russia Down the Rabbit Hole

When the first Ukrainian politician first sets foot back in Ukrainian Crimea, what will he say? Picture for yourself the airport, the plane. They roll out the stairs. What will he say on the tarmac? Something deep and meaningful?

More like, "We'll bring bread."

That's all he'll need to say. Because a Russia that loses Crimea, will be a country running short on both food and security.

The return of Crimea is both easier and more difficult than the return of the Donbas. Easier because the peninsula is not soaked in blood—the blood that sacralizes a conflict. There aren't family photos draped in mourning on the shelves. There is no generation growing up whose fathers died in the trenches.

It will be harder because Russia will hold onto Crimea until the bitter end. It probably won't be possible to actually discuss the fate of the peninsula until large global upheavals have taken place.

If those upheavals result in a collapse of Russia's economy and the crisis spirals out of control, a situation could emerge in which the Russian elites become eager to normalize relations with the West just to salvage whatever they can. Then they would agree to return to the 2013 status quo and just forget 2014 and everything that followed.

And so, the only thing the Ukrainian politician arriving in a returned Crimea would need to say is the sacramental: "We will bring you bread." If that phrase isn't relevant, he won't be coming back to Crimea.

No one can predict Russia's future.

For instance, there is no longer a Russian opposition. It was destroyed and replaced by dissidents. Dissidents don't fight for power—they just try not to join in the chorus. They try to keep their hands clean and avoid signing collective letters in support of the government's actions. They just try to survive in a country that goes against everything they believe in. The dissident doesn't fight the system, he just tries to avoid interacting with it. Dissidence is a form of internal emigration chosen when actual emigration is either not desired or not possible.

There is also no longer a functioning media system in Russia. The large outlets became propaganda outlets back in the 2000s. Independent outlets have been bought out or shut down. A small liberal reserve of dissent doesn't impact anything. Western social media networks have become the only remaining islands of resistance, and so the Russian government will now go to war against Youtube and Facebook. The Russian train is in the station and there's no question about which way its headed.

We can debate about exactly what set Moscow on this path. Maybe it was the rising oil prices at the start of the 2000s that untied the Kremlin's hands. Or the first Maidan, when Russian authorities started worrying about a Western invasion. There's the fate of Muammar Gaddafi, which persuaded the Kremlin they should never make concessions to Washington. And the 2008 invasion of Georgia, which demonstrated Europe's weakness.

Maybe it was the second Maidan, which the Kremlin took as a declaration of war. Or the occupation of Crimea which cut off Russia's path to the West. Or the sanctions, which Russia interpreted as the start of a siege. The fact is that none of those nuances matter anymore. What matters now is what comes next. And we have no reason to expect any major changes in direction.

At some point in the life of any country, an escalator effect can take place in which it is no longer possible to remain in place. The state will either move up and evolve, or move down and degrade. Something like that happened in 2014, when the Russian invasion forced the Ukrainian government to make significant-changes.

These changes took place against the wishes of the elites and against the will of the oligarchs. Nonetheless they were unavoidable, because without them, it was impossible to imagine the survival of an independent Ukrainian state. Kyiv was forced to become part of the "collective West," because Moscow had cut off their path to the East.

Since then, Ukraine has stayed on the up escalator. Sure, the authorities relapse occasionally and head back in the opposite direction. Still, for now, the logic of events is forcing the country to change. Maybe more slowly than it could. Maybe less enthusiastically than we'd like. But even though Kyiv is taking a meandering path, the trajectory is clear. It's easy enough to see if you compare our current priorities with the pre-war period.

Meanwhile, Russia continues its journey on the down escalator. The authorities are purging dissent. Thought crimes earn prison terms. Any form of protest has been declared a form of foreign intervention and each new round of legislative action increases the fines and prison sentences.

It's not difficult to imagine what Ukrainian success could look like. We'll become just another Eastern European country. One with uniformly enforced laws and reformed institutions. Of course, the power of inertia isn't going anywhere. There will still be plenty of backward-looking thinking. But it will still be a country much closer to the average European mentality than neighboring Belarus.

It's much harder to imagine Russia's future. The depths of its degradation could exceed even the boldest of forecasts. No one knows how this journey ends. Or what Russian citizens will accept as "normal" ten years from now.

Some inflection points change everything.

The Loneliness of Victory Day

The comedy show KVN could call itself "international" with no exaggeration.

Each season teams from various countries would come together. Young people from Ukraine, the Caucasus, Central Asia and the Baltic countries would compete for prizes. KVN reflected the immediate post-Soviet reality, when participants had more shared experiences than differences and the topics for jokes didn't require translation or additional context.

Actually, the show can still play the role of social mirror. Now it reflects the post-Soviet drift that took place before our eyes. The Club's geography gradually shrank until it fit neatly within the borders of Russia itself. Now it's a program where Russians compete against Russians. There are occasionally some token foreigners in the mix, but it's former "internationalism" has faded into oblivion.

By all accounts, Russia's May 9th "Victory day" celebrations will be next.

Every country has a day on which they celebrate the agency of the people. A holiday for citizens to declare, "we did it." Bastille Day tells the story of how the French got rid of their king. Independence Day in the US celebrates how Americans gained their independence from the English. May 9th in Russia makes similar claims — but there is one "but."

The Russian holiday celebrates the victory of the government. It is statism embodied, the concept that not only is nothing "against the state" permitted — neither is anything "outside the state." The governmental power vertical is the alpha and omega of everything. Any activity receives the right to exist only after official approval. Any independent expression of individual agency is viewed as a threat. It will be either co-opted or eliminated.

That's exactly what happened with May 9th in Russia. It is no longer a day to celebrate the accomplishments of the people, but a day to celebrate the state. The ultimate justification of its entire existence. May 9th and the victory over fascism is the heaviest weight on the moral-ethical scales that outweighs anything that happened before May 9th and everything that has happened since. May 9th can be used to justify repressions, deportations, imprisonment, executions and massacres. It provides the universal refutation. Any attempt to discuss the brutality of the Soviet regime will come up against this argument which puts an end to any further attempts at reflection.

May 9th has become a key source of legitimacy for the state—far too key for the Russian government to relinquish control of it. It should come as no surprise that in recent decades the state has fought anyone who tried to challenge their monopoly on the story.

Here's the thing: in the Soviet-Russian tradition there have been two approaches to commemorating this date.

The first was the official, state celebrations. Flags, parades, portraits of military leaders, big stars displayed on epaulettes. According to this style of commemoration, the war was won by the government, the leadership and the generals. Big numbers. Massives scale. The power vertical and the system.

The second approach is the exact opposite. It is intimate and personal, focused on individual experiences. The war writing known as "lieutenant's prose" falls into this bucket as do diaries and personal stories that had no place for Stalin or Zhukov, but plenty of space for grandmothers and grandfathers.

The state always fought the second approach. It made every effort co-opt and nationalize it. Yury Bondarev softened the ending of his novel, *The Battalions Are Asking for Fire,* and was rewarded with literary fame. Director Andrei Smirnov shot dozens of inspiring propaganda films in exchange for the lyrical *Belarus Station.* The government clung tightly to its interpretation of the events of May 9th—it certainly wasn't going to allow anyone to challenge the primary justification of its existence.

The same fate befell the "Immortal Regiment" movement. It began in 2012 as an alternative to the official pathos. Opposition station TV-2 came up with the idea and encouraged people to replace the usual banners and slogans with portraits of their loved ones who had died in the war. Three years later, the Russian state revoked their broadcasting license and took over the "Immortal Regiment."

The Kremlin does not recognize the right to anything private. Greatness can exist only within the power vertical. If you want to feel powerful, turn to the state. In exchange for your loyalty, you will be allowed to stand under the umbrella of its might.

Of course, this approach dooms Russia to loneliness. Russian Victory Day is following in the footsteps of KVN. Less and less "internationalism." More and more isolation. Not a surprise.

Moscow has turned May 9th into a political loyalty test. Swear fealty to the state and we'll describe your contribution to the victory over Germany. We'll inscribe you in the list of the winners.

As a consequence, Russia's neighbors increasingly seek out their own language to describe the events of the Second World War. All because the Kremlin sells its version as part of a package deal. A deal that has less to do with the past than it does with the present and the future. Their deal includes all the Soviet baggage of "brotherly peoples," "we can do it again" (i.e. march on Berlin), and the mentality of the "besieged fortress." In Moscow's version, they hold the monopoly on victory. The current inhabitants of the Kremlin have declared themselves the direct successors to the previous inhabitants, which passes the mantle of victory directly to them.

Moscow has been turning its version of the "Great Patriotic War" into a state religion for decades now. This state religion has its own rites, its own host of apostles and saints, its own pantheon of sinners and demons. Any deviation from the official version is heresy and will be punished by excommunication.

Meanwhile, the Western rituals to mark World War II are seen as an alternative sect, a sort of Catholicism in contrast to Moscow's Orthodoxy. The boundaries between the two are clearly outlied and any crossing of the lines is seen as encroachment.

Moscow perceives the "Reform movement" of its closest neighbors as apostasy, a sort of "Uniate" church in which the rites may be Eastern, but the self-awareness is Western. And of course, anything that was once "ours" and chooses to become "other" is always more painful than that which was never "ours" to begin with. This fact explains why Moscow regularly addresses Kyiv in terms they would never use toward Paris or London.

And if Moscow doesn't like the fact that fewer and fewer true believers attend its annual communion ritual, it has only itself to blame.

People and World War II

There's an Imperial War Museum in London. The first floor is World War I. The second floor World War II. Then comes peace and security after 1945, including the Cold War. The top floor is dedicated to individual heroes.

The First World War gallery matches our normal expectations for a museum exhibit, with a detailed chronology, displays dedicated to the largest battles, descriptions of the different military branches, an exhibit of complex methods for killing other humans.

Guns, tanks, ships, planes, battles, statistics. Everything you would expect to see based on our own museums at home. The logic of large numbers and global processes. The only difference is that it's more interactive and engaging.

As you head up to the second floor, you expect more of the same. Particularly because Britain could certainly claim to have "won" both wars. The country didn't fall apart like the Austro-Hungarian Empire. It didn't collapse into revolutionary chaos like the Russian Empire or the Kaiser's Germany. It was never occupied — unlike most of the European continent.

Britain did not put the island's population through the meat grinder of concentration camps. It didn't go mad for far-right or far-left rhetoric. It fought when it was outnumbered and when it's opponents were outnumbered. London has every right to a linear description of the Second World War. An exhibit similar to the one on the first floor: state, diplomacy, military-industrial complex.

But they did the exact opposite.

Their exhibit on the largest war of the 20th century begins with a model of an ordinary home. This was the home of the Allpress family: head of household William, a train driver; his wife Alice, a homemaker; and their ten children. Two of their sons fought at the front: one in the air force and the other in the infantry, from Dunkirk to Normandy. Two of the daughters served in the Auxiliary Fire Service, watching for fires and extinguishing

German incendiary devices. Another continued to lead her private life and worked in a factory.

There is an interactive model of the house and a few feet away a reconstruction of their bomb shelter, built according to government-approved standards. Inside the bomb shelter, you can hear the sounds of an air raid, sounds familiar to any Londoner who lived through the war.

You pass through reconstructions of the rooms of their house. In the kitchen, you'll find typical groceries of the time. In the bedrooms, there are gas masks, clothes and linens. Historic posters hanging in the hallway urge citizens to conserve food and electricity.

The history of the Second World War is told through the history of just one British family. In essence, the museum visitor lives through all six years of losses and victories alongside this one average family from the outskirts of London. Honestly, it's extremely powerful.

In Ukraine, we're still figuring out how to talk about World War II. Ukrainians wore the uniforms of various armies. Many lived under multiple different governments during that period. They fought side-by-side and against each other. Sometimes the winners turned out to be the losers. And sometimes the losers won in the end. Unlike the British, we don't have the luxury of a linear perspective on those years. That war put our lands through a meatgrinder. And the people along with the land.

Maybe the fate of the "little man" could become the universal denominator that reconciles the range of numerators. Everyone had different victories and they didn't always belong to the people who achieved them. But the struggles were somewhat the same for everyone.

Who knows, maybe someday we'll see a Ukrainian World War II memorial in which the stories from different regions could be gathered under a single roof. And it would turn out that the experience of an engineer from Donetsk, a peasant from Kherson, a Crimean Tatar farmer, a priest from Lviv and a person from Uzhgorod are not so different as we've imagined.

Monumentalism is convenient for empires. Individual biographies are swallowed up in the monumental, the global squeezes out the private. But if you want to understand what people lived through, you have to look at the details.

The things we all have in common.

Viral Diplomacy

There are two ways to unite.

The first is on the basis of shared values. This is how the European Union is organized. 27 nations, many of whom fought each other not so long ago. They formed a common market and the Schengen zone and shared governing bodies. They have agreed to limits on their national sovereignty in favor of shared sovereignty.

But geography won't get you in. Or at least, geography isn't enough. Entry requires that you demonstrate a commitment to shared values. Democracy, human rights, and a willingness to play by the same rules. A European address isn't enough to make you part of the "collective West." You have to actually *be* the West, meeting the ethical *and* economic criteria. This is why we refer to countries far from Europe as part of the collective West. Australia, for instance.

The other main way to unite is by facing a common foe. A global threat can erase the differences between rivals and make them allies in the battle against a new challenge. World War II is one example—the threat of the Third Reich tossed the USSR and US into a shared trench. It should come as no surprise that Russia is drawn to repeating that experience.

After the September 11 attacks, Russia offered its assistance to the US. A logistics hub was established in the city of Ulyanovsk to support the transit of US soldiers to Afghanistan. American bases were established in Central Asian countries. The battle against international terrorism united Moscow and Washington for a while.

Then the Velvet revolutions in Georgia and Ukraine reawakened Russian suspicions. Moscow began to suspect the West of encroaching on its "sphere of influence." Not long afterwards, we see Putin's 2007 Munich speech and the invasion of Georgia in 2008.

Even after that, Moscow continued trying to sell the West on an alliance against a "greater evil." In 2015, after the annexation of Crimea and the invasion of the Donbas, Putin tried to offer the US and Europe a deal on the floor of the UN General Assembly. The essence was pretty straightforward: "The Islamic State is a threat to the world and we must join forces against it." Putin declared Islamic terrorism a "new Hitler" and hinted that Russia was prepared to open a second front against it.

In that scenario, Ukraine is assigned a role similar to pre-1939 Finland. Before the Germans invaded the Soviet Union, the Soviets had already seized 11% of Finland's territory. World War II then overshadowed that aggression and those lands remained under the control of the Soviet Union after 1945. Moscow was undoubtedly expecting something similar in 2015, imagining that going into battle against a common enemy would lead to an indulgence regarding the occupation of Ukrainian territory.

The West ignored his proposal. First Barack Obama, and then Angela Merkel, declared that the greatest threats to the world were Ebola, Russia and ISIL. And both of them identified the Russian factor as a greater threat than terrorism. The message was loud and clear: we are not going to unite with you against a "greater threat" because you *are* the "greater threat."

The Kremlin tried playing the same card again during the pandemic. This time they offered a united front against Covid. The coronavirus was slamming every country without exception, vaccine makers couldn't keep up with demand, and Moscow began to push its "Sputnik V" vaccine to anyone who would take it. Pharmaceutical diplomacy. Medication as a pretext for conversation and dialogue.

Russia was counting on Covid-19 to outweigh Crimea and the Donbas. They believed the pandemic would force the West to turn the page on those events. They hoped that approval of the Russian vaccine would open the borders of the European Union to

Russians earlier than to people from countries without vaccines. That's not how it played out.

Moscow had gone to war against the West seven years earlier. There were too many broken dishes and too little trust left between them. The Kremlin had made the very image of Russia toxic and made people look for the "Russian trace" in domestic problems.

It's going to be hard for Moscow to find a new "Hitler" for Europe that would help it "make a [plea] deal" with the West. There's one basic rule of selling your allies on a battle against a common threat: don't become the greatest threat yourself.

Knockin' on Europe's Door

Peace with Russia is impossible. No matter how much people want it.

Europe wants peace. The same Europe that desperately wants to turn back the calendar to 2013, when they didn't have to wring their hands over sanctions, Crimea, the Donbas, or arguments about the North Stream pipeline. When they didn't need to spend money on the army or chip in for NATO.

Ukraine wants peace. The same Ukrainians who don't want to change their business models. The ones who go on tour in Russia. The ones who justify the decisions that benefit their wallets with the rhetoric of "fighting for peace."

The people in Russia's employ want peace, both the people officially on the payroll and the ones who take money under the table. The people who assured themselves that values and valuables always coincide. The ones who want to get back to their comfort zone, the one that permanently disappeared in 2014.

There's just one problem. Why do people think that Russia wants peace?

Eventually, every politician is held hostage by his own world view. Sooner or later, he starts to measure reality by his personal standards. This is why elections should function to rotate the elites. They should regularly transfer the levers of power to people who grasp the zeitgeist and the shifting demands of the electorate. Regular transitions of power can facilitate competence.

Any country with a regular transfer of power will change because the moods, hopes and demands of the people change. This is easy to see in Ukraine, where many people's preference for prosperity outcompetes their preference for sovereignty. But here's the thing: nothing changes in Russia. There is no transfer of power and there won't be anytime soon.

Vladimir Putin has been sitting in the Kremlin for more than two decades. He has become accustomed to the fact that governments, regimes, and structures change around him, but he remains. Public sentiment doesn't dictate his views; he lives in his own reality. A reality that has little in common with the reality of the average Russian.

Putin actually started his first term talking about a Europe united all the way from Lisbon to Vladivostok. Instead there was the Rose Revolution in Georgia and the first Maidan in Ukraine, his Munich speech and the repression of the Bolotnaya protests in Moscow. Now he is hostage to his own world view. A world in which the West constantly wages war again Russia—denying its "sphere of influence" and refusing to view Moscow as the capital of an empire. From Putin's perspective, it was the West who started this war: the West destroyed the USSR, the West seized the Baltic states, the West interfered in Georgia and Ukraine. And so Putin is just "restoring balance," "responding to events," and "hitting back."

Why would he want to end the war when he views compromise as defeat? Why would he want to restore a peace that doesn't feed his imperial fantasies?

So long as the Russian president doesn't change, Russian politics won't change. For Putin, contemporary history is just one long chess game in which he plans to restore the empire, defend Russia from the West and inscribe himself in the history books.

In every other country, economics can influence politics and public opinion shapes political rhetoric. That's not how it works in Russia. In fact, it's the opposite. The entire economy is just a piggy bank for the realization of one man's dream.

Ukraine's politics would change with a new president and new parliament. Europe's politics would change if the voters decide the threat from Moscow has been exaggerated. But we have no grounds to suppose that Russia will change.

Russia won't change so long as the same people remain in power—the people who believe in the "Dulles Doctrine" plans to destroy the Soviet Union and constantly quote conspiracy theories. The people who talk about preemptive nuclear strikes and claim that every protest is orchestrated from outside. The people who claim that strength is weakness, black is white, and the inevitable can be avoided.

Why would they want to return to the 2013 status quo when their birth trauma dates to 1991?

Resources for the Empire

"The largest separated nation." This is how Putin has described ethnic Russians who found themselves outside the borders of Russia in 1991. In doing so, he condemned his compatriots to loneliness.

Millions of ethnic Russians were left behind foreign borders following the collapse of the Soviet Union. Not only in Ukraine, but in all the former Soviet republics. And they suffered almost the same fate in all of those places.

In an ideal world, a diaspora becomes a conduit of soft power for the mother country. They become a power center that is fully integrated into their new homeland and serve as "ambassadors" for their native country. We can see this in the Ukrainian diaspora in Canada, the Armenians in France or the Jewish diaspora around the world. Nothing of the sort has happened with Russians abroad.

They didn't become "trendsetters." They didn't make plans for the future. They didn't lobby for their own interests—interests that wouldn't be perceived as hostile to their new homes. None of this is hard to explain.

The only role Moscow saw for the diaspora was the role of irredentists. Russian speakers abroad would serve as the pretext for "unification" within the boundaries of a new shared state. For 25 years, the Kremlin has done all it could to maintain this lever of influence.

It didn't take much. All they had to do was block the integration of Russians into the political culture of their places the lived. The very idea that Russians might align their interests with their new homelands, rather than with Moscow, was perceived as betrayal.

The Kremlin never wanted Russians to adapt to their new circumstances. On the contrary, they wanted ethnic Russians to be as isolated as possible. Then, for years, they could capitalize on their claims of defending the "persecuted and wretched." They couldn't even comprehend the idea that Russian-speakers might be patriotic Ukrainians. The very thought was terrifying. Moscow viewed Russian speakers as actual Russians who must be loyal to mother Russia. Anything else was a threat.

"Overseas Russians" were encouraged to view their nationality as granting rights without responsibilities. The Kremlin assigned them the role of a sort of "Baba Yaga," a threatening hag opposed to everything. Their role was limited to nostalgia and nothing more.

And so, Russian parties independent from the Kremlin never emerged in the post-Soviet states. The only groupings which did emerge were oriented toward the Kremlin and formed a disloyal "fifth column" within their new nations. They were just lobbyists for Russian financial interests and sales agents for imperialist superiority. Anything else was viewed as a threat by Moscow.

The Donbas demonstrates the consequences. That same Donbas which Moscow has now been "defending" for years. With Kremlin support, the entire region has been turned into a bridgehead whose only purpose is to create problems for Ukraine. The quality of life of the "Russians" in the occupied territories is irrelevant to Russia.

The Donbas has proven one simple thing: the Kremlin has assigned the role of "imperial compost" to its foreign compatriots. Their interests are secondary to the interests of the Russian leaders. Moscow isn't fighting for them, Moscow is using them to fight. Citizens exist for the empire. And it's never reciprocal.

The invasion of the Donbas also set another important process in motion. Moscow was certain the south and east of Ukraine would rush into its warm embrace. They were confident that every speaker of Russian would automatically support the "Russian World." This expectation was entirely wrong.

The very thing Moscow always feared finally happened following the invasion of Ukraine. Russian speakers have now fully integrated into Ukrainian society, freely choosing their new homeland over the old one. The Kremlin can no longer count on anyone lobbying for their interests: the new identity required the loss of the old one.

The next census is likely to offer plenty of surprises.

3 War

Not Political

I remember going to the Azov region in August 2016. One car, three passengers and a trunk stuffed so full we could have survived a sudden blizzard.

We arrived late one evening in the town of Melekino near Mariupol. We quickly got settled in someone's home and then went out to the beach at dusk. The sea was warm, the sand was still warm, we had wine and cheese. Our only worry was the approaching rain. Frequent thunder claps suggested a storm was moving in. At least, until we looked up. The sky was filled with stars without a cloud in sight. We weren't hearing thunder – it was artillery. A bit to our east.

You could feel the war in Melekino. The windows of abandoned resorts stared blankly out onto the streets. Sand was encroaching on the beach hotels. The little old ladies there didn't like cameras. The moment you took out a camera, they'd ask you to put it away. They said that as soon as someone starts taking pictures something happens. "And nothing has happened in a long time, let's keep it that away."

Melekino was sobering.

The war is never far away now. Just six hours away by train or ten by car. Our comfortable life here in Kyiv is only possible because it was halted there in the front line towns and villages whose names we learn from the military bulletins. The only reason we don't feel the war in the capital is the efforts of the people who experience every day here.

I remember my pervasive sense of disorientation in February of 2014. I distinctly remember that feeling – a sense that my normal world had turned upside down. Friends leaving Crimea would switch off their phones and then turn them back on once they reached mainland Ukraine. There was a thin green line of people in Ukrainian military uniforms separating mainland Ukraine and the peninsula.

I lost the ability to make plans a few years back. My planning horizon has shortened to six months. Even that is excessively optimistic. In 2014, I didn't try to see beyond the next week. And even so, my situation in Crimea was quite comfortable compared to what awaited my friends from Donetsk.

When I talk about my shortened planning horizon, people tell me I'm being neurotic. That it's a consequence of what I've been through. That it's a form of trauma which interferes with my ability to draw appropriate conclusions and assess risks. I'll probably agree with them. As soon as the war is over. But for now, it's a bit premature to say who has a better grasp of reality.

We're like survivors of a car crash who tell everyone they need to buckle up. Reminding them that seatbelts are not optional or "bonus." That wrinkled clothes aren't too high a price for personal safety. And we keep hearing the same response, "Stop trying to scare us."

I keep hearing "Oh, the Kremlin won't invade." They've already taken everything they can. They went as far as we let them. That going forward they'll fight completely differently and there's no reason to expect a repeat of 2014. It gives me déjà vu. That's exactly what I kept hearing before the annexation of Crimea. "There's no reason." "They won't dare." "The world order." I didn't just hear it—I said it myself. The next thing I knew, there were Russian flags flying over the Crimean parliament.

The war is still happening regardless of what you want. It is still happening even if you decide to fill in the trenches. It will still be here regardless of whether your favorite politician seems to remember it.

The only thing under your control is whether the politician does remember. Because the issue here is the political narrative which voters can influence, pollsters can measure and politicians must address. If the war doesn't exist for your political idol, it probably doesn't exist for you either. Just like it didn't exist for me before February 25th, 2014.

Now I can't get away from it. Neither can you, by the way. The war isn't going anywhere, it's not going to disappear or dissolve or fade into oblivion. No matter who we elect or who leads the country — it's still here. Just six hours by train. Or ten by car.

Not far at all.

Not the War We Imagined

This isn't at all how we imagined war. And when it started we weren't ready.

We didn't form our own version of what war is. It was forged by books and movies. Books and movies that we inherited from the Soviet Union. When we talk about war, occupation and abuses of the civilian population, we are picturing the classic Soviet films depicting the first half of the 20th century.

How do we imagine war? Blitzkrieg, massive battles with hundreds of thousands of soldiers, "everything for the front, everything for victory," air raids and partisans. How do we imagine occupation? Tanks, men in black uniforms, terror from the first scene to the last, mass shootings, torture.

In Soviet cinematography, there was one war and one war only: World War II. There was no room for nuance and no space for "compromise." For someone who was raised on those images, war is fought against the threat of extermination. If you lose, it will cost you your life. If you don't die in battle, then you will die later anyway in a concentration camp.

In that kind of war, the enemy is evil and incapable of compromise. Battle offers the only chance of survival. In this confrontation, the stakes are your life. If you lose, you die — so retreat isn't an option.

In reality, that kind of war is the exception, not the rule.

Most wars have much more utilitarian goals. Countries fight for spheres of influence and access to resources. Someone starts a war to maintain domestic political stability — or to destabilize someone else. There is no shortage of variations — it is actually rare for a conflict to include total genocide against the local population.

A key characteristic of "non-total war" is the fact that the average person always has the option not to participate. His personal survival is not directly tied to the outcome of the war, so he can afford to make his own assessments. There's nothing surprising in that approach.

In total war, your life is always at stake. Indifference is not an option when your very survival depends on the outcome. Defeat equals death — a price no one is willing to pay.

In any other kind of war, the stakes appear far less dramatic. The geopolitical calculations of invading Afghanistan means little to the average Soviet citizen. American pacifists couldn't understand why their compatriots were dying in Vietnam. British citizens had serious doubts about the necessity of fighting Argentina for the infinitely distant Falkland Islands.

In this sense, Ukraine is no exception. For all its brutality and amorality, the Russian invasion has little in common with World War II.

The Kremlin's goal is not the physical extermination of all the inhabitants of the conquered territories. Moscow will be perfectly satisfied to have Ukrainians agree that they are part of the "triune Russian people." They just have to accept the Russian version of history, swear allegiance to their "shared spiritual bonds," and renounce any claims to sovereignty.

The Kremlin's conditions look very simple. Admit that you're "Russian" and receive all that the empire has accumulated over the centuries of its existence. Deny your identity and you gain the right to Tchaikovsky, Pushkin, Lermontov and Tolstoy. We'll even preserve your national culture as folklore, with some colorful national costumes. And accept the Russian cult of the 17th century Pereiaslav Agreement, in which Ukraine supposedly freely offered up total subjugation to Moscow.

In that sense, the stakes of the current war turn out to be more about the upper levels of Maslow's hierarchy. It's not a war for physical survival, but for issues of identity and self actualization.

The average Ukrainian faced a difficult choice. On one side of the scales: a risk to his home comforts, increased government expenditures, general anxiety, and possible death following military mobilization. On the other side of the scales are the categories of independence, sovereignty, symbolic values and a national liberation struggle. The elements on the first side of the scales are entirely clear and tangible — they belong to the first two levels of the pyramid. The elements on the other side are more abstract — they belong to the upper levels. Of course, if a person hasn't reached those levels in personal life, they are unlikely to accept their significance unquestioningly.

As a result, while the average person can easily grasp the negative consequences of war, the benefits of victory are far less clear. A bird in the hand may still be better than two in the bush — particularly when you can't quite make out those birds in the bush.

This is the key aspect. If public opinion dictates the political agenda, then the government will always focus on tactical, short term issues. Immediate priorities don't always align with strategic goals. The right decisions won't always be popular.

This is the key weakness of democracies vs. authoritarian regimes. The Russian leadership isn't dependent on voter sentiment. They can allow themselves to disregard other people's wishes and focus on their own. They don't have to be conservative in their choices of means or methods; their war against Ukraine can stretch into years and billions of dollars.

Meanwhile, each new Ukrainian government has to pass the same exams again and again. Tests for consistency and foresight. Common sense and responsibility. It's very tempting to give into short-term desires — thus tossing everything that could give the country a future into the dustbin of history.

Leaving the next generation to begin everything from scratch.

Territory is Secondary

Any Ukrainian politician will tell you that we "don't trade in territories."

Theoretically, that should be reassuring. The words should inspire confidence that Kyiv won't agree to a redrawing of our borders. That returning the blue and yellow flag to the occupied territories is still a priority.

In reality, those words aren't reassuring at all. Since the start of the hybrid war, Ukraine has ceased to be a hybrid state.

It's tempting to invent your past based on the present. Hindsight helps us to smooth the corners, level the roads, soften the contradictions. But here's the thing, pre-war Ukraine could boast of any number of things, but not genuine sovereignty.

Ukrainian independence was not achieved in 1991 due to our own efforts. Our national liberation movement had far less mass participation than those in Poland or Lithuania. Those countries actively tried to escape the Soviet prison to gain their independence. In contrast, Ukraine gained freedom just because the prison collapsed.

That could explain why the next 23 years were a period of hybrid independence. Because when we get something for free, we don't value it as much as what we win on our own. The country got stuck in some in-between state for the first two post-Soviet decades, trying to make sense of its own existence.

"Non-aligned." "Multi-vector Doctrine." "A bridge between Europe and Russia." The Ukrainian choice consisted of a refusal to choose. The decision to preserve its "borderland," in-between status. Its "hybridity," if you please.

And so 2014 became what 1991 should have been. The year of a victorious uprising. The year of the invasion. The year of the armed independence struggle.

It was actually Moscow who put an end to Ukraine's "multi-vectorality." Moscow forced the country to answer foundational questions. Moscow forced us to cut the Gordian knots and make decisions. The previous balance was violated, and that allowed Ukraine to finally Ukrainianize itself.

Sovereignty is our greatest acquisition of recent years.

Ukraine gained the right to determine its own future independently. To select history textbooks without submitting them to Russian politicians for approval. To ignore shouts from Moscow and disregard voices coming out of the Kremlin. To follow the classic path of any colony at the moment it separates from the imperial center. Ukraine set out on that path later than her neighbors to the west, but better late than never.

And when Ukrainian politicians claim that their priority is territorial integrity, that's worrisome.

Because the Russian invasion of the Donbas wasn't a war for territory. Moscow doesn't need Ukraine's eastern regions, it needs the whole former Soviet republic as a controlled, secondary, buffer state. The Kremlin's real goal is to hand the Donbas back to Kyiv as a Trojan horse to serve as a bridle for Ukrainian sovereignty. Then Kyiv's dejure control of the country would be balanced out by Moscow's de facto control through the Donbas.

If Ukraine genuinely decided to regain the Donbas, it could be achieved rather quickly. Just grant the region autonomy. Legalize the militants through amnesties and elections. Moscow would then hand control over the border to its proxies and retain influence over the entire region. And if the "borders" are a "priority," the politicians will report a "historic end to the stalemate."

Of course, they won't mention what it will cost us.

This isn't a war for territory, it's a war for sovereignty. Some people see the frontline as a bridgehead for the liberation of the Donbas. But as long as Russia continues to expand, it would be more accurate to describe it as a line of defense. It's purpose is to ensure that Kharkiv and Odesa don't meet the same fate as the "Luhansk People's Republic."

If Moscow ever sees an opportunity to exchange the occupied east for control over all of Ukraine, they won't hesitate. Particularly if the deal includes an end to sanctions, to their pariah status, to the label of "a threat to peace." If Kyiv's priority becomes the return of territory at any price, we will quickly find ourselves back in our hybrid past. Without Crimea, to be clear. We'll have our own political "Chernobyl," that Moscow will use to destroy any Ukrainian hopes for the future.

Sovereignty is more important than territory. It must serve as the control weight against which Kyiv calibrates every decision. It is sovereignty that Ukraine is fighting for. And Moscow has been attempting to eliminate it from the moment we gained our independence.

Ukraine has zero reason to give up the Donbas or Crimea. It also has zero reason to agree to a mechanical reintegration, if

Moscow demands that we hand over the future of our country in return.

The Price of Capitulation

It's common to compare Ukraine to Israel. The comparison goes that, like Jews, the Ukrainians have to establish their statehood with a powerful adversary right next door. Although it is appealing, the comparison is faulty.

In some ways, the creation of the state of Israel was easier. There were no close emotional ties between Israel and their neighbors. There was no question of their adversaries' intentions. The goal was physical survival.

Prime Minister Golda Meir expressed the entire logic of Israel's existence thus: "We intend to remain alive. Our neighbors want to see us dead. This is not a question that leaves much room for compromise." The Jews simply had no choice. They could win and build a successful state. Or they could lose and die.

This is probably the most significant difference between Ukraine and Israel. Moscow's goals are different from those of Israel's neighbors. Moscow doesn't want to wipe us from the face of the earth or throw Ukrainians into the sea. The Kremlin's minimum goal is to transform Ukraine into a protectorate, deny its right to self-determination and prove that it doesn't really exist. The maximal goal is to make Ukrainians admit that they're actually Russians.

So our main issue isn't physical survival, but identity. Plenty of people are willing to sacrifice that. After all, it's easy to sacrifice what you don't have. Particularly when you harbor the illusion that your life won't actually change much in case of defeat.

Some theoretical Ukrainian common man might comfort himself with the illusion that nothing terrible will happen to him personally. That if Ukraine loses, a ceasefire will take hold, the military obituaries will stop appearing and the military budget will return to its more modest pre-war levels. Investment will follow, the Russian markets will open up and our economic partnership will resume. Based on these illusions, our imaginary common man will flatly dismiss any and all objections, insisting that the "personal" is more important than the "collective."

Proponents of this approach don't grasp that identity and language are only part of the story. He doesn't realize that his prized economic well-being is also at stake. Ukraine is also fighting to leave behind the world of dysfunctional economies and rigid, ineffective political systems.

Russia could fake competence only due to high oil prices. It is actually high oil prices that form one of the two true "spiritual bonds" holding the country together. The nuclear arsenal is the other. Those are the two items that protect Russia from the centripetal forces of dissolution. The moment oil prices started to fall, we saw their attractive social reality start to crumble.

The Russian social contract looked pretty appealing in the 2000s: sacrifice your political freedoms in exchange for a higher standard of living. That ended when oil prices collapsed.

It quickly became clear that although the creature comforts disappeared, the lack of political freedoms remained. In fact, the Russian government announced a unilateral withdrawal from the old social contract. Now Russians were offered a different deal: give up political rights *and* a full refrigerator in exchange for making Russia "great." Of course, you can't directly feel that "greatness," or eat it or deposit it in your bank account.

And that intangible acquisition of a "great Russia" came along with the same old ineffective political model. The one that views doubt as rebellion. That makes foolish decisions in a patriotic fervor. Modern Russia is a country whose citizens bear costs that they haven't agreed to and can't object to. All because back in the 2000s, they voluntarily agreed to give up their political rights and make do with personal opinions at home, instead.

Ukraine is not just fighting for identity, language and history. Ukraine is fighting to change the rules of the game. This battle isn't only with an external aggressor, but also with our own ineffectiveness multiplied by corruption. The battle will be a long one, progress will be marked with setbacks, but while we may argue about the speed, the direction is no longer in question.

There are no alternatives to this path. If we capitulate to Russia, we won't gain a thriving society in exchange for our identity. Losing this fight would mean losing our chance at a comfortable existence. People in Russian protectorates don't live better than people in the capitals. In today's Russian Federation, internal discussions always come down to where to cut costs first. The answer is never Moscow.

A Russian victory would mean the destruction of Ukraine's future. The windows of opportunity will close. Our attempts to create a state that serves its citizens will fail. Russia doesn't have the money to make its conquered territories into showcases, so Kyiv's capitulation would mean not only a failure for the current generation, but the next generation as well.

Which is why Israel had it easier in some ways. They never had any illusions about what awaited them if they lost. We can't compare the two countries until Ukrainians shed their illusions as well.

Yugoslav Scenarios

Slobodan Milosevic was a forerunner to Vladimir Putin. The Serbs who were left outside the borders of Serbia in the break-up of Yugoslavia were no more than a resource to him. He used them to maintain influence over the former parts of Yugoslavia that were striving for independence.

Wars broke out in two of the new states: Bosnia and Croatia.

Bosnia and Herzegovina was populated by Muslim Bosniaks, Catholic Croatians and Orthodox Serbs. In 1992, Bosnia's Serbs, with support from Milosevic, declared the creation of the Republika Srpska in Bosnia, which bore a striking resemblance to the later DNR [Donetsk People's Republic]. Psychiatrist Radovan Karadžić became the political leader of this Bosnian breakaway state. Yugoslav general Ratko Mladić was the military leader. The government in Belgrade took essentially the same position as Moscow has with Ukraine: public diplomatic support and covert military support. Military equipment, ammunition and volunteers flowed across the Serbian border into the "unrecognized republic."

The meatgrinder lasted for almost four years and claimed more than 100,000 lives. It ended with a scenario not so different from what the Kremlin is imposing on Ukraine today. Under the Dayton Accords which ended the war, the West insisted on the preservation of the "Republika Srpska" as a distinct entity within Bosnia. Its representatives are guaranteed one third of the seats in the national parliament and the enclave received veto power over all decisions. The powers of the central government were curtailed in favor of regional structures.

As a result, modern-day Bosnia and Herzegovina enacts the fable of the swan, the crawfish and the pike: unable to compromise, unable to develop effectively. The governance structure has proven cumbersome and inefficient. Unfortunately, the fact that Milosevich has been dead for years now doesn't change the status quo. His creation, intended to allow him to hold onto Bosnia, lives on, despite the death of its author.

Ukraine should take a good look at Croatia's experience, too. War broke out in Croatia shortly after the collapse of Yugoslavia, too. In 1991, Croatian Serbs formed the "Serbian Krajina" within Croatia—yet another variant of the DNR. The enclave received the same support from Belgrade. However, the Croatians, unlike the Bosnians, didn't permit the rebel republic to be reintegrated into the government under someone else's rules.

There were certainly attempts. In January of 1995, Peter Galbraith, American ambassador to Croatia, proposed the Z-4 plan. The Z-4 plan would have granted autonomy to some of the rebellious areas and re-integrated others. Croatian president Franjo Tudjman found this plan unacceptable, although he officially promised to consider it—at some point.

Although negotiations took place, their primary purpose was distraction. The leaders in Zagreb waited for their moment, when Belgrade would begin drowning in its own problems. Four years later, that moment arrived.

In 1995, the Croatian army carried out two military operations: "Operation Flash" and "Operation Storm." Flash resulted in the return of the Serbian enclave of Western Slavonia to Croatian control. Storm brought the remainder of the "Serbian Krajina" under the control of the central government. There are still mixed interpretations of these events: in addition to the restoration of territorial integrity, it also resulted in numerous refugees and civilian casualties.

Ukraine is at a crossroads. One road leads to a repeat of the Bosnian scenario. The other, to the Croatian. If we take the first road, we lose the right to determine our own future. If we take the second road, we will live in an ongoing state of hybrid warfare with intermittent escalations. But who ever said that war could be any different?

A Different Point of View

"What are you getting all worked up about, he just has a different point of view. He just wants peace. You need to talk with him."

No, I really don't.

A long time ago, I believed in compromises. I believed that people behave rationally. Then the Russian army came to me in Crimea. Then they went to the Donbas and started shooting my illusions, a few at a time.

It turned out that the whole post-Soviet discussion wasn't about whether Ukraine would be neutral, pro-Russian or pre-Western. It was about whether Ukraine would exist at all. And neutrality was actually just an intermediary step to becoming "Russian."

"Russian" is in quotation marks for a reason. The Donbas has shown that you can dream of Russia but never actually receive Russia. After the occupation of Crimea, the average pro-Russian person tended to believe in the "Crimean scenario," in which a foreign army sheds relatively little blood to bring you your pension in rubles rather than hryvnia. But now that eastern Ukraine has been turned into a new killing ground, only an idiot or enemy agent can suggest compromise with Russia.

Only someone with no sense of self-preservation could dream of the "Russian World" after seeing what they've accomplished in Donetsk and Luhansk. Ukraine's surrender would not result in a return to the "Yanukovych era." Losing now would mean a return to the "Motorola era."

For 23 years we lived as a non-aligned border state. Year after year we reached agreements with Moscow and made compromises. The problem is that there is no compromise that will satisfy the Kremlin. They require a buffer, and have no interest in the lives of the people who form that buffer. The Donbas illustrates that fact very clearly.

History does offer some axioms that are as straightforward as math. Three is greater than two. Seven times seven is forty-nine. There's no point in trying to have a discussion with someone who denies it. Some ideas are toxic. Some people will never grow up. And chronological age isn't the issue.

People have a variety of motivations. One person may have grown tired of personal responsibility and wants someone else to lead with a strong hand. Someone else is nostalgic for their youth and good erections. Another person may believe in the "decadent West," or miss their status in the old bureaucracy. But there is no form of nostalgia which makes sense if it destroys the future.

I'm not talking about *Homo sovieticus*. I'm talking about people who want me to have a serious discussion with them. Who believe that their perspective has equal value. Who want to make their perspective a legitimate element of public discourse.

It doesn't matter what their motivations are. Maybe one person sees his task as defending the weak, forgetting that those "weak" are backed by one seventh of the world's land mass. Someone else may have served Russia's satellite territories for so long that they've cut off any other form of employment. Some of them are still collecting Russian money. And some people are just fools.

Discussion is not possible, no more than you would expect an oncologist to compromise with a charlatan. The oncologist's victory means survival. The charlatan's victory yields an obituary. Under the law, the person who believes the earth is flat is equal to the one who knows the earth revolves around the sun. But it wouldn't occur to anyone to put them on a talk show to discuss their differences. And no one is going to hire a flat-earther to teach school.

War severely narrows the field of what is permissible. Before Crimea and the Donbas, we could still discuss Ukraine's future. All those years when Moscow and Brussels were competing for Kyiv. Now there's no more room for discussion. Either you resist the aggressor, or you refuse to acknowledge that they are the aggressors. In which case it would be best to follow the example of propagandist Anatoly Wasserman and—

Get the hell out.

The Nostalgia of Scumbags

Today's pro-Soviets are far more dangerous than actual Soviets were. They don't even pretend to be decent human beings.

A Soviet citizen could genuinely believe that there was no mass repression in the 1930s. Or that the Katyn massacre was carried out by the Wehrmacht rather than Soviet execution teams. They could believe that punitive psychiatry was just Western slander. Or that the Communist Party was actually building a state of universal well-being.

I mean, what is it we want from the Soviet everyman? Pressed as he was between work and home, between the waits for basic household goods and constant food shortages? The informational iron curtain was extremely powerful—all alternate versions of reality were strictly cut off. The surrounding reality had been built before he was born and the propaganda system was finely honed before he arrived to question it. The average Soviet person knew no other reality. As soon as cracks appeared in the information embargo, the Soviet Union started coming apart at the seams.

Now a post-Soviet person longing for the USSR—that's a different matter entirely.

The new everyman is carrying around the baggage of the 1990s. The same '90s when the archives were opened. The first interviews with dissidents appeared. Information about the mass repressions, arrests, and murders became available. When no one could continue to doubt the scale of Soviet repression.

The post-Soviet person didn't even need to seek out information about the system built in the USSR. That information went mainstream in the 1990s, screaming from every screen and every headline. The repressions formed the main topic of election campaigns and a central part of the national agenda.

A Soviet person could defend the Soviet system out of ignorance. But the post-Soviet defender chooses to do so. The Soviet everyman could reject accusations against the regime because he didn't believe them. The post-Soviet person chooses to defend the indefensible.

The post-Soviet person can't claim ignorance. Can't claim that he doesn't have any information about the scale of repression. On the contrary, he does know, and hides behind an insidious "but." "But at least we had space travel." "But at least we had stability." "But everyone was afraid."

All those "but"s are just attempts to justify personal comfort despite the repression of others. He's convinced himself that his own life was quite comfortable in the previous reality and he's entirely prepared to offer up other people's lives to regain it. Cynicism has taken the place of naivety. Ignorance has been replaced by amorality.

The post-Soviet pro-Soviet person has deliberately rejected the truth. Has voluntarily put blinders on. Is prepared to put his own personal comfort on one side of the equation and other people's lives on the other.

And what's more despicable than that?

A Made-up Soviet Union

Pro-Soviet nostalgia is not a longing for the past. It's a longing for a past that is entirely invented. Because the dreamer wants to return to a reality that never existed, she will always remain dissatisfied.

"Kielbasa for 2.20," "vodka for 3.62," "empty shelves but full refrigerators," these formulaic memories are surprisingly resilient.

Their Soviet Union comes straight out of films by directors such as Leonid Gaidai and Eldar Ryazanov. Films in which the hapless Shurik always triumphs over bumbling ne'er-do-wells, the police always catch the smugglers in the act, and the height of injustice is when the pianist Basilashvili wins the beautiful Gurchenko away from Mikhalkov.

The reality of daily life in the Soviet Union has been wiped from people's memory banks. Three decades have erased the negatives and allowed people to invent their own past. And in that imaginary past, there are no interminable lines for groceries, no bribes or shortages. Politicians are wise and the state is caring.

They still talk about how the Soviet Union was the most literate country in the world. There's no sense in pointing out that the full bookshelves and lines at the theater are just more indicators of shortages. In this case the shortage was entertainment: the lack of options meant that people bought up books and theater tickets.

I'm not even bringing up freedom of speech—the people who long for the Soviet Union still don't see its absence as a problem. But even this consumer paradise they've nostalgically invented for themselves is only sewn from the popular films "The Irony of Fate," "The Girls," "Operation Y," and "Moscow Does Not Believe in Tears." If you try to show them the bleakness of "Little Vera," they'll be deeply offended.

These same people go to the polls year after year to vote for outdated slogans. They refuse to understand that the Soviet world wasn't viable even in 1991—that's why the state collapsed. They keep dreaming of the past and thus deny their children a future.

The problem is that even if their dream comes true, they'll still be dissatisfied.

They believe in a Soviet Union with all of its flaws filtered out. Even if you could take them back to the 1970s, they won't believe it. The hardships and deprivations aren't recorded in their memory. They wouldn't believe in the authenticity of what they saw and would decide they'd been deceived.

Their misfortune is that they are a priori a protest vote. The only platform they'll vote for is one in which the future becomes a jumping off point for resurrecting the past. The past we see in classic Soviet films, the past that never existed.

Their nostalgia is actually for an age, not an era. The two have become blended to the point of being indistinguishable: a person's memory of her own youth, that sense of broad horizons and infinite possibility is projected onto the political system. But no reconstruction of the past can return their health and strength, so they'll still be sullen and resentful.

It's pointless to try and win them over. Nothing you do will ever be enough. Anything you achieve will be dismissed as half measures. Even a complete historical reconstruction (impossible, of course) wouldn't satisfy them, because they're dreaming of an invented past.

So don't bother casting your pearls.

The Rules of Propaganda

In the 20th century, censorship consisted of controlling access to information. We believed that the truth could conquer the dragon and that authoritarian regimes could be torn down by facts. It turns out that the game is played by entirely different rules in the 21st century.

The internet was a death sentence for previous forms of censorship. So a new approach came to replace them. The new approach buries the facts in a pile of information garbage. It erases the line separating truth from lies. It teaches consumers to doubt the evidence of their own eyes.

We hear categorically opposed points of view and we obediently repeat, "The truth is somewhere in the middle." No, the truth is where it is. And it doesn't change its location just because of new lies. Although that's what the inventors of alternative realities want us to believe.

This all makes the twentieth century look pretty patriarchal. Back then, the information wars were conducted according to the rules of the First World War. The trenches were firmly established, as were the zones of influence. Direct fighting took place solely along the peripheries. The USSR had its own priorities "for export." The ideological complex included "internationalism," "state management of the economy," "social equality," and "universal employment." But then came the 21st century and the rules changed.

Now the Kremlin isn't so much trying to export its own values, as attempting to undermine everyone else's. They blur the very concept of fact. They clog the media with fakes and manipulate public opinion. The tactics of positional warfare have been replaced by sabotage operations.

Russian propaganda isn't trying to prove the superiority of the Kremlin. On the contrary, they are trying to show that everyone is the same. They want to bury the truth under a mountain of lies, with heaping servings of conspiracy theory. They demonstrated this approach exceptionally well during the annexation of Crimea, the invasion of the Donbas, and the downing of MH17. The calculation is simple: the higher the pile of information garbage, the harder it is for facts to gain any traction.

We're accustomed to viewing censorship like a boarded-up door. Like a lock, blocking access to information. The new reality has changed the rules of the game. Now censorship means dozens of mutually contradictory versions that leave the viewer utterly confused. It is a clamor that prevents us from distinguishing truth from lies, relevant information from deliberate distractions, facts from fakes.

This is exactly what today's Kremlin is betting on. They aim to torpedo institutions and trust. They nurture voices on the fringes and invest in chaos. For any topic, they will pile on additional versions whose only purpose is to bury the truth.

"The moon was invented by the Freemasons." "The moon is made of Swiss cheese." "The moon is a man-made disc nailed to the firmament." These claims are all intended to silence those timid voices reminding us that the Moon is a satellite of the Earth. The main problem is that there's no antidote to this strategy.

The history of human weaponry has generally been a contest between arms and armor. The stronger the ammunitions become, the thicker the armor. But we have no armor against information warfare. If you even bring it up, you'll be accused of censorship.

We typically think of information as a commodity and imagine that the laws of supply and demand will bring the system into balance. We believe that all points of view have an equal right to exist. We are rightly concerned that the stick of censorship will become a boomerang sooner or later. This concern is then exploited by people who use the media as a weapon.

The rules of the market work when there's a market. That's no longer the case for the media. The people who follow journalistic rules work side by side with those who don't acknowledge any rules. New investors are here to harvest indirect dividends: political, social and electoral advantages.

In addition, facts are dry. They appeal to reason. In contrast, information noise and media hype sell themselves through emotions. In this battle, the person who is most entertaining defeats the one telling the truth. Distortions are more appealing than facts for the same reasons that junk food is more appealing than a healthy diet. It's time we started warning people about the age of junk information.

Calls for fair competition sound rather dubious if you take into account that authoritarian countries are spending billions to promote their own agendas. And so, this new reality poses some unfamiliar questions. For instance, where to draw the line between propaganda and journalism. Or whether we can impose consequences for the use of fakes and distortion.

We don't have answers to these questions, but that doesn't mean we shouldn't be asking them. Contrary to the old sayings, the truth will generally lose out to the lie. The one telling the truth is limited by its contours. On the other hand, the liar has an infinite realm of possibilities. The new reality has destroyed the old rules.

There's no point in burying our heads in the sand to avoid that reality.

Censoring Common Sense

I used to believe in the marketplace of ideas. Then it turned out that actively making sense of your surroundings is a choice made by adults, and societies can be infantile.

In recent years, the limits of personal freedom have become a central issue. Does war justify propaganda? Does the invasion justify censorship? At what point does the collective good start to impinge on personal freedom?

This debate flares up every time we discuss information policy. Many people sincerely believe that humans are rational beings. It sometimes seems as though this belief dates back to our pre-war past, when we valued Ukraine not so much for the existence of something good as for the absence of something bad. The wide-open Ukrainian marketplace of ideas wasn't so much a manifestation of freedom of thought as it was of the country's indifference to its own fate.

Then came the war. Now we're trying once more to answer the central question: can a wide-open society remain open when faced with aggression from a closed one?

An open society lives with competing ideologies. In wartime, these peacetime policies become a fatal flaw. The Kremlin has at its disposal a finely honed system of propaganda with an annual budget of over a billion dollars. Their broad media network advances the Kremlin's interests from Moscow, and sometimes from within Kyiv itself. Russia also pays public figures in Ukraine, who work diligently to earn their rubles.

Pre-war ethics told us to focus on fair competition. To create our own information space, rather than limiting anyone else's right to expression. Don't censor, just inform. But here's the thing: David only beats Goliath in old stories. In real life, David becomes food for unscrupulous predators.

We can see now that the idea of "rational choice" doesn't always work. It turns out that even mature developed democracies can fall for populist ideas. The past is seeking revenge on the future all over the world. And even high standards of living don't seem to offer a reliable defense.

Reality is what we think it is. And so the competition today isn't for reality, it's for the right to describe reality. In peacetime, you can try to correct your errors. In war, there are no second chances. We don't have the luxury of arguing with people who want to defend the rights of "Little Russia" to exist. Compromise is impossible. Their victory would be an eraser, erasing our shared future. And we can see in Donetsk and Luhansk what happens when the "Russian World" takes over.

Growing up isn't always about age. Gray hair is no guarantee of wisdom. People can remain infantile for their entire lives and act against their own best interests. And if the fate of the occupied territories hasn't caused a person to reconsider their convictions, they just aren't capable of reconsidering anything.

Memory Lessons

Whenever Ukraine attempts to defend itself, pro-Russians behave as though the annexation of Crimea never happened.

They go on about freedom of speech and censorship, human rights and pluralism as if we were still living in 2010. As if we still lived in a world where the word "Crimea" conjures up images summer vacation and "the Donbas" means debates about the size of coal subsidies.

Before the war, Ukraine lived according to competing discourses. Two centers of influence were fighting for the future. The West worked with civil society. Russia focused on political elites. The two sides went head to head in elections, but there was no question of a "fight to the death."

Before the war, there wasn't a frontline, so you couldn't really cross it. We could talk about competition and solidarity, about a shared set of rules and equal opportunities. Everything changed the instant "frontline" lost its quotation marks.

Pro-Russian parties in Ukraine lost their right to be a part of the mainstream in spring of 2014. The instant Russian troops set foot on Crimean territory. The instant occupation forces began their invasion of the Donbas.

Moscow's complaints about a Ukrainian "junta" can be refuted by the reality that the Kremlin's advocates continued to be part of Kyiv's political life. If Ukraine were anything like they describe it on Russian television, the party of revanche wouldn't have had a chance.

But no, the Kremlin's proxies were confident in their impunity. Confident that they could avoid responsibility. Confident that they could continue the project they'd begun before the war: the demolition of Ukrainian statehood.

There is one minor adjustment. Recently they're agitating less *for* Moscow and more *against* Europe. Not so to promote Russia's rules of the game as to demolish the Western rules. Specifically, the ones that are designed to fight corruption and create a solid foundation for development.

The pro-Russian elements traded in distrust and cynicism, lies and hate. They drowned facts in fakes and tried to rewrite reality. Their picture of the world simply didn't include the annexation of Crimea and occupation of the Donbas. Although there were plenty of stories about "external control" and groundless Russophobia. Of course, their whole revolt against Western influence was no more than an attempt to hand the reins to Moscow.

They were relying on people with no principles and useful idiots. The first group would do the dirty work. The idiots would cover up that work with debates about the marketplace of ideas and freedom of speech. Both groups did their best to avoid any mention of the spring of 2014.

Any mention of the occupation of Ukrainian territory kicked away any remaining ethical foundation they hoped to stand on. Any mention of the Russian invasion undermined their attempts to seem part of the Ukrainian political landscape. They tried to make their existence in Ukraine after the start of the war seem normal. In reality it was just an unfortunate misunderstanding.

They could participate in Ukrainian debates—until the annexation of Crimea. They could discuss the future of the country—until the invasion of the Donbas. They desperately want us to forget the context here. They want us to forget everything we know about them. They want us to stop looking back so they can regain their prewar legitimacy.

The legitimacy the Kremlin destroyed in 2014.

Pecunia olet

The task of journalism is to inform the public to ensure fair elections. If we remove the word "fair" from that phrase it immediately loses its flowery idealism. It also comes closer to Ukrainian reality. Whoever funds the media sets the agenda.

For journalists, professional solidarity has trained us not to air our dirty laundry, and so we've created our own Achilles heel. We know that whoever has access to hearts and minds will determine the future. And just try to convince me that the war on this battlefield is less important than the war on the frontlines.

We've spent so long fearing the word "censorship," that we've lost the ability to call things by their proper names. To distinguish between journalism and propaganda. Between opposition and sabotage. We've accepted the fact that Ukrainians place no emphasis on personal reputation: you can take money from crooks and still consider yourself a decent person.

There are two major factions in the Ukrainian media. The first group consists of the genuinely Ukrainian media. They may be pro-government or opposition. Self-supported or subsidized. Partisan or neutral. Boring or neutral. Professional... and not so professional. Outlets with journalistic standards and those without. The second group is composed of media outlets actively working to erode Ukraine's statehood. They are either directly funded by Moscow or by the Kremlin's representatives in Kyiv. They offer high salaries and generous budgets. They may vary in their degree of professionalism, but their owners certainly don't want Ukraine to win this war.

Of course, many of the people working for the pro-Russian media will claim that they are the ones maintaining professional standards and that they aren't involved in anti-Ukrainian propaganda. But you would have to be very naive to suppose that everyone supporting revanche will openly call for friendship with Moscow.

On the contrary, any media company serving Moscow's goals will attempt to shield themselves from any such accusations. They'll try to hire people with good reputations whose very presence serves to legitimize the rest of the content on the platform.

In fact, their job is to be publicly pro-Ukrainian: they're the spoonful of sugar that helps a hostile agenda go down.

It really is more convenient not to concern yourself with where the money comes from. To just consider yourself part of the opposition without noticing that you're sitting on the other side of the trenches. To believe that you don't need to take responsibility for the media outlet employing you. To reassure yourself with the thought that "they're all the same anyway." Of course, it certainly doesn't hurt that those pushing ideas of revanche will pay wages an order of magnitude above the market rate—excellent anesthesia for any pangs of conscience.

And you can always take comfort in the fact that the Ukrainian public has the memory of a goldfish. You can always just leave that line off of your resume. After all, pecunia non olet.

Not true. It does stink.

Ukrainian Barricades

When the fate of the country was being decided under bombardment in the east, there was only one significant divide in society. Do you want an independent Ukraine or not?

In 2014, the question of values was something like the story of Cossack induction from Taras Bulba: "Do you believe in Jesus Christ? Do you believe in the Holy Trinity? Show me how you cross yourself! Alright, go join a battalion." Instead of questions about whether you believed in Ukraine, the question was who you wanted to win the war. The answer to that question created a simple two cell table on the map of the country. Ukraine or Little Russia. Sovereignty or vassalage.

And then everything changed. The main test question was the same, but it no longer answered every question. New cells were added to that first two-square grid.

Do you support European values or not? Low taxes or a welfare state? The right to bear arms or a state monopoly on violence? Same-sex marriage or homophobia? The list could go on ad infinitum.

None of these questions are relevant on the frontlines: in the trenches everyone is fighting for their dream of the future. The contours of that dream tend to be pretty vague. Although whenever the fighting dies down a bit, the contours start to firm up. Our desires start to take shape. And then it turns out that all these people who recently thought they were fighting for the same thing, discover that their neighbor's dream has no space for them.

Perhaps everyone is equally eager for Kyiv to win. But one person is dreaming of taking down the oligarchs, another imagines the "Polish model," a third is a libertarian and the fourth is a total anarchist. The fifth wants to see legal recognition of domestic partnerships, a sixth wants to become a nuclear power again, the seventh wants a third Maidan and the eighth wants to see the region of Kuban transferred from Russia back to Ukraine.

We have a habit of labeling anyone who doesn't agree with us as "conservatives" and "agents of the Kremlin." Sometimes it's absolutely true. But not always.

Ukraine's contradictions are non-linear. They're like tables with cells of varying sizes. When you overlay one on top of the others, you understand that there aren't just two bunkers in the country, but far more. It also turns out that people with varying perspectives on the present and the future can create all sorts of unexpected combinations.

In theory, this should come as no surprise. The country is trying to come to agreement with itself at an accelerated pace. This is never an easy process, particularly if you take into account the fact that Ukraine is taking a crash course in something that other countries have worked on for decades. The new discussion is just beginning.

We are going to live through a dramatic period: the old social contract is gone, the new one has not yet been created. We only have the broad outlines: break out of the post-Soviet context, defend ourselves from the former imperial center, make the country livable. We've united around what we don't want. Now we will have to divide ourselves along the lines of our preferred future.

That may be the hardest part.

Lost in Translation

Journalism is a form of negotiation. We attempt to explain the country to itself. The war creates the contours of identity based on certain foundational questions, but even people who answer those questions in the same ways are actually very different people who want different things. The conversation is an attempt to understand the people who've unified within those basic contours. The moment we stop negotiating is when things start to come apart at the seams.

The problem is that Ukraine has changed since 2014, but we still don't have the language to describe our new reality. And so a wartime logic prevails and we start suspecting treachery from the person sitting next to us in the trench. And then, instead of trying to talk it through, we deliver a verdict. Labels are the weapons we use to defeat compromise. They're born of lack of nuance. A descriptive deficit. A willingness to perceive differences as absolutes.

Before the war, the gap was between "pro-Russian" and "pro-Ukrainian." That all changed after the annexation of Crimea and invasion of the Donbas.

The pro-Russian camp shrank. A considerable number of its supporters stayed in the occupied territories. And then the pro-Ukrainian camp, now left alone in the marketplace of values, began to break up into different categories, including what we might call "left" and "right."

The left wants civil liberties and democracy, dialogue and decentralization. They don't accept the right of the state to regulate public life. They believe in the marketplace of ideas and the individual's ability to make the right choice in that free market.

They view any discussion of a "strong hand" with suspicion and worry that the "emergency powers" associated with the war will outlive the war itself. They view the state as a leviathan which must be kept on a strict diet so that its appetite doesn't grow.

On the other side of the barricades we find those who want to mobilize society. They believe that the Gordian knot must be cut, not untied. They believe that society can be infantile and it is the province of adults to make choices. They are certain that the social priorities of wartime are different from those of peacetime.

Each camp has its own collection of symbols and banners. For one group, the value of freedom is always more important the interests of the state. Others believe that at certain points in history, compromise may be necessary to ensure the survival of the state. Some believe that a political nation must be nurtured through discipline. Others are prepared to dispute that point.

The biggest problem is an almost total lack of communication between the two camps. We don't even have a proper vocabulary to describe our opponents. And so a primitive reflex kicks in, one developed before the war, according to which supporters of Ukraine are convinced that anyone who disagrees with them is an agent of the Kremlin, whether overt or covert. That's why any divergence of views leads to accusations of bribes or collusion.

Until recently, Ukraine and Russia were joined like Siamese twins. Unsurprisingly, almost anyone's biography can reveal awkward photographs or inconvenient lines in their resumes. In light of the fact that there genuinely are many Kremlin agents operating in Ukraine, this creates a pervasive atmosphere of suspicion. Particularly since the pro-Russian forces today paint themselves as part of the "opposition."

And of course Russia invests in both camps. The left is useful to Russia since their priorities can weaken commitment to the public good during wartime, prioritizing the individual over the collective. The right is useful because they can be used, for instance, to challenge the state monopoly on violence. And it's not just Russia — other players are also willing to invest in these camps to advance their own vested interests.

None of this changes the central point: the pro-Ukrainian camp has lost the monolithic character which characterized the first twenty-three post-Soviet years, the one which was forged in battle with those who viewed Ukraine as a colony of Russia.

The war brought the old conversations to an end and gave birth to new ones. No more negotiating with people who want to make Ukraine into a Russian colony. Now we begin the negotiations between differing visions for Ukraine's future. We're going to have to learn new ways of being in this new reality.

In the Trenches

Let's imagine that Moscow decides to leave the Donbas. The soldiers withdraw, the collaborators flee, the Ukrainian Army regains control of the border. And that's when our shouting match begins.

One group of pro-Ukrainian, patriotic citizens, including many frontline veterans will begin talking about how "the Donbas is ours" and must be returned. Another group, just as pro-Ukrainian, just as patriotic, also filled with veterans, will say they weren't fighting for the return of the Donbas, but to defend Ukraine from the "Russian World."

Virtually any aspect of a "peace settlement" runs the risk of creating internal battlelines.

Amnesty for collaborators? Some will say yes, it's time to turn the page. Others will be opposed, equating cooperation with treason.

The rebuilding of the Donbas? Some will see it simply as national development. Others will deem it reparations that Ukraine is paying rather than the aggressor country.

"Special rules" for the region that appear to favor Russia? Some will see it as a natural stage in the "return of the territory." Others as a voluntary renunciation of sovereignty.

An end to the active phase of the war will lead to discussions of what kind of army we need, which will lead to conversations about bloated military budgets and the need to reduce them.

And then comes the discussion of whether to maintain sanctions on Russia. Some people will say that Ukrainian goods need access to the Russian market. Expediency and economic logic will be presented as justifications to restore financial ties.

Similar rifts will affect every aspect of the peace process. Some people will view this as a sign that we've returned to our pre-war version of "normal." Others will see it as a rejection of the new normal that emerged in Ukraine after the invasion.

If we're going to define "normal" according to the 2013 status quo, territorial integrity is the highest priority. Seek compromise, stitch things up, negotiate.

If "normal" is going to be based on more recent events, then sovereignty is the highest priority. We're fighting a war for independence, not for square miles. That means the trenches along the front line are much more than a staging ground for liberating the occupied territories—they're also a line of defense protecting Ukraine from the criminal chaos that has prevailed there.

Sometimes peace is harder than war. Each of these discussions has the potential to divide people who just recently stood shoulder-to-shoulder on the same side of the barricades. Each side carries before them the banners of those who died at the front, those whose memories will be invoked at every turn, "They didn't die so that…" It's always convenient to turn the dead into ideologues. They won't object.

Victory doesn't always fill in the old trenches. Sometimes it digs new ones.

The Belarusian Mirror

For 30 years, Ukraine has compared itself to her more successful neighbors.

There are plenty of success stories. The Baltic states. Poland. The Czech Republic and Slovakia. We compared our economic reforms with Poland and got depressed. We compared our self-awareness with Lithuania and felt discouraged. Our neighbors were charging ahead and, in comparison, Ukraine looked like hopeless failure, mired in a kaleidoscope of contradictions.

And then came the protests in Belarus. And Belarus suddenly became another mirror for us. Except this time, the mirror was far less discouraging than we'd gotten used to.

If we look at Belarus, we can see the progress we've made. We can also see the pitfalls that we successfully avoided.

For instance, not so long ago many of our fellow citizens saw Aleksandr Lukashenko as a model politician. In any listing of the most popular foreign politicians he was routinely near the top, which led some people to wax poetic about the charms of having a single, consistent ruler. For "continuity." For "consistency."

But it turned out that the whole round dance of Ukrainian presidents was our insurance against dictatorship. No homegrown guarantor managed to put down deep enough roots in his position to completely appropriate the nation. No Ukrainian head of state had the opportunity to completely clear the field of competitors. Regular changes in governance kept the government responsive. Even if the virus of Messianism did penetrate to the president's seat, it didn't have the opportunity to take hold. The one president who tried it ended up in Russia.

Moreover, Belarus demonstrated the idiocy of any Ukrainian dream of a "state hegemon." The government in Minsk maintained control over the industrial foundations of the Soviet inheritance, and then proceeded to use it to hold the whole country hostage. The leviathan of the state had no competitors. No one could dispute its right to power and no alternative power centers existed.

During the Maidan, it didn't even occur to anyone to identify Yanukovych with the country's economy. Calls for a new president didn't include calls to violate our financial stability. The government and the economy in Ukraine are not so interwoven as to be indistinguishable. That's not how it is in Belarus. During the Belarusian protests, opposition Telegram channels called on the protestors to withdraw their money from the banks to collapse the national currency. They quite accurately believed that the stability of the regime relied on the stability of the system. Meanwhile, Ukraine's decentralized economy meant the protestors could fight political abuses without starting a crusade against the economy.

In addition, Belarus's lauded stability turned out to be dependent on life support from Russia: Moscow controls the switches. It is Moscow who decides whether this holdover of pseudosocialism will live or die depending on Belarus's loyalty. If Moscow ever stops the payments, the resulting deluge will make the Ukrainian economic crisis of 2014-15 look like a light ripple. While the Ukrainian everyman may well express class hatred toward Ukrainian business, it is actually private enterprise which provides the margin of safety that our neighbors lack.

Belarus offers Ukraine a different mirror. In contrast to the Polish, Lithuanian or Czech mirrors, we don't see only our failures in this one. We can also see the magnitude of our progress. If we take a good look, we can see that our imperfections are the flipside of our virtues. And that what we generally see as shortcomings are actually our insurance policy against dictatorship.

Sometimes the best way to understand yourself is to peek into your neighbors' windows.

Triumph of the Antimaidan

Belarus also illustrates what the consequences would have been had the Maidan failed.

At some point, a protest becomes a bicycle: when it stops, it falls. The only thing that matters is the ability to respond to challenges as they arise. The regime and the protestors steadily up the ante. The first one to throw their cards on the table is the loser.

There was never any guarantee that the Ukrainian protests would be successful. At any particular point in time, the people determined its fate. The people who went out into the streets. The people who brought medicines and food. The people who protected the protest from hired thugs and goons. In the post-Soviet space, the idea of silent dissent is pointless. The group that wins the standoff gains the right to draw the ethical contours of the nation.

The people who lost on the Maidan are still trying to play a game of "what if?" They talk about the violations of procedure and disregard for democracy. They blame the Maidan for the loss of Crimea and the Donbas. But they're just trying to distract attention from reality: the Maidan is the only thing that stopped Yanukovych's usurpation of power.

It almost happened in the winter of 2013. People in the president's offices were already working on the final draft. A proposal was ready to have parliament select the president. There were suggestions of raising the minimum age for candidates. If it weren't for the protests, Ukraine's fourth president might have been her last.

If the protestors had lost on the Maidan, we would have seen the Belarusian scenario play out: activists facing the threat of jail, opposition forced into emigration, the independent press destroyed. Russia wouldn't have needed to invade Crimea or the Donbas — it would already have had control of the entire country.

All of that would have become inevitable, because Yanukovych's revenge on the opposition would have cut off any possibility of cooperation with the West. And so he would have fallen right into the Kremlin's outstretched hands. Just like Lukashenko. Ukrainian opposition activists in exile would have given interviews to European television stations. Brussels would have voted for sanctions against Yanukovych's Party of Regions. None of it would have changed anything.

When today's Kremlin supporters in Ukraine blame the Maidan for our loss of territory, they're rewriting the narrative. In the fall of 2013, there was no center of power that decided to start the Maidan. There was no individual waiting at the switch to "turn on" the street protests. Of course, this is in complete contrast to the catastrophe of Crimea and the Donbas where the decisions were made by one man sitting in the Kremlin. What did we achieve? The answer is easy — we drove out the usurper. Everything that followed is due to the Kremlin's attempts to take advantage of the situation.

It should come as no surprise that attitudes toward the Maidan have become a litmus test of values. The litmus test that identifies "ours" and "others." The war put the Antimaidan group outside the bounds of the acceptable and removed any claim they had to legitimacy. Removed any right to their own opinion and voice.

The example of Belarus shows us what Ukraine's fate would have been if the Maidan had failed. That doesn't necessarily mean Ukraine would have lost any chance to break out of post-Soviet orbit—or that Belarus has. But it's impossible to guess how long we would have had to wait for a new window of opportunity to appear. And if the moment had come again, war would still have become inevitable then.

Empires don't like to give up what's "theirs" without a fight.

The Pleasures of the Periphery

The post-Soviet space is something like a solar system. In the center is the largest object: the Russian Federation. The other countries revolve around it. Quite close, say in the orbit of Mercury, we find Belarus. Slightly further out, toward Venus, is Armenia. Further still is Kazakhstan. And in the farthest orbit is Ukraine, which is trying to move into the neighboring solar system.

This is nothing new. Thirty years ago the Warsaw Bloc planets began to orbit in the next system over. The Russian Federation is terrified of seeing a repeat of that scenario, so Russia focuses on keeping the remaining states within its gravitational field.

This attempt to maintain the status quo forms the cornerstone of contemporary Russian politics. It is the source of all these "traditional practices": from the "spiritual bonds" to the Soviet nostalgia. They simultaneously broadcast all the supposed problems plaguing the planets who left for the other system, claiming that those countries are now eking out a miserable existence. That in the old system they were frontmen, but in the new one they're provincials.

The funny thing is that they're not entirely wrong. But it's also the best proof that they made the right choice.

Yes, it's true that the Baltic states played a special role in the Soviet Union. The European atmosphere that was unavailable anywhere else in the USSR enchanted the unsophisticated Soviet tourist. The flair of uniqueness, bohemianism, and exoticism made plenty of Soviet citizens dream of moving to Riga or Tallinn. The Baltics were right next door and yet completely different.

After they switched solar systems, the Baltic states turned out to just be provinces of Europe. Their architectural and civilizational accomplishments no longer stood out. Now they were competing with Barcelona and Bruges, not Sochi and Yaroslavl.

But that transition from frontmen to provincials is just one more proof that they made the right choice. It illustrates the gulf between the two solar systems. It's like the difference between first class and the others: what one system considers deluxe, is just normal in the other. The comparison hardly benefits the first system.

The same fate awaits Ukraine. Russians love to reminisce about Kyiv's "special role" in the Soviet solar system. They warn us that we'll be irrelevant and provincial if we move to the other orbit. They point to the Baltic states and tell us we'll be outsiders like them. That's fine.

That's fine, because that is how it will be. When Ukraine switches orbit, it will indeed be one of the peripheral planets. But in the modern world, the most efficient interdependent systems win. And it's far better to be on the periphery of a functional system, than the frontman for one that's deteriorating.

On the Other Side of the Iron Curtain

The outlines of a new iron curtain are taking shape right before our eyes. But this time, unlike in the 20th century, Ukraine is lucky enough to be on the other side of the trenches. In the last century, we were in the same situation as East Berlin. Now we have every possibility of becoming West Berlin.

Russia has fully switched to Cold War rhetoric. And in their minds, Ukraine has already been moved to the category of the alien and hostile. Russian citizens now give us second place in their list of enemies. Right after the US. Right before the European Union.

We should celebrate this transformation. The further apart we drift in mentality, the fewer illusions we will have. The wider the emotional gap, the clearer the boundary. And in this new war that Moscow has decided to declare against the West, Ukraine will not accept the role of bridgehead or supply wagon for Russia.

If we look to Belarus, we can see the consequences of failure on this front. Our neighbor has not been so fortunate as us, they haven't traversed the path of maturation and emancipation that Ukraine has. Now their entrenched dictator is keeping Belarus tightly locked inside Russia's orbit. Mobilizing for war with the same old West. Still on Russia's side.

The war with the West means a war on values. A war against democracy and dignity. Against freedom and personal initiative. And countries that go to war against the West rarely support the development of their own populations. Most often they become monsters living not for their citizens, but off their citizens.

The entire history of the twentieth century is direct proof of this. The Soviet Union meant the triumph of the gray and obliging, ingratiating and identical. And now history is going for a second round. With one difference: the geography of the battlefield has changed.

Ukraine managed to jump out. Yes, the border is still right there. Yes, some Ukrainian territory is still under occupation. But if things had gone differently, the theater of war would be at the Ukraine-Poland border rather than the Ukraine-Russia border.

And that's what gives us a chance. Our choice of trench determines the rules of the game. Choosing a side in this war means choosing our values. We will have to learn new things, inherit principles and gradually change the rules we live by. There's no alternative. Because any other alternative will be on the other side of the Iron Curtain.

If we hold out, our future has a chance of defeating our past.

The Enemy of My Enemy

Honestly, we lucked out in terms of enemies. Some people support us more because of who we're fighting than who we are.

How can Ukraine win the war? The correct answer is that we won't—not alone. Not even the information war. Russian state media produces content in over twenty languages reaching Europe, Asia and both Americas with a budget of over a billion dollars. Here's another question for you: how many Ukrainian sites even have an English language version?

If you think that the average editor of a Czech/ Romanian/ Italian media outlet is going to "google translate" a Ukrainian site, you're mistaken. Honestly, how many Ukrainians read European publications using a browser translator? There's no sense in overestimating our hardworking colleagues abroad. They consume content they can understand. And Ukraine doesn't create any for export.

Our problem is over confidence. We consider ourselves part of the West and are confident that Europeans feel the same. But for many countries in the West, our problems are hardly a top priority.

Don't rush to outrage. What do we know about the conflict in South Sudan? The one that has killed 200,000 people? But that's Africa, you answer? Well, yes. And until quite recently, all the world knew about us is that we have two world boxing champions.

Our only advantage is geography. In the imagination of the West, the Donbas and Crimea are simultaneously far away and close by. Far away — "somewhere in the East, in the former USSR." And quite close, because it's still on the European continent, somewhere "between Moscow and Warsaw."

Our beloved Europe still sees us as the third world. In the twenty-three years leading up to the war, we did nothing to change that perception. We spun our wheels and consumed what we already had, without creating anything new. Now we're reaping the harvest.

For us, this is an existential issue. For them, it's just another sad story taking place somewhere "out there." They identify with people inside their vision of Europe. And whoever is outside that vision receives only the dregs of empathy. To be honest, we don't have much interest in "outsiders" either, do we?

The time the world is willing to spend on us is directly proportional to our interest in the world. If we want the average person in the West to see the war as anything more than another abstract problem, we have to become "insiders."

Our enemy is the only thing that saves us. Russia is trying so hard to be the USSR, that it's starting to convince people. Syria, the American elections, the poisoning of the Skripals, hacker attacks, explosions in the Czech Republic. Moscow is doing the work that Kyiv can't afford. If Russia had limited the conflict to a bilateral one, we would have been forgotten. But Russia has decided to go global.

From the very start of the war, Ukraine has described the war not as a confrontation between two countries, but as an attack by the Kremlin on the West. No one really took it seriously at first — is Ukraine really the West? But now, due only to Moscow's assiduous efforts, we have become fully inscribed in the global context.

In the face of this beast that is "enormous, disgusting, a-hundred-maws and barking[1]" we've attracted more sympathy. We're a natural barrier. A border wall. A bulwark against the East, which is rattling its nuclear relics and dreams of the past because it fears the future.

Our integration with the West remains dependent on our adversary. It is situational, something accomplished by Moscow, not Kyiv. Victory will come when we are genuinely accepted as part of Europe. When we break out of the swamp we've been drifting through for the last twenty-five years. When we are united with the West on the basis of values, and not just because we're sitting in the same foxhole together.

The Grass is Always Greener

Most Ukrainians can name a country they like to compare Ukraine to. A country that serves as a benchmark to define some imaginary norm. We constantly compare this imagined standard to our actual life just so that we can complain about the problems in our own country.

---

1   Radishchev, 1790, wikipedia. Tr. note.

We criticize our life for its failure to live up to the heroic epics. We're angry that corruption and inefficiency are still rampant. We complain about the roads, taxes and bribes. We hate the kickbacks, delays and backroom deals. And when we point to the example of other countries, we imagine that their path to freedom and sovereignty was smooth and without potholes.

The only problem is that we actually have no idea what they went through.

Do we want to be Finland who fought off the Soviet Union, built a comfortable standard of living and created one of the best educational systems in the world? Of course we do. We talk about how the Finnish Army beat the Red Army in the Winter War, defended their independence and won their right to sovereignty.

It's the story of a 3.5 million-person David against a 190 million-person Goliath. It warms the soul and makes us believe in miracles. But is Ukraine really ready for the Finnish scenario?

Finland's pre-war defense spending ranged from 16-25% of GDP. Men, women and adolescents completed military training — half a million people. It's only the passage of time that makes the Soviet-Finnish war look like an unqualified victory for Finland. In the spring of 1940, things looked very different.

Finland lost a quarter of its army — 70,000 people killed in battle, injured or missing in action. Finland lost 1/10th of its territory and evacuated 430,000 people from occupied territories.

Yes, Finland successfully defended its independence, but still it was essentially a satellite of the Soviet Union after World War II. Finnish foreign trade was tied to the Soviet market. And not just trade — their foreign and overall economic policy also enjoyed only limited sovereignty. The collapse of the Soviet Union set off a domino effect and Finland went through an economic crisis which it took a long time to recover from. Finland didn't join the EU until 1995.

A Finnish scenario for Ukraine would mean legal renunciation of the occupied territories and recognition of them as part of Russia. The evacuation and resettlement of residents of Crimea and the Donbas. Ukraine's return to Moscow's economic orbit. Giving up NATO and the EU. Are we ready to pay that price?

The "promised land" is referenced even more often as a model for Ukraine. Israel, who valiantly defends itself against everyone. Israel, who has won wars and carved out the most comfortable oasis in the Middle East. We'd like to be like them and copy their recipe for success.

The recipe is clear enough. Mobilize 40% of the able-bodied population into the army and auxiliary units. Lose 4,000 out of 30,000 soldiers in the fight for independence. Yes, the Israeli army quadrupled during the war for independence, but in relative terms, their losses were many times greater than what Ukraine has suffered.

The "Israeli experience" includes Orthodox Jews protesting military conscription. Extreme conflict between the "left" and "right." The regular army vs volunteer units. The sidelining of "difficult radicals" — who survived the Holocaust, by the way. Fierce arguments over whether to accept reparations from Germany.

The "Israeli experience" included allocating a third of the national budget to national defense. Rationing that lasted until 1959. A complex distribution system affecting groceries, household items and even electricity. Energy rationing controlled by the state, with officials going door-to-door to ensure compliance. The Standards Institution. Hyperinflation that reached over 400% a year at one point.

No one built a military-industrial complex *for* Israel. It was developed in response to an arms embargo and the threat of sanctions. No one built an economy *for* them. In fact, the Israeli economy thrived not so much thanks to the government, but despite it. Corruption scandals, indictments of political and military leaders, double standards — all of these Ukrainian flaws were also characteristic of Israel during its formative years. In fact, Ukraine is doing quite well right now in comparison.

We love to look to others for examples. But all these historical analogues only work because of our ignorance.

We have only the vaguest conceptions of what the struggle for independence was like in these countries we aspire to emulate. We compare their wartime experiences with where they are today and imagine those two points are connected by a smooth historical autobahn. Nothing could be further from the truth.

It's very simple to propose some other ideal country as an example for our own. But that ideal is always imaginary. In reality, every "recipe for success" included what we see around us right now. Blood, sweat and tears. Betrayals that look like victories. Victories that turn out to be betrayals. Reforms and relapses. Mistakes and treason. We are deep in the dark tunnel of state building — with any luck our grandchildren will be the ones to make it out the other side.

Our daily reality now is very similar to the experience of those countries we see as having "made it." The only difference is that we're still at the beginning of the path. The trials we've been through so far are only a tenth of what Israel and Finland passed through.

Our frustration is the result of inflated expectations. We refuse to believe that the construction of an effective state takes generations. We want our bright future right away. We don't accept the costs and crave lightning-quick progress.

The fact is that we're in the middle of the story right now. And whether we are ever held up as a good example depends on how the story turns out. If we lose, then our problems will be read as a recipe for failure. If we win, those problems will be added to the list of preconditions in the encyclopedia entry for our victory. We will be seen as proof that the path to sovereignty is inevitably a torturous one, just as it was for the countries we admire. But our current starting conditions don't guarantee any particular outcome. Neither victory nor defeat.

Everyone knows that the grass is always greener and the neighbors' kids are smarter, more polite and more athletic. But that's just an illusion.

Our Grandfathers Fought

Ukraine is a country with a long history and a short memory.

There's this old joke where some tourists come across an old hideout in the Carpathian mountains. A hundred-year-old man crawls out with a machine gun.

"Praise God. What's happening in the world?"
"There's a war on, grandpa."
"Who are we fighting?"
"Moscow."
"And where exactly?"
"In the Donbas."
"Well, then... our boys have made some good progress."

The unexpected twist at the end is often what makes a joke funny. But if the ending of this joke seems funny, then history has bad news for us. Because the only way this ending could be an "unexpected twist" is if you found 2014 unexpected.

For someone with a Soviet memory, war between Ukraine and Russia is unimaginable.

For the people who became refugees following the Russian invasion, it was like a knife to the back. A betrayal.

For apolitical Kyivites, the war is a historical anomaly that must be corrected.

But for the old man in the joke—it's only logical. It's all the same war. Against the same adversary. For the same reasons. Only on the other side of the country.

We are each hostage to our own memory. And individual memory is short—70 years at best. A historical perspective can frame the events of our lives in ways that can seem logical or incomprehensible.

In 2015, a Polish colleague described the difference between his country and mine. He told me that in Poland, the period from 1991 to 2014 was seen as a brief historical respite. A pause during which they would need to mobilize society, implement reforms and strengthen their defenses. Because for them, Russia's "normal" condition is that of an empire determined to expand, absorbing other regions in the process. So, its neighbors have to be prepared for the fact that Russian "Thaws" are always short-lived.

But Ukraine believed the opposite. We mistook a weakened Russia for the new normal. We imagined that the age of empires was over and done. And so, we wasted those two decades.

It's a good example of how historical memory works. It could help us not to fool ourselves. Teach us to see windows of possibility and use them. The events of the last several years could serve as a good inoculation for us. But only if we decide to place these events within the broader context.

It's not all that hard. We lived for hundreds of years with colonial status. Spent the last two decades in a transitional status. Then the phantom pains of the empire provoked their invasion and our war for independence. There's nothing new here. It all makes sense.

As long as we insist on seeing what's happening as a historical departure, we lose. As long as we imagine that there is space for compromise, we lose. As long as we claim that a "militant minority" is responsible for the war, we lose.

We can only start winning when we start to view everything taking place from the perspective of the old man in the joke. The one for whom war with Russia wasn't news at all. Who recognized this "new" war as simply a continuation of one that started way before 2014.

And then we can understand his optimism. Because if you look at a map of Ukraine, then our guys really have made some good progress in the last 60 years.

4 The Media

A Fake Future

We love to invent ethical placebos to convince ourselves that truth and justice will prevail over lies and manipulation. In reality, genius and villainy are frequent bedfellows, and there is no guarantee that truth will conquer lies. The battle between facts and fakes is raging now, and the outcome remains uncertain.

Jokes about the "world's second oldest profession" are popular with people who don't realize that journalism is only five hundred years old. It is a product of "the Gutenberg galaxy," the world created by the printing press. Not just journalism. In his book "The Gutenberg Galaxy," Marshall McLuhan writes that Protestantism, capitalism, individualism, democracy, and nationalism were all made possible by to the invention of the printing press. The world as we know it is a product of a publishing culture that emerged five hundred years ago.

In the following centuries, changes in journalism kept pace with changes in the world itself. In the mid-seventeenth century, the first print ads appeared. In the mid-nineteenth century, paid advertisements became the foundation of the business model. Then everything changed again when we suddenly discovered that we're now living in the "internet galaxy."

In 1993, there were 130 websites. In 2007, that number had reached 1.2 billion. Today, approximately four billion users use 45 terabytes of data. The internet is not just a means of communication: it has changed the very nature of communication. Over the course of centuries, humanity became accustomed to viewing the world through the keyhole. Technology has blown the doors wide open and we are all standing at the threshold, battered by the winds of information. Now we have to learn to live in this new reality.

Initially, the arrival of the internet looked like the ultimate victory of freedom over censorship. Everyone would be able to communicate with everyone, released from the vise grip of governmental control. Instead, institutional censorship was replaced by voluntary censorship.

People turned out to be less rational than I imagined and more inclined to rationalize. First form an opinion, then seek out information that confirms it. The information space came to consist of non-intersecting bubbles where everyone lives in their own information realities. Instead of being a space for everyone to communicate with everyone, the web has splintered into isolated interest groups whose members see only what supports their beliefs. They only learn of the existence of other perspectives from public opinion polls or election results.

Communications have changed. Technology has deprived the media of its unique role in mediating between speaker and listener. The institutional buffer has disappeared, and traditional forms of censorship are far less effective. Of course, the censoring of fakes has weakened right along with the censoring of truth. Anyone can find exactly what they want on the internet and it may have nothing to do with reality.

So, it turns out that facts don't always triumph over fakes in the modern age. In fact, they frequently lose badly in the contest.

Emotions are like the crude oil of the human soul; whoever can extract them can get rich. Fakes are inherently appealing because they have nothing to do with rationality. Their function is to construct the reality their adherents want to see.

Facts are dry and mathematical. Fakes are vivid and emotional. You have to grasp the broader context to understand a fact. A fake provides its own context, often a picture of the world with a heavy admixture of conspiracy.

Fakes don't just sell well. They also reproduce at an alarming rate.

Russian journalist Leonid Bershydsky has written that most people want information primarily to maintain small talk. He writes that, "People tend to discuss either what directly concerns them or issues that allow them to appear smart and well-informed. No matter how much media advertises its importance for informed decision making, they actually are mainly just helping their readers maintain small talk. The most obvious benefit a publication can offer its readers is the opportunity to shine in conversation, to avoid looking like an idiot, and to be in the loop about whatever the topic of the day is."

But who said conspiracy theories don't make good small talk? In this sense, the demand for fakes or facts depends directly on the level of the audience. The less an interlocutor knows, the lower the bar, and the less chance a boring fact has against a bright, shiny lie. As a result, we once again find ourselves in a situation where the astronomy of facts loses out to the astrology of fakes.

Facts used to come in a package labeled 'respectability'. Apparently that's not enough anymore. With well-to-do Western countries increasingly voting for populists, it is clear that fakes sell much better than accurate descriptions of reality.

This creates a host of new challenges. Maybe truth just has terrible marketing. Maybe we need to devote more thought to how to package it. Otherwise, we run the risk of offering a quality product that nonetheless loses in the battle for the mass consumer. And those consumers enjoy the full range of electoral rights. They will define the future of the country no less than university professors.

Large institutional media in developed countries have already been looking for answers to these new challenges. They create interactive, playful products and experiment with various formats. They create different content for different platforms. They learn to sell facts to new audiences. They work on their "packaging" and have no issue with the word "marketing." But even that doesn't protect the developed countries from the hucksters of stupidity.

In the past, news had to pass editorial review before it could reach an audience. Today, those barriers are gone. And in this new reality, trading in emotions is far more profitable than trading in actual knowledge. Demand now determines supply in the media market.

Well, it won't be boring. Fortunately. Unfortunately.

Get to Know the Country

One thing was quite different during the analog age. If you took any democratic country and presented its media landscape and the public as a fraction, the numerator would include a range of people with varying beliefs, income levels, education levels, and social status. But they were equal in their shared picture of reality. This was because the denominator included a relatively small number of media sources.

Television channels and print media might have differed in their target audiences, editorial positions, party preferences and values promoted, but only within a limited range because the number of outlets was inherently limited. And since they were relatively few in number, they all followed some shared professional guidelines and universal values. The media was an institutional mediator between content producers and consumers. The only way to reach an audience was to convince an editor of the value of your perspectives. The Internet eliminated that reality and has given birth to a new one. We now live in an era where anyone can speak directly to their audience, with no intermediaries. The blogosphere is the offspring of social networks and online platforms.

Until recently, any nut who believed the planet was flat was doomed to solitude. He could imagine that he was the only one who knew the truth and everyone else was either hypocritical or deluded. Now the Internet has given the nutcases the opportunity to find each other, create content for each other, and promote their ideas. The Internet has allowed disparate freaks to come together and create political demand. And the market responds with political supply.

Media "for all" has been replaced by media "for us." Even Facebook indexes the news feed based on our preferences and we're shown more from authors whose posts we "like." Everyone else eventually disappears from our feeds. And so, each of us exists in an information reality different from that of our neighbors. Rather than becoming a communications platform for everyone-with-everyone, the internet and social networks segmented the information field, and society along with it. Dialogue has ended and we now live in a world of endless monologues.

Ukraine is no exception. We are bewildered when we read polling results—"Who are all these people?" Then we just accuse the researchers of corruption and assume they've been paid off by a political campaign. Once again, we fall prey to our habit of viewing ourselves as the norm, assuming that everyone else shares our view of reality.

All of this presents a rather formidable challenge. A state's viability depends on the mutual trust of its citizens. If they trust each other, then by extension, they can trust the processes governing the system. If I believe that my neighbors are not so different from me, that we have more in common than not, then I can recognize their right to vote as they please. But if I view my neighbors as strangers whose interests conflict with mine, then I have no reason to trust their choices. Or the election results.

And no, Ukraine isn't the only one dealing with this. Even the most stable countries, the ones we always looked up to, are dealing with this crisis. The old boundaries of identity have blurred. New ones are emerging before our eyes. It becomes difficult to talk about a shared vision when our descriptions of reality don't even match. The mismatch results in the most bizarre phobias. And these are the conditions under which Ukrainians must reach an agreement about our future and our identity.

You know, history has a rather strange sense of humor.

The ABCs of Manipulation

In the early 2000s, Russian spin doctor Oleg Matveychev published the book *Ears Wag the Donkey: The Uses of Political Technology* [untranslated]. The author described how to win the battle for public opinion and the most effective methods for manipulating the media.

He emphasized the role of self-fulfilling prophecies whereby expectations influence behavior; shaping questions, in which voicing the question is more important than the actual answer; and the deliberate use of fake smear campaigns so that revelations of actual wrongdoing lose their power in a morass of absurdity.

Matveychev notes that journalists are particularly easy to manipulate, simply due to the reactive nature of the profession.

Journalists are congenitally incapable of recognizing the overarching agenda due to the nature of their work. They take pride in their ability to creatively present a situation, changing black into white, or white into black, but they have little comprehension of what it is they're actually painting or whose interests it serves. The difference between journalists and good spin doctors is the same as the one between painters and architects. However, the painters don't imagine that if they paint the other person's house black it will fall to ruin, or if they paint their own white it will stand for a hundred years. Also, journalists frequently have trouble even recognizing which house is theirs.

Matveychev writes that setting the agenda is more important than how you cover it. He gives an example describing mayoral elections in a small town. The incumbent mayor had a 30% positive approval rating and faced a dozen other candidates, including a local businessman who violated local norms by refusing to pay for positive media coverage. The jilted journalists decided to take revenge. They enthusiastically provided blanket coverage criticizing his every step. The mayor hoped that his 30% approval rating would allow him to coast to a win while the rest of the votes were spread among his opponents. Instead, the businessman won with 40% of the vote.

The journalists had successfully convinced 60% of voters that the businessman was bad. But they failed with the other 40%. And they had created the sense that there were no other alternatives: the only question was choosing between the mayor and the businessman.

Similar outcomes aren't always the result of chance. The media is reactive by nature, so why buy off a journalist if you can manipulate them instead? It's easy enough to create events for them to report. It doesn't matter how they carry out your agenda as long as you're the one setting the agenda.

Modern man lives in a state of permanent referendum. He must constantly determine whether he agrees with this or that fact or statement, whether he is in favor or opposed.

This means that the main battle is actually for the ability to set the agenda. Here we are talking about issues on which people are asked to have their say. For example, in the 1980 US presidential election, Reagan and Carter were neck and neck. It was impossible to predict the winner. But then, on the eve of the election, the hostage crisis dominated every channel, and foreign policy became the most important yardstick for Americans. Foreign policy was Reagan's strong suit and he won.

Matveychev writes that *"When you see dozens of comments with different opinions, don't get too excited thinking you're dealing with a free press. The main thing isn't the comments themselves, the 'for' or 'against' — the main thing is the questions that are being raised in those comments."*

He writes that a request for comment is one of the easiest ways to blow up a topic and bring it to the top of the agenda. When a top official is asked to comment on an issue, it triggers a chain reaction and then additional media and pundits begin engaging with the same topic.

The commenter doesn't have to have a broad audience to push forward an issue; the value of information has long ceased to depend on the value of the original source. Any random freak can launch the news, as long as his information makes it to the audience.

"The value of information doesn't lie in the source of the information, but in how rapidly it can reproduce. Information isn't knowledge or facts, it isn't a finished product with inherent value. Information is a stimulus to action or the means to justify action. Its value lies solely in action."

Although, the value of information can also be inaction. Whether you go vote for the candidate—or you stay home. Whether you attend the protest—or sit it out. Whether you donate to a project—or scroll on by.

And it doesn't really matter what the source of the information is. Because information is like a virus that saps our motivation and dictates our actions and it doesn't matter whether it's good information or false. Even when the lie is disproven, it leaves a sour taste behind.

In 1999, Boris Berezovsky was promoting Vladimir Putin's presidency. Yevgeny Primakov was considered one of his main rivals and Berezovsky's media outlets relentlessly attacked him. Journalist Sergey Dorenko from Berezovsky's ORT station was one of the most persistent.

In addition to claiming that the 70-year-old Primakov would "sell" Russia to the West, Dorenko suggested that Primakov's age was a problem. Despite the fact that people knew exactly who Dorenko was and who he worked for, that didn't lessen the effectiveness of the "thought virus" he had unleashed. Berezovsky's team had successfully changed the agenda, making the future president's age an issue in the election.

Up to that point, voters had considered the candidates based on their professional qualities and experience. Now age was added to the list of relevant traits. Initially, the topic was secondary, but once it made it to the agenda, it became central. Primakov's staff responded by emphasizing the health and efficacy of their candidate. But that only made things worse. They played right into someone else's agenda and it was impossible for Primakov to become younger than the forty-five-year-old Putin.

Something similar happened in the United States when 73-year-old Ronald Reagan was running against 56-year-old Walter Mondale. When Reagan was asked about his ability to manage the country, he stated "I am not going to exploit, for political purposes, my opponent's youth and inexperience." Reagan won because he changed the agenda to serve his needs. Primakov lost because he let someone else set the agenda.

The French are convinced that Muslims make up 25% of the population of modern France, although the actual number is 8%. We live in a world with a massive gap between reality and what people believe. The battle isn't for reality anymore; it's for the right to describe reality.

To say that particular actors are investing in a particular agenda is no conspiracy mongering. It's a basic political strategy that's been in use for decades.

You don't always have to be vulgar in your efforts to buy public opinion. You can buy public opinions with a bit of flair as well. Journalists can be caught due to the "reactive" nature of the profession and their habit of following whatever's "newsworthy." Pundits and public figures can be manipulated by their dependence on anonymous sources, leaks, and insider tips. As for the regular person, the usual "where there's smoke there's fire" and "it's not that simple," will generally suffice.

By the way, Matveychev left his career as an election consultant shortly after the elections. He went to work in the Presidential Administration. After all, who said politicians are the only ones who can hire spin doctors? Why not the government itself?

Follow the Money

We love to say the truth will win, but it's not necessarily so. The one who successfully promotes his version of the truth wins.

We still imagine the clang of metal when we hear the word "war." We still imagine that battles are fought for square miles. The actual battlefield is no longer reality, but our perception of it. So, if you don't keep your media army well-fed, expect to lose.

The Ukrainian media can be divided into five categories based on funding sources.

State media. In Russia, the largest media outlets feed from the government trough. In Ukraine, it's the opposite. Only a few media outlets receive government funding and its often insufficient to accomplish their tasks. State media are the "poor cousins" in the media market.

Western funded. This category includes two groups: grant-funded media and local bureaus of international news organizations. They can get by without looking for advertisers, choosing quantity over quality, or relying on clickbait. They constitute a certain "daily informational minimum" for the Ukrainian consumer. In the land of television, they play an important part, but not the key role.

Russian funded. These media outlets offer the most toxic content and most repulsive delivery. Sometimes they promote the Kremlin's picture of the world, other times they just undermine the Ukrainian one — it depends on the needs of the moment. Some of their presenters provide pure propaganda while others focus on attacking Ukrainian perspectives. Still others just drown the viewer in manufactured chaos, destroying the very concept of facts.

They play at respectability by inviting famous media personalities onto their shows. They paint themselves as the "opposition" and hide behind "freedom of speech." Their ultimate goal is to dismantle Ukrainian sovereignty and promote capitulation to Russia. Of course, their task is simplified by ambitious Ukrainian commentators who are so eager to be on television that they don't care whose agenda it serves.

Corporate media. This group dominates television. In the past, when an industrial conglomerate gained control over a given resource, they would then defend their power through the creation of a multi-tiered system that included forming their own political parties and media outlets.

The focus of each station depends on the current relationship between the owner and the government. Some follow their owner's lead and actively participate in political games. Others actually try to master various business models. Ukraine is still largely a "television" country in which most people get their information through the TV screen, so this category still holds the key to mass consciousness.

Audience funded. Any media outlet that wants to actually operate as a business is going to need the audience pays their bills, either directly (through donations or subscriptions) or indirectly (through advertising). Unfortunately, this model is rarely successful in Ukraine. The advertising market is very limited, there is intense competition with corporate-controlled media, and readers aren't accustomed to paying for content.

In addition, Ukrainians view information primarily as "entertainment," when it's actually a matter of national security. The

Ukrainian viewer is prepared to pay money to meet their basic needs, but an "accurate picture of reality" doesn't fall into that category. As a result, the country consistently votes for populists and upstarts. And we don't seem to learn from our mistakes.

It's understandable to some extent. Ukraine is a poor Eastern European country. Research suggests that the demand for quality information appears in countries when ⅔ of the population have annual disposable income of $7300 (with purchasing power parity). And, it has to stay at that level for at least ten years. Until this standard is met, citizens generally won't spend money on information.

We continue to think of war in twentieth-century terms. Unfortunately, that perception is not grounded in reality. And since thoughts determine actions, we can be conquered without resorting to tank formations.

Who's paying for your content?

Club Rules

Each season, Ukrainian voters eagerly welcome fresh faces at the polls without ever noticing that the usual suspects are standing right behind them. Politics is still a seller's market in Ukraine.

To get his message across to voters, a politician relies on three types of resources: organizational, financial, and informational. In other words, a team, money and communications.

Let's say you've managed to build a strong team. Let's say they're willing to work for free. Let's say that you've garnered support in multiple regions of the country and opened offices in key districts. That's just the tip of the iceberg. It is necessary but not sufficient.

Next, you'll run up against a problem with the second resource: finances. Without money, your campaign is dead before it's even started. Door-to-door canvassing may be good enough if you're hoping to win a seat in local government. But if you're running for national office, you're going to need hundreds of hands. And hands have mouths to feed. Campaign staff, outreach, pollsters—if you think it's cheap to campaign, that mistake will cost you dearly.

And even if you win the lottery and manage to get your campaign tents on the streets, then you'll come up against a problem with the third resource: information. Because television is still the main source of information for the majority of Ukrainian voters. And the TV audience are the most consistent voters. And the financial-industrial groups control access to the largest stations. If you want those stations to support you, you'll have to reach an agreement with their owners. And they have their own priorities.

As a result, any "new face" in politics faces a dilemma. The candidate may be entirely honest, unblemished, and uncompromising. He may have an excellent team and reform platform. But, if he wants access to money and media for his campaign, he's going to have to turn to one of the major financial-industrial groups. And they will only invest in him if they expect to receive dividends on their investment. Your new idols are going to have to pay those debts.

Electoral demand for "new faces" in politics is good, but not sufficient. If someone wants to meet that demand, he has to make the potential consumer aware of his "offer." And that requires serious investments. Getting those investments will require some compromises.

And this explains why we repeatedly find ourselves in a situation where the demand for "new faces" doesn't open their path to political success. Before you toss your hat in the air to celebrate your brand-new idol, take a look at whose hands are lifting him up.

The Party of the Majority

If you can't find anything to watch on TV, that just means you're not the target audience. It's no cause for celebration.

Television is still the main source of information for much of the country. That's the majority for whom the content and the ads are made. The consumer demands of this majority are the "mainstream" that you want to reach.

If you don't watch television, that just means that you are in the minority. Sure, you can take pride in that fact, but it really just means that you remain a minority. Meanwhile, the majority decides your future.

Advertising executives know as much about the country as pollsters. They track the response to various programs on a daily basis. Sex. Age. Region. Content that doesn't gain viewers disappears from the airwaves. Of course, there are exceptions if we're talking about political content or what serves the owner's interests. But the bulk of the content is always based on demand. And if you think you've washed your hands of television, that just means that television has washed its hands of you.

Users of social media become convinced that they represent the mainstream and the norm. They're not. Ukraine is still an analogue country and the most consistent voters still sit in front of the blue screen. If you want to better understand their worldview, you'd better try blowing the dust off your television.

Maybe you would find answers to some of your burning questions. For instance, why politicians don't talk about you. Why their political platforms don't respond to your priorities. Why there is so little demand for what you hold dear. And so much demand for what is irrelevant to you.

Maybe you would understand why no one comes to consult with you before the elections. Why the daily political menu is filled with dishes you never ordered. Why you have to vote again and again for the lesser of two evils. Why your vote is less a vote "for" and more a vote "against" people with entirely different priorities from yours.

Sure, you can take pride in the fact that the minority is often the most progressive group. Celebrate that you're focused on the future. Just keep in mind that none of that matters in the actual election. Everyone's vote is equal and it doesn't matter who marks the ballot any more than it matters which wallet you pull out to pay your bill.

If you want to understand the country, you need to get off social media sometime and turn on the television. It's sobering.

The Microphone

Should a racist get airtime? What are the limits of the permissible in a debate? Does every opinion need to be heard? The answers to these questions divide Ukraine into two groups: those who prioritize "legality" and those who prioritize "legitimacy."

From the perspective of "legality," everything that isn't forbidden is allowed. Everyone has the right to the podium regardless of their background, competence, or proposals. Supporters of the Kremlin can talk all about "freedom of speech." Criminals can critique corruption. Those who are nostalgic can debate decommunization.

From the perspective of "legitimacy," you have to earn your right to be on the podium. Equal rights in the eyes of the law does not mean access to the microphone. An approach based on legitimacy keeps Flat Earthers off the airwaves. A media outlet that gives equal time to oncologists and psychic healers rapidly becomes irrelevant.

The first approach claims mass media as a space of total freedom without responsibility. Freedom, because they're prepared to platform anyone, regardless of reputation. Without responsibility, because they transfer all responsibility to the audience. "Our viewers can listen to everyone and draw their own conclusions."

The second approach demands responsibility from the media. Editors are expected to take a position based on values and accept responsibility for their work. While a pop star and a Crimean Tatar dissident may be equal under the law, they have entirely different levels of legitimacy. That's why Mustafa Dzhemilev's perspective deserves more serious attention.

One of Ukraine's most pressing problems is the almost complete absence of the institution of expertise. This applies to everything, from movie reviews to political commentary. A person can say any idiotic thing on air, and there are absolutely no consequences. It won't impact his reputation, because there is no tradition of attention to reputation. The audience doesn't care about a person's previous mistakes, so they can keep right on making them.

We don't have professional associations that will revoke membership for incompetence. Want to be a political scientist? Just call yourself one. Private stations are like vacuum cleaners — if you can show up on time, they'll put you on the air. Everyone provides commentary on everything.

And so, the editorial board faces a choice. They can serve as a filter and decide for themselves who to put behind the podium. Or they can stay out of it, relying on the letter of the law. And the law doesn't say a thing about professional or ethical competence.

As a result, Ukrainian political shows are like having a conversation with a cabbie. Everyone offers their opinions about our development as if they were discussing a sports team. This is despite the fact that common sense would dictate that economists should be discussing the economy and that reading a Wikipedia article doesn't provide an adequate foundation for discussing relations with Mexico.

Obviously, the producers are free to invite whoever they want, as long as that person hasn't been banned from the airwaves. But that means they accept the risk to their reputation. And the producers decides whether their guest gets a soapbox for preaching or is called in to confess their sins.

"Journalistic standards" doesn't imply a free pass. On the contrary, the idea of standards is entirely about responsibility. The skill to make decisions. The ability to grasp the situation. The ability to foresee consequences — not just for themselves, but for the polis and its citizens.

The Earth is round. Planets revolve around the sun. Vaccinations prevent illness. Ukraine is a victim of Russian aggression. Two plus two equals four.

Responsibility means telling it like it is.

Professional Standards

There is one important thing to understand about journalism in Ukraine.

In our country, journalists don't dictate the rules of the game. The owners do. And you have just one choice: don't take part in a war if you don't want to win.

The annual budget of an average television station is less than that of a single army battalion. And yet the return on investment is significantly higher. Why flatten the landscape with tank tracks if you can plow it with thought viruses?

There is always a gap between reality and perception. Just hammer some wedges into that gap to achieve your desired outcome. Why kill people if you can convince them instead? Ukraine goes to whoever successfully imposes their agenda.

For the most part, Ukrainian media is not set up as a business. The average consumer isn't accustomed to paying for content and isn't likely to start. Even if they did start paying, the potential profits from manipulating the media will always be immeasurably higher than the potential income from subscribers. And that's why we each have only one decision under our own control. Leave in time.

We can choose where to work based on the employer's reputation. The lines in your resumés show your level of squeamishness. The number of zeros in your paycheck indicates the price of your conscience. More zeros mean more anesthesia.

That's why the only thing that really matters in your job search is your picture of the desired future. Yours and your employer's. If they match, you're in luck. If not, keep sending out resumés. Or try to convince yourself and everyone else that "it doesn't really matter. They're all the same anyway." Plenty of journalists choose the latter route. It's the easiest way to make peace with your new position. The easiest way to doze off without drinking yourself to sleep. You can always take comfort in the fact that reputation doesn't matter in our country. People will forgive and forget. Meanwhile, your bank balance looks good.

You can also bargain for the right to your "personal opinion." Boast of your own hygiene in someone else's bordello. Carefully avert your eyes from the fact that your media tugboat is pulling the country onto a reef. Assiduously bat away the thought that your "personal" freedom of speech is just the cheese in the mousetrap for a gullible audience. In the end, it doesn't really matter who's at the helm: a committed charlatan or a useful idiot. The outcome is the same.

Editors never control the editorial policy. A journalist's entire career is a series of shifting alliances made with different media owners. Our consciences don't require anesthesia if we're aiming for the same outcome as the owners. But when we're not, then we face a choice. On one side of the scales: a fabulous income. On the other: a couple of old-fashioned ideas like self-respect.

We're mercenaries. We don't have the ability to form our own army. We'll never have enough resources for that. An independent editorial policy is only possible through grants—and there are never enough of those to go around. So all we get to choose is which flag to fight under.

There are plenty of unprincipled people in our ranks. They love to say there's no difference between flags. When it's time to go—they stay. When it's time to speak—they fall silent. And they try to recruit us, too—sometimes successfully.

Because it's easy to get tired. Of the ethical dilemmas. Of the short-term planning. Of constantly measuring your goals against your employer's. Meanwhile, an inner voice reminds you of your age, the need for stability, family obligations. You start using your children as justification for your choices. And you start to invest in your "personal" future at the expense of our common future.

That's the fork in the road I fear the most. It's bound to show up in my life sooner or later. I'm afraid I won't notice. I'm afraid I'll make the wrong choice. There won't be many arguments in favor of the right choice.

Our country's future is one of them.

5 Changes

The Impossible Becomes Possible

I have a recurring nightmare in which I wake up and it's 2013.

I already know what's coming: Yanukovych won't sign the association agreement. The students will be beaten. The Maidan will start. The storming of the Maidan by the riot police, Molotov cocktails, snipers, the Heavenly Hundred, the president will flee Kyiv.

Crimea will be annexed and our military units there surrounded. Our ships will be seized. My former friends will take oaths to the occupying government. My future friends will leave for the mainland. The Ukrainian army will contemplate its tanks, wondering whether they will either drive or shoot.

Then comes the Donbas. Igor Girkin. Volunteer battalions. So many military obituaries, we can't remember all the names anymore. In July, the invaders will shoot down the Boeing jet. Then comes the battle for Ilovaisk. The first Minsk agreements.

More battles. Debaltsevo. Minsk II. Russian fairytales about radioactive ash and crucified toddlers. The news reports become more gripping than feature films.

I know all this in the summer of 2013. But what will I do with this knowledge? Who will believe me? The minute I say, "and the ex-president of Georgia will be in control of Odessa oblast," my friends will be calling me an ambulance.

The only thing I can do in 2013 is buy dollars at a good rate.

Before the Maidan, who imagined a war with Russia? Who would have believed that the annexation of Crimea and the occupation of the Donbas were possible? "Invasion" was a word used by weirdos and outcasts. The rest of us believed in the power of the Budapest Memorandum and Rinat Akhmetov's ability to defend his interests.

In the middle of 2013, who would have believed that Yanukovych would be gone in six months? Two thirds of the country expressed an unwillingness to go to protests, the opposition couldn't put together a mass demonstration, and the only political excitement was whether there would be a second round of voting in the 2015 presidential elections.

At the beginning of the Maidan, who could have predicted Poroshenko's presidency? Yatsenyuk, Tiahnybok and Klitschko were the faces of the revolution and there were no extra spots in the triumvirate. Poroshenko's victory looked about as likely as the restoration of Yulia Tymoshenko.

Everyone ages. And now we're not talking about pre-Maidan Ukraine. Just imagine you're a Ukrainian waking up in September 2016. Now tell your friends what to expect in three years. When you finally find that television remote and show them the comedian who will be their future president—what reaction will you get? And how long before that proverbial ambulance to the psych ward shows up at your door again?

Nothing is over the top. Nothing is too much. In our reality, there's no such thing as a "bold prediction." We compete to make the most outlandish assumptions—and then the future arrives to wash our sandcastles away. We're used to that ritualistic "everything is just like always," but in reality, there's no "everything" and there's no "always." Angels and demons trade places, idols become anti-heroes, and red lines are there just to show you where to cross.

No one is linear. People change every day—and our attitude towards them changes, too. What did we think of Ihor Kolomoyskyi in 2014? How did we view Ilya Kiva in 2015? How did our attitude toward Mikheil Saakashvili change in 2016?

It's hard to find any continuity in our zigzags, much less any logic. There are no linear plotlines, and no character is purely good or evil. The plot doesn't promise us a victory, and reality demonstrates that the world is ruled by interests, not ideals.

The people we see as heroes today could adopt different roles tomorrow. Today's favorites could fade into oblivion tomorrow. Today's prophets are tomorrow's clowns and lunatics may prove to be visionaries. Nothing is predetermined and only the dead have finished biographies.

The Lessons of August

Six years before the start of the Russian-Ukrainian war, there was the Russian invasion of Georgia. Today, we see 2014 as a logical extension of 2008, but let's be honest. How many of us at the time saw the Russian-Georgian war as a precursor to a Russian-Ukrainian war?

29% of Ukrainians saw Georgia as the aggressor in that war. 25% saw Russia as the aggressor. And 20% thought both sides were responsible. This data comes from a Razumkov Center poll taken immediately after the Russian invasion of Georgia. Informative, isn't it?

We love to reinvent ourselves with hindsight. But the fact is that we were different from who we are today. In the best case, we relied on "It's not so simple." In the worst, "It's their own fault." Three-quarters of Ukrainians held Georgia wholly or partially responsible.

Just over a year after the Russian invasion of Georgia, Tymoshenko and Yanukovych were facing off in the second round of Ukraine's presidential elections. Georgia wasn't even on the agenda. And we can't just blame this on the candidates. After all, the campaign offices based their work on public demands. And there was no demand for defense.

Calls to modernize the army were designated as alarmism. Calls to prepare for defense were scaremongering. Naval exercises in the Black Sea remained unchanged: preparation for a potential attack against a "third state" and the fight against illegal armed groups. "Illegal armed groups" was a reference to the Crimean Tatars. Meanwhile, Russia's Black Sea Fleet was treated as an ally.

The Russian-Georgian War really was a forerunner of the Russian-Ukrainian War, but not in the ways we think.

We complain about the shortsightedness of our Western partners. Their weakness. Their inability to accurately assess the risks. But we were exactly the same in 2008.

We complain that the Russian invasion hasn't resulted in total isolation of the aggressor. We're upset that the world is still trading with Moscow, still buying Russian gas, and still selling them everything else. But were we ready to defend Georgian sovereignty at the price of Ukrainian profits?

We judge moral relativism. We demand that people don't compare the victim with the aggressor. But where was that principled stance in 2008?

I'm no exception. I was part of the majority too. And so when the anniversary of the Russian-Georgian war rolls around, it's an annual reminder to myself of how I've changed.

We like to condemn faults in our friends that we shared until quite recently. If you want to understand the logic of Europeans today, just remember yourself yesterday.

This war has another lesson for us. Georgia was never a part of the "Russian World" in the ways that Ukraine was. Georgian is a completely different language family. They have their own separate church. Their own history, culture, and traditions. It would be hard to talk about "one nation" or "one people" in referring to Russians and Georgians. Yet none of that protected them against invasion by Russia.

That's because while language, religion and identity are important aspects of the imperial ideology, they're not sufficient. They can complicate the aggressor's task, but not stop it. The empire bases its appetite on potential benefits and won't be stopped by cultural differences.

The only thing that will stop an invading army is your own army. And that army's sense of identity will determine whether they're prepared to open fire.

Just look at Crimea.

Peacetime Rules

After independence, Ukraine was split into two groups. Those who treasured the country's existence and those who took it for granted. In 1991, the first group voted for independence for the sake of Ukraine. The second group voted for independence to avoid subsidizing Central Asia.

The former group was smaller, but managed to advance their agenda. Over the next 23 years, they moved from west to east, gaining more and more regions. The second group grew steadily smaller: both in terms of numbers and territorial reach. They took a defensive approach. They couldn't assimilate their opponents, but did all they could to slow their movement east.

The Maidan emerged from the first camp. But after winning the elections, they had to take into account the people in the second camp—the people who were still flying flags glorifying the same old Soviet Union and "Great Patriotic War," dreaming of a "strong hand" and an empire. After the Orange Revolution, it didn't take more than two years for reaction to set in. And just five years later, Yanukovych was elected to replace the reformer Yushchenko.

Then the war overturned everything.

During peacetime, "private" agendas are prioritized. The individual takes precedence over the common. The citizen over the state. Personal freedom over collective ideology.

But war demands a "collective" agenda. The common good becomes more important than the private. Society outweighs the individual. The survival of the state becomes the highest priority. Only war gives the state the right to take a private citizen, put him in a soldier's uniform, and send him to the trenches.

It was only peace that allowed Ukraine to remain lax and loose. Only the absence of war permitted the Kremlin to cultivate its acolytes in Ukraine. When they unleashed the war, Moscow brought the period of "diverse perspectives" to an abrupt end. There was no longer any ethical foundation for any vision promoting a pro-Russian Ukraine.

It's not solely because part of the pro-Soviet electorate were in the occupied territories. The arrival of war also gave the "common good" the right to interfere in "private" lives. As a consequence, new laws made the use of Ukrainian mandatory in some educational and mass media spaces; new, less Soviet symbols for the army were introduced; changes were made to public spaces; street names and textbooks were finally decommunized.

The military invasion destroyed any existing equilibrium between those who looked to the West and those who looked to the East. It transferred moral authority to the first camp and knocked the ground out from under the feet of the second camp. The eastward movement of the Ukrainian "west" is only accelerating and Moscow is helpless to slow the process. The old banners and slogans have been discredited; new ones will take their place.

The great irony is that Moscow started this war in order to maintain the previous Ukrainian equilibrium. Instead, they destroyed it. As long as this war continues, there will be fewer and fewer opportunities for supporters of the Russian Federation in Ukraine.

Peace would be the only way the Kremlin could slow this process. Peace would force Ukraine to face the difficult questions: her past and future, trajectory and personal rights. Peace would make private life the priority again rather than the common good. And that's the only thing that could stop the Ukrainization of Ukraine. The Ukrainization that became possible only after the invasion of Crimea and the Donbas.

The war for the "Russian World" is destroying the Russian world. The war against the "Ukrainian World" is strengthening the Ukrainian world. The best way for Moscow to win this war would be to stop the war. If you want to weaken Kyiv, stop attacking them and then they lose their status as heroic defenders.

But the people in Moscow cosplaying at being epic war heroes can't grasp the meaning of that gambit.

The Virtual Stepan Bandera

Anybody who can find Ukraine on a globe has an opinion of what the country should be like. Unfortunately, those opinions generally have very little to do with the actual Ukraine. This is true in Moscow and Warsaw, on the Ukrainian left and the Ukrainian far-right.

People have trouble parsing the new symbols the state has adopted. Streets are named after Roman Shukhevich and monuments erected to Stepan Bandera. One group calls them freedom fighters, another views them as fascists. The same goes for the chants shouted in the streets and the colors of the flags that hearken back to the Ukrainian Insurgent Army. The left is outraged by the use of these "fascist" symbols. The right is bewildered: how can these "right-wing" symbols have become mainstream, yet the hard right still can't even get enough votes to hold a seat in Parliament?

In reality, none of this should come as a surprise.

For a long time, Ukraine was a battlefield between two projects. On the one side, the Russian and Soviet empires. On the other side, Ukrainian ethnic nationalism. But then came the Revolution of Dignity.

Today's Ukrainian political project was born on the Maidan. It's about values and beliefs. It emphasizes the patriotism of action. The war made this transition inevitable: identity is now determined by who you support in this war. And what you're willing to do to achieve victory. Mother tongue, blood, and soil all moved to the back burner.

But there was no set of symbols ready-made for this new Ukraine. So Ukraine picked up the banners of the nationalists in their battle against the empire. They used what was available.

And that's how Stepan Bandera and Roman Shukhevich turned up on Ukrainian streets. Their reincarnation was inevitable—they symbolize the armed struggle for independence. All the talk of the reincarnation of "ethnonationalism" or "proto-fascism" represents a failure of understanding. The adoption of the symbols doesn't suggest the adoption of the methods. The only relevant parallel is our common goal—independence, not our methods.

The Ukrainian left prefers its heroes pure as driven snow. They refuse to acknowledge the emotional aspects of war. If Russian propaganda had chosen someone else to obsess over, let's say Yevgeny Konovalets instead of Stepan Bandera, then it's entirely possible we would have a Konovalets Prospect in Kyiv today. Every action creates a re-action. If your adversary fights against some symbol, that symbol is likely to land at the center of your pantheon.

The Ukrainian ethnonationalists found themselves in a different trap. The new Ukraine has appropriated their aesthetics without adopting their ethics. In 2013, "Slava Ukraini!" was used primarily by people who supported an ethnic vision of Ukrainian identity. Eight years later, it has moved firmly into the mainstream. It is part of the civic nation, and can be heard on the lips of all citizens, regardless of whether their names end with Ukrainian suffixes.

Ukraine's neighbors to the West have fallen into the same trap. Poland's objections to the new names and banners also represent an error of optics. They can't grasp the fact that the past serves as a source of symbols, not a roadmap for state-building.

The symbols no longer represent narrow ideologies. Identity of form does not indicate identity of content. For modern Ukraine, Roman Shukhevych and Stepan Bandera have ceased to be actual historical figures, and have become pure symbols of the fight for independence without regard for historical context.

We will probably have new names in Ukraine's pantheon of symbols after a few more decades. Ukraine will have heroes who have withstood the test of time to become moral authorities. Some of the people dying today will be our national heroes tomorrow. That's inevitable for a country that is busy building a nation in real time.

There's just one little thing we have to do first. Win the war.

Cultural Politics

Every now and then some Ukrainian popstar genuflects toward Moscow and society erupts.

There's always a two-stage reaction to these scandals on social media. First comes the outrage over whatever was said: "What a scumbag!" Then comes the outrage over the outrage: "don't we have more important things to worry about than what some musician/director/actress has to say?" Sometimes there's a third stage: "Well, he's just an idiot anyway." But of the whole array of responses, the most ridiculous is the attempt to separate culture and politics.

There is no culture outside politics. In the broadest sense of the word, "practicing politics" means to determine the rules of social life. Politics defines the norm and deviations from it, separates the acceptable from the unacceptable. Every single one of us is part of that process one way or another, regardless of which box you check on the ballot or even whether you show up at the polling station at all.

A refusal to be political is just another aspect of your public position. If you're "not political," that just means you've delegated the right to determine your future to someone else.

After all, being a public figure shows us that rights always come with responsibilities. It is their public status that gives them the ability to earn lots of money, travel, and just generally live large and express themselves everywhere. But those things come with a price tag: people will react to every mistake you make, and the reactions will be much more harsh than if you were a private person. And the claims that a famous star is entitled to complete privacy are ludicrous. The very reason the country pays attention to a star is that she is not a private person.

Public figures help establish the "boundaries of the normal." They set the trends in style, music and behavior. A celebrity can legitimize his perspective among his fans. But Ukrainian society also has the right to delegitimize the celebrity.

The country has changed, but Ukrainian show business hasn't caught up. Maybe this is because during the twenty-three years before the war they became accustomed to living like the Eloi in H.G. Wells' *The Time Machine*. They took it for granted that their daily reality was constructed of entirely different materials from the reality of their audience. So when the war started, many of them decided not to notice.

After all, the Soviet era had trained them to believe that you aren't a real star until you move to Moscow. And so year after year we keep seeing the names of Russian cities on the tour schedules of Ukrainian performers. We keep hearing "we all need peace." Day after day we observe these desperate attempts to straddle the fence.

It's hardly surprising. If they acknowledged the current situation, they would have to move outside their comfort zones. It's far more enjoyable to continue serving as god parents for each other's children, chartering jets for parties and cursing abstract concepts than it would be to (God forbid!) get into an argument with an actual person.

In interviews, many Ukrainian stars continue to address their audiences on both sides of the border. They don't seem to have realized that Ukrainian and Russian audiences are no longer the same or that something that pleases their fans in Moscow, won't go over well in Kyiv.

The more you avoid reality, the more likely it becomes that reality will avoid you.

Our Children's Flags

The ideas of political scientist Benedict Anderson offer a clear explanation of why Ukraine needs its own, separate Orthodox church.

Anderson's book *Imagined Communities* explores the nature of political nations and the stages of their formation.

Anderson wrote that any society larger than a village is an "imagined" community. The participants can't know everyone individually, and so intragroup interactions begin to function with an entirely different set of rules.

Cities, states and empires became possible only when humanity underwent a cognitive revolution—one in which people began to create imagined realities.

Imagined realities are like agreements that people make about who they are and the rules of the game governing society. These "myths," these collective assumptions, formed the foundation which allowed *Homo sapiens* to become ascendant. Myths provide the structure for humans to cooperate in large groups.

The Crusades were organized by groups of Catholics who had never met. Strangers within a country are united by a flag, an anthem, and a belief in the existence of their nation. Thanks to the fact that people continue to believe in the value of paper money, you can exchange paper rectangles and metal circles for food and goods.

The entire modern world is actually a web of myths capable of uniting people along various lines. Religious myths unite people who share the same beliefs. Our belief in money allows the entire system of banking and credit to function. Our belief in human rights allows us to create more humane laws in modern societies. These myths are united by the fact that they live in the collective imagination.

We tend to think that reality is either objective or subjective. There is actually a third form of reality: intersubjective. Intersubjective reality is built on trust and the cooperation of large numbers of people. Nations are one form of intersubjective reality.

Our entire civilization is built on intersubjective realities. It is these intersubjective realities which make some societies models to emulate, while others move to the margins of history. The difference between North Korea and South Korea can't be chalked up to biology or geography. The difference lies in each country's picture of the world. We have created imagined communities and have become part of them.

But here's the thing: these realities can't always co-exist easily. Sometimes they are mutually antagonistic. A revolution is fundamentally a change in myths. One paradigm of self and worldview is exchanged for another. The current war between Ukraine and Russia is, among other things, a battle between two versions of Ukraine. The Ukrainian version and the Russian one.

Russia wants Ukraine to live according to the Kremlin's vision of its past and future. Our former colonizers want the Russian myth and Russian interpretations to dictate reality here.

In order to survive, Ukraine must offer its own vision of itself. That vision is made up a variety of elements that include: our own interpretation of history. Our desired future. Our expectations. And our own institutions: social, governmental and religious. These differences draw the outlines which protect us from attempts to convince us that we don't exist.

Sure, you can dismiss the idea of intersubjective realities and collective identities. Perhaps you are a modern and sophisticated "citizen of the world" without any social preconceptions. You may say that a 21st century nation should not be concerned with the church or religious identity. None of that changes the need for

Ukrainian self-definition. The litmus test for significance should be the potential outcomes in case of failure.

It's not biology that differentiates the quality of life in different countries. After all, we're all 98% monkey and 70% water. Quality of life is determined by which vision of reality predominates in a given society. What the society accepts as normal and what is unacceptable. Which collective myths we believe and which rules of behavior we follow. If we want to pursue our own vision, we have to defend ourselves against attempts to impose one from the outside.

In 2019, the tomos from Constantinople finally recognized the Ukrainian Orthodox Church as autocephalous, formally ending its subjugation to the Russian church. This added another section to our defensive palisade. It can't guarantee our success or victory, but it does give us the opportunity to determine our own future.

Rather than leaving it to those who want to replace our collective myth with their own.

History Does Not Tolerate the Subjunctive Mood

The autocephaly of the Ukrainian church is in the category of things that can't be reversed.

NATO has only existed since the mid-20th century. If we calculate the birth of the European Union from the date of the Maastricht Treaty, it appeared only in the early 1990s. Ukraine aspires to join both, but who can say with any certainty how long either of them will last?

We can't predict the fate of the Schengen Agreement either. It is approaching 40 years old, but the pandemic has already introduced changes to the usual routine. The EU Association Agreement and visa-free travel in Europe for Ukrainians look like victories, but who can say how durable those treaties will be?

In comparison, the tomos affirming Ukrainian autocephaly begins to look like the most significant turning point of recent years. There is no expiration date for that decision. The horizons of the church extend further than secular ones. The fact that the decision on Ukraine's autocephaly references events of the 15th century offers additional confirmation of that reality.

The tomos doesn't just consolidate Ukraine's movement away from the former imperial center. It doesn't only change the balance of power in the Orthodox world. It also offers a historic "save point" from which we can rebuild if we ever need to.

We could lose to our adversary. Or to ourselves. We could fall under occupation or slide into authoritarian rule. But no one can reverse our religious independence. Not us, not anyone else.

This is why Ukrainian autocephaly changes the symbolic landscape within Russia itself. It's not just about the baptism of Rus. You have to understand that the whole 17th century schism of the Russian church was actually a consequence of Ukrainianization.

Back in 1912, church historian Nikolai Kapterev wrote that the Russian schism was a direct consequence of the Pereiaslavl Agreement of 1654 and subsequent attempt to unite Ukraine and Russia. At that time, the orthodox church in Ukraine was under the direct ecclesiastical jurisdiction of the Patriarchate of Constantinople. Kapterev wrote that, "In Moscow, the Orthodoxy of the Little Russians and the Greeks aroused strong doubts simply because the rituals practiced in Southern Rus were the same as those practiced by contemporary Greeks, and differed from those practiced in Muscovy."

Essentially, the Russian state forced the Russian church to align its rites with the practices of Kyiv and Constantinople. Kyiv and Constantinople didn't have to make any changes. This explains why there were no "schismatics" in Ukraine. The 17th century Russian church was forced to adopt the Ukrainian-Greek rite.

"Two Romes have fallen, the third stands, and there will be no fourth." Moscow loves to present itself as the Third Rome, the successor to Constantinople. But that famous 16th century formulation attributed to Philotheus, a monk of the Yelizarov Monastery, isn't actually unique. Both the Serbian tsar Stefan Dushan and Bulgarian tsar Ivan Alexander, each of whom had family ties with the Byzantine dynasty, had declared themselves the successors of Rome two centuries earlier. The city of Tarnovo, capital of the Bulgarian state of the time, was also referred to as the new Constantinople.

The tomos actually eliminates two pillars of the Russian state. It's hard to consider yourself the "Third Rome" when the Second Rome (Constantinople) demonstrates its existence by continuing to issue decrees. Particularly, if it demonstrates its existence by granting autocephaly to the very church Moscow tried to "digest" centuries earlier, putting its own believers through the meat grinder in the process.

The collapse of the "Third Rome" claim directs us to another key point: Russia as a successor state to the Golden Horde rather than Constantinople.

You can find plenty of information in Karamzin's history of Russia to show how Moscow absorbed the Mongol inheritance. In this part of the continent, the monarch was far more authoritarian than European kings. This was a legacy of Genghis Khan's efforts to hold together the motley lands and tribes of the Mongol empire. Giovanni de Plano Carpini had already described this phenomenon as early as the 13th century.

A rigid hierarchy and the demand for "great power" status are also inherited from Genghis Khan. The state is sacralized as a supreme value and its subjects exist for the benefit of the state rather than vice versa.

Post-Mongol Russia was characterized by serfdom and the total subjugation of subjects to the ruler. All forms of self-rule were eliminated. The sacralization of the autocrat prevented the development of strong institution or any idea that the ruler was subject to the law. In Western Europe on the other hand, the Magna Carta initiated the slow, but steady movement towards an entirely different form of state.

It's not hard to understand the motivations of Russian ideologists. They prefer to claim succession from Byzantium rather than the Golden Horde, finding that more prestigious. But in reality, when Moscow took over the territory of their former masters, they also took on the structures of internal governance. While claiming descent from Constantinople, post-Mongol Russia implemented the political practices of the Horde.

So, yes. The independence of the Ukrainian church is far more significant than any political calculation. It is an example of how symbolic changes transform political possibilities. The future belongs to whoever controls the interpretation of the past.

The Age of Experiment

The Ukrainian conversation about the future is actually a debate about what kind of imaginary community we want to create. And it comes down to the question of whether we can cheat historical logic.

Years ago, I read all the sci-fi novels by the Strugatsky brothers. In their novel *Hard to Be a God*, a flourishing Earth sends its agents to other planets as "progressors." Their job is to help backwards alien societies pass more quickly through their medieval periods. The idea fails. It turns out that the ladder of social evolution is rigid and you can't skip rungs. Nothing actually changes until a society climbs every single rung.

I remember that story whenever people start talking about Ukraine's future. Ukraine is playing catch up, going through the stages of nation building that our neighbors completed one hundred years ago. All our arguments end up in the same place: is there a "shortcut" to achieve what other European countries have done over the last century?

The 20th century saw the collapse of empires. The empires broke up into nation states and those new nation states created their own myths. They formed their own national imagery and developed their own interpretations of history. Some, like the Baltic countries, later fell back under imperial control for a time. Nonetheless, those decades of self invention had actually created a point of no return. Even years of Soviet occupation couldn't eliminate their traces.

None of these processes touched Ukraine. We remained a colony for the entire 20th century. Our window of possibility for nation-building didn't open until 1991.

By that time, our neighbors no longer had to even think about who they were and why. Ukraine plunged into the debate a hundred years late. So now the conversation comes down to whether a country can skip over several rungs on the ladder, or whether it has to climb up each one in order.

A nation becomes a nation via a national myth—a shared image of its history and its heroes, values and symbols. A nation is born in the moment it begins to imagine itself. And it dies when someone else's interpretation replaces its own. A nation is defined not by borders, but by what its citizens believe. Or don't believe.

Ukraine only began to imagine itself quite recently. This process intensified after the Russian invasions of 2014 forced each citizen to come up with their own answer for who they were and why. And Ukrainian public opinion split again.

On one side of the barricades stood those trying to build a solid symbolic wall of new beliefs, aesthetics, and ethics to separate Russia from Ukraine. They celebrated the newly independent church and an independent view of history. They cheered the removal of Soviet monuments and the renaming of streets. They looked to the experience of the countries around us, pointing out that there were ready-made models for state-building available and we didn't need to reinvent the wheel.

Their opponents declared those examples hopelessly outdated. They declared that those things were just old news from a hundred years ago, that collective identities were secondary and that universal human rights were more important than any national mythology. They believed that modern humanity has devised more universal methods of coexistence and there was no point in latching onto ideologies from the era of Pilsudski and Mannerheim.

It's hard to argue with them—the modern world really has gone beyond the framework of traditional borders. Western civilization has become diverse, free and multicultural. The traditional outlines of "imagined communities" sometimes seem to infringe on personal freedom.

There's just one "but." Everything we like about the modern world grew on the foundations of national identity. Everything we're drawn to comes from discussions Ukraine didn't participate in. Before they drew together in new organizations, the "imagined communities" of the West had time to separate and come to an understanding of themselves.

You might suppose that the modern Western world has become so appealing despite its recent past. But what if it became that way not despite it, but because of it?

Symbolic Achievements

In Ukraine, the reform of symbols is often counterposed with reform of the economy.

People say that the fight against corruption is more important than decommunization. That tax reform is more significant than the color of our uniforms. And they conclude that the celebration of what has been "accomplished" is just a ruse to distract us from what has *not* been accomplished.

It's easy to fall hostage to that logic for any number of reasons.

First of all, there's no actual contradiction here. Reforms of symbolism and institutional reforms are not an "either-or" situation. The one has nothing to do with the other. It's not as though there are some finite "resources for reform" that will get used up in one sphere or the other. Decommunization won't hinder tax reform. It won't help it either. They're two entirely separate processes.

Secondly, people operate from a belief that the government uses reforms in the sphere of symbols (new holidays, placenames, historical narratives) to hide the absence of progress in the sphere of institutional reform (reform of the courts, the prosecutor's office, taxation). The instant we accept this perspective, we fall into a trap.

In any area, the success of reforms is determined by the level of resistance. Supporters of change are always battling those who want to maintain the status quo.

Before 2014, wide-sweeping transformation of the symbolic space was impossible because there was a well-established lobby who opposed meaningful change. After 2014, the war and occupation changed the balance of power. The marginalization of the pro-Russian lobby opened a window of possibility, through which a whole range of symbolic changes could be made. By invading, Moscow actually eliminated the restraints that had allowed the Soviet legacy to remain on protest banners and street names. The supporters of change triumphed over the lobbyists for the status quo, and stylistic renewal accelerated everywhere.

Institutional reforms have lagged for related regions. In terms of institutional structures, the position of those who support the status quo hasn't changed at all. The bureaucrats who control customs, the prosecutor's office and the courts haven't gone anywhere. The war and occupation have not shaken their foundation. This explains why progress has been so much more difficult in those areas.

It's not that symbolic changes have been chosen over institutional changes. They're just two parallel processes. In each case, the effectiveness of reforms is determined by the balance of power. And there's no point in comparing and contrasting the two. Changes in one area are not achieved at the expense of the other.

And if you're upset at all that has *not* been accomplished, that's no reason to rail against what *has* been accomplished. After all, frustration is an emotional response, not a logical one.

Toxic Fantasies

Ukrainian civil society is like a boxer who was expecting a knockout victory against the old elite in the first round. But our opponent performed well in the clinch and now we'll have to fight all twelve rounds.

This is why disappointment is the most common descriptor. The reforms are too slow. Corrupt officials haven't been replaced. The rules of the game haven't changed enough.

Successes are seen as inadequate. Accomplishments are perceived as cosmetic. Evidence of progress is seen as a lie. Some of this skepticism is warranted. Reforms have not transformed Ukraine into "another Poland." The thing is, that outcome was never on the table.

Not only has Poland spent the last twenty years reaching its current status, the Poles also had a memory of full-fledged statehood from the 20th century. Even behind the Iron Curtain, they retained the right to private property. The Poles never disagreed on whether their capital was in Warsaw or Moscow. They never debated whether they needed independence.

In Ukraine, all of those discussions took place. There were plenty of people who didn't see any value in independence. The country's sovereignty was seen as a resource that could be bartered for various perks. That situation only started to change after the Maidan, Crimea, and the Donbas.

So now we're paying the price for our own short-sightedness. For two decades of just drifting. For our inertia and indifference.

You don't go from couch potato to sprinter overnight. You have to overcome obstacles to achieve results. Even weight loss is a complicated process of strict discipline and hard work, self-restraint, discomfort and fatigue. There is always the risk of failure and relapse. Why would anyone imagine that reforming an entire state should be simpler than a personal weight-loss battle?

Some would say that engaged citizens can drive change. That's true. But the engaged portion of society and the more passive masses are like the locomotive and the carriages. The locomotive may determine the direction, but the carriages provide inertia. If that isn't taken into account, the whole train can go off the rails.

Frustration is born of unrealistic expectations. The more sober a look we take at our options, the less likely we are to succumb to disappointment. Even if successful reforms don't transform Ukraine into Poland. After all, successful reforms didn't transform Poland into Germany either.

You can't get rid of those 20 years of inaction after the collapse of the Soviet Union. We will continue to lag behind other countries. The war in Ukraine's east will continue to negatively impact our equilibrium. Proximity to Russia robs Ukraine of stability.

Nonetheless, our frustration with the pace of reforms doesn't change the reality: we don't have any alternatives. There is no "third way" that can promise a "happy ending." Magic formulas for creating superheroes only exist in the movies. In everyday reality, the only options are diet, exercise and tight discipline.

The best way to avoid disenchantment is to avoid enchantment. It's only in fairytales that Ilya Muromets can lie on the stove for 33 years and then jump up to vanquish his enemies. In real life, he'll have to deal with bedsores and atrophied muscles.

A Vaccine Against the Tsar

You could debate forever about what, exactly, makes Russia what it is. Each new answer will build on the previous one. But the alpha and omega of any description of Russia's essence must take into account the concept of monopoly: in politics and economics, decision-making and charting the future. It's no coincidence that the cacophony of Russian voices in the 1990s took place at a time of low energy prices. The Kremlin power vertical was able to reassert itself when high oil prices returned and protected Moscow from any need to be competitive.

In the 2000s, Russia essentially turned into one big oil and gas pipeline. Every other aspect of society lived off the bounty of the pipeline. There was more than enough money to permit inefficiency. To keep the country on life support. To offer welfare to both government employees and private business. The pipelines were enough to support it all, and the whole country either directly serviced the pipeline or served the people who earned their money from it.

Ukraine's oligarchy was different because there is no single dominant resource. There was no single export commodity that could support everyone. So, instead of a single power vertical, we had several that competed for influence. That reality gave rise to all those aspects of Ukrainian reality we take such pride in. Parliament. Mass media. Rival power centers.

Another reason that a Russian-style monopoly on political power was impossible in Ukraine is that there was no monopoly on money. Economic competition nourished ideological diversity. It allowed Yanukovych to hang onto power and it prevented the country from collapsing when he fled. Because in addition to the "Alpha dog," there were other people in the country who had their own interests to defend. At a certain point, some of their interests aligned with the interests of the Maidan. Both the people in the streets and the financial-industrial cartels needed Ukraine to survive.

During the winter of 2013 and all of 2014, people's interests were aligned. Still, the battle against a common enemy, be it Yanukovych or the Kremlin, couldn't offer a complete alignment of objectives. The Ukraine that went out on the Maidan wanted reform — reforms that definitely wouldn't suit the oligarchs.

The fight for reforms is a fight against monopolies. Ukraine knows that economic monopolies give rise to political monopolies: dependent subjects are loyal to the person who signs their paychecks, which weakens their ability to make independent choices in the voting booth. This is why the people who benefit from economic monopolies seek to undermine reform efforts.

The advantage for Ukrainian civil society is that there are several different oligarch dragons as opposed to Russia's one big Dragon. But they're still dragons. Agreements with the West play the role of the sword: they agree to keep feeding the dragon only if it switches to a vegetarian diet. Each new package of financial assistance will arrive only if the monster agrees to rein in its appetite and range.

The West is offering Ukraine an alternative to paternalism. The offering includes diverse interests, the development of market forces and open competition, and a system of checks and balances. These are the things that can make politics and economics multifactorial and create an environment in which no single group of interests holds a monopoly on political power.

As people become less dependent on the government or on particular oligarchs, the level of political competition will increase. As Ukrainians develop their own economic interests, they will make their political choices more carefully. This is why small business and private companies hold the keys to the future. If any group gains complete control of the state or the economy, we will remain poor.

Free markets and economic reforms are just one step in the acquisition of independent thought. Independent thinking emerges from concern for personal benefit. Only economic motivations will cause the voter to pay attention to election platforms and demand accountability from politicians.

None of this could have happened without the war. The war has destroyed the previous matrix according to which Kyiv alternately took money from Moscow and Brussels, without fulfilling its commitments to either, always threatening to run to the other camp. Now that it's impossible to accept money from Russia, the elites are forced to ask for loans from the EU, agreeing to self-castration in the process.

None of which is to say that they won't do all they can to undermine change. That they won't try to carve out personal exceptions to the new rules. That they won't nurture dependents, who will look for handouts via the ballot box. But they're less ubiquitous than they once were.

The recipe for success is actually quite simple. Competition, diverse interests and individual economic motivation are good. Monopolies, concentration of resources and paternalism are bad. The formula for prosperity already exists. So do the scenarios for failure. The war just raises the stakes.

Either Ukraine's future history textbooks will describe our success or they won't exist.

The Anatomy of Corruption

Do you know why it's hard to defeat corruption? Because everyone loses, but just a little. Only a few people gain, but it's a lot. It all depends on the specifics of the organization. Some ministries and agencies spread just a thin layer of corruption, while others offer a thicker slab.

It's one thing if a corruption scheme earns 500 people a hundred thousand hryvnia a month. It's another matter entirely if just 20 people benefit, each of whom makes tens of millions. The first example is easier to fight. Challenging the second is downright dangerous. That's because the more dispersed the benefits are, the harder it is to organize to defend them. The effort expended will be directly proportional to the benefits or costs available. If a person loses money regularly, but not too much, he won't go out to protest. If a corrupt politician is making a fortune off you, he'll defend the scheme to the bitter end.

The entire history of humanity comes down to this confrontation. On the one side is the free market which acts on everyone, but in a scattered and indirect manner. On the other side, groups of private interests which may be small, but are highly motivated and therefore powerful. Each such group makes money by working against the market and the common interest.

Everyone loves to complain about corruption. It has to be defeated. There's just one little question: what are you personally willing to invest in that process? How much effort are you prepared to expend to defeat the groups that are feeding off you?

It's like de-oligarchization. The Ukrainian leaders on the Forbes list went to great lengths to make their way up the social ladder. They made it through the brutal natural selection of the 1990s. If you want to take away their influence and resources, you'd better be prepared to put in as much effort destroying their influence as they invested acquiring it.

You can certainly say that the government should be the ones leading the fight against corruption and monopoly power. After all, under normal conditions the state exists to defend the public interest. But in distorted conditions, it defends the interests only of certain castes.

Here's the thing: in order for society to rely on the government, we would have to own it and consider it ours. But Ukrainian voters aren't even willing to pay market wages to the people who are supposed to be defending them against the dragons. Then they're surprised when Lancelot starts collecting his paycheck from the dragons.

Of course, you can cite numbers and claim that millions of people are eager to fight corruption. But the thing is that just the pure number of participants in the political process doesn't mean much. It is not so much the number of participants that matters as their level of organization.

A disorganized mass has no power. When they organize, they do. Power always belongs to the organized minority. If you want to compete for power, organize. Or join up with people who already have.

An infantile society awaits miracles, rainbows and butterflies. They want kindly wizards, free ice cream bars and the instantaneous victory of truth and goodness. But reality belongs to people who put in the work.

And that's it.

The Formula for Evil

There are many definitions of evil. Most general is that evil is the appropriation of the common good.

A pickpocket doesn't just steal a wallet. He steals public safety. He appropriates it, diminishing the common good for his own personal benefit. In that sense, he is no different from a drunk driver.

Corruption, monopolies, bribes are violations of the rules of fair competition. I have to pay a little extra on the top for every transaction. The costs are spread out so that everyone pays a little more, while one particular person makes a lot more.

So evil begins with the appropriation of the common good. The destruction of a common resource. The privatization of what belongs to everyone.

The quality of a government can be seen in how many "common goods" it provides: clean parks and safe streets. Fair competition for business and public procurement. Efficient administrative services.

One cigarette butt tossed on the ground is a deduction from the total sum. The person who builds his garage on a playground is no different from the monopolist who sells services at three times the fair price, using his personal access to government officials to eliminate his rivals.

The thieves generally describe this theft of public resources in altruistic terms. "It's for my children." Or "it's for my family." The formulation of self-justification is always the same: the thief hides his responsibility behind empty phrases of care for his loved ones.

The entropy of the state begins at the moment when there are more people willing to privatize the common good than people working to create it. This is how collective ethics work. If the logic of "dividends" wins, the country goes to pieces. If the ethics of investment wins, the state becomes a source of growth.

This is one of the central challenges of modern Ukraine.

On one side, you have all the people living according to the old habits of using up whatever is held in common and privatizing collective assets. They don't view the country or the state as belonging to them. They feel no loyalty beyond their own family. Thus, they will only invest in their private benefit, while taking what they need from everyone else.

They're all stealing from the people on the other side. The ones who pay their taxes. The ones who try to follow the rules. The people who are trying to change the rules that favor those in the first camp.

The people in the second camp are likely to serve in the army or teach in the schools. They might create jobs or write code. They might work for the government or create art. But their world doesn't end at the doorstep of their own apartment. Their world is something that is shared, it doesn't belong to them personally, and they're willing to invest in it. Even if someone else keeps trying to appropriate it.

We win when there are more people in the second group than in the first. And we lose if we agree to justify our greed with the word "family." Our own family.

A Philosophy of Treason

"They're all the same" and "nothing ever changes anyway." Those words aren't diagnoses, they're admissions of guilt. And the people who use them are telling you exactly who they are.

A society ceases to be viable when its level of cynicism skyrockets. At that moment it begins to fall apart and is no longer able to respond to external stimuli. No shock is great enough to elicit collective feelings of grief, or unity, or solidarity. Society becomes atomized into a mass of individuals without shared ties. And that's when you can do whatever you want with that society.

"They're all the same anyway" unites everyone in disunity. The person saying it is justifying his own inertia. He is advocating for laziness and a lack of moral fiber, a lack of motivation to leave his comfort zone and change anything. People without ideals use this phrase to deny the very existence of ideals to people who actually have them.

And the person who tells you "they're all the same anyway" has just unmasked himself. Cynicism as a worldview cannot coexist with higher motives. It is based on a deep disbelief in the best in man, in a willingness to consider only the worst in a person. For any particular person, it's just a projection of their inner world onto the world around them.

The irony is that the contemporary Russian system is entirely based on the refusal to believe in values. Russia keeps repeating that lies and deceit are the alpha and omega of the world order. They claim that Russia isn't breaking the rules or crossing red lines, it's just doing what everyone else does. That's why it responds to accusations about Crimea, or repressions, or their hypocrisy in the Donbas with the simple phrase, "you did it, too!"

The worldview based on distrust regards the breaking of norms as the actual norm. Cynicism is the highest virtue. It requires the bearer to squint cynically and arrogantly when anyone speaks of "overcoming" something. Yeah right, "we know all about that," "you're not going to change anything." As soon as someone delivers that dismissive verdict, you should know they're confessing their own shortcomings.

Any given individual is small and measures others by his personal standards. He takes his views and convictions as the norm, as the yardstick by which others can be measured. And for him, the world starts to "change" only when he does something new himself. Something that pushes him outside his usual boundaries. Something that changes his core understanding of the world.

The way we depict the world around us is a mirror of our own perceptions. The way a person represents his surrounding reality is a reflection of his inner world. A difficult person lives in a difficult world, a light-hearted person in a light-hearted world, a kind person lives in a kind world and a stingy person lives in a stingy world.

So, if someone tells you that "nothing changes anyway," you're talking to a person who doesn't change. They need to stop generalizing that to everyone else.

The Fight for the Indifferent

Ukraine is in a state of constant expansion, expanding itself within itself.

The entire history of our country is the competition between two different projects: Little Russia vs Ukraine. At first, the primary alternative to the imperialist vision was an ethnic one. Ethnic nationalists fought the communists, led partisan battles in the forests and wrote books in emigration. But in the last few years, a civic Ukrainian identity has come to replace the ethnic project of Ukraine. A political project based not on blood and soil, but on values.

Multiple languages resounded on the Maidan. The last names of its participants indicated a whole patchwork of ethnic identities. The people who joined the volunteer battalions and the ones who showed up to support them didn't all remember Ukrainian lullabies from childhood. It felt like a miracle to a lot of people. Social mobility emerged, the windows of opportunity blew open, words took on weight and a political nation was born.

But first impressions are deceiving. Society is actually like an ocean: even the biggest storm only reaches the top twenty meters of the sea. The deeper water remains calm even in the strongest tsunami. Waves of mobilization created deeper and deeper layers that broke through the dense depths of inertia. In every corner of the country volunteers and veterans appeared, activists and engaged citizens. But still, right alongside them, there were still people who weren't inclined to change. People who were focused on the values of daily survival. People for whom the refrigerator is still more important than the flag.

And newborn Ukraine immediately had to address another problem that may be no less ambitious than it's fight against the external aggressor. Ukraine needed to engage the indifferent.

Indifferent people don't go out on the Maidan. They don't volunteer to collect supplies for the army. They don't live for the future. They value inertia and habit; they have no interest in changing themselves or the world around them. They take themselves as the norm, and so they argue that "everyone is the same." Mutual distrust both divides them and unites them. Everything beyond their own doorsteps is "alien." They don't believe in any "common good" and they will appropriate it when they see it.

They view the current war as a battle between two external players, one of which is more or less familiar from the Soviet past. One player offers them a power vertical to lean on, a boss who knows what's best, easy paternalism which relieves them of any responsibility. The demands of their daily life are too pressing to think about the future.

The other player wants to tear down everything that's old and familiar. To talk about things that are complicated and unfamiliar. This new project wants them to take responsibility and get involved. It demands that people leave their comfort zones and give up the comforts of nostalgia. This new project demands effort, but they're not accustomed to that and aren't prepared for it. It criticizes both their present and their past. It diagnoses and prescribes treatment. And then it meddles in the realm of the intimate and personal, expanding the reach of Ukrainian as the official state language and removing symbols of the past.

The first project is Little Russia. The second is Ukraine. The first is led by Moscow. The second by civic society.

The battle for the indifferent is unceasing. The new Ukraine, the one born on the Maidan, is constantly expanding into new territories. Into rural areas and industrial centers. It is trying to convert power verticals into horizontals. To force people to unlearn their habits of expecting wishes to be granted by golden fish or delivered on silver platters. To make them change and think about logical consequences. It also has to deal with the old elites constantly trying to maintain the old patterns using new rhetoric. The elites have zero interest in giving up their nice warm seats to those who are scrambling to reach the top of the social pyramid.

Ukraine's greatest foe is inertia in thought and action, habits and perspectives. So the biggest debate is between supporters of "leave us alone" vs "things can't go on like this." On top of that, the Kremlin is still on the battlefield, as ready as ever to plunge Ukraine into a state of suspended animation. Although it is no longer able to advance and is now forced into defense. Its highest ambition is to hold on to the dregs of the Little Russian concept.

The most ambitious project of the post-Soviet space may be unfolding right before our eyes. People who talk about delays in the reform process don't comprehend the scale of what is happening. We have to fight against the elites who "can't," and the masses who "don't want to." Centuries of habit bolster the enemy camp. Kilotons of distrust. Kilometers of inertia that permeate the Ukrainian sea from the surface all the way to the bottom.

In essence, Ukraine is trying to traverse a path within a few years that has taken other countries decades. We must establish new social habits. Agree on new social norms. Neutralize hostile energies and assimilate neutral ones. The country is now divided into the people who are building a new reality, the people who are trying to preserve the old one, and the ones who don't care.

Everyone has to choose a side.

L'État, c'est moi

The only way you'll work effectively with the state is if you recognize it as your own. This has become yet another line of demarcation in Ukraine.

Ethical systems are often born of family memory. You may not remember your grandfather who was sent to the camps for telling the wrong joke, but your father does. And your father will teach you that any form of cooperation with the power vertical is taboo.

In the USSR, there were two significant modes of existence outside the state structures. One was the prison subculture, which was deeply infused with the spirit of non-cooperation with the state. The other was the dissident subculture, which viewed itself as outside the bounds of any "official" culture. When they were sent to prison, the dissidents absorbed the experiences of the criminal subculture.

After 1991, those experiences continued to be the norm in the new post-Soviet countries. People kept their distance from the government. Anyone who cooperated with law enforcement was viewed as a stool pigeon. Reporting anything to the authorities was considered snitching.

When a society doesn't recognize the government as their own, they will do all they can to keep their distance from it, correctly believing that representatives of law enforcement are best avoided.

This was the case in Ukraine right up until 2014. Then, with the outbreak of war, many people discovered that the state also represented a homeland. And the people who decided to change the rules of the game went inside the system: as volunteers in the army or in government agencies. The Berlin Wall between vertical and horizontal power structures finally fell. Even if only at a local level.

In reality, the inertia didn't disappear. Neither did a tradition of mistrust nurtured over centuries. So Ukrainian society remains divided among those who consider any form of cooperation as treachery and those who perceive it as a normal relationship between the people defending the state and the ones being defended.

Ten years obviously isn't enough to destroy centuries of social tradition. Particularly not for a society that for decades has become accustomed to perceiving a man in uniform with authority as a representative of an alien and hostile power.

The tradition of "non-cooperation" with the authorities isn't limited to prison ballads. It was also nurtured in the stories of the dissidents, who were subjected to repressive measures for the slightest of reasons or no reason at all. To this day, those dissidents will offer up mockery of government representatives as the most entertaining form of conversation.

This is another ethical line fracturing contemporary Ukraine. On one side—the people who stormed the Reichstag. On the other—the people who still keep their distance from the power structures. It is a battle between those who now believe the state belongs to them and are willing to invest in it and those who still see it as external to themselves and distrust it.

In essence, it is being determined right now whether future generations of Ukrainians will be listening to Russian pop radio. Whether they will consider the institutions of the state as their own. Whether they can begin to see the law as a path to actual justice.

Don't be too quick to respond skeptically. After all, jokes about Soviet-era traffic cops have disappeared along with the traffic cops themselves.

A Land of Castes

"Court releases corrupt official from custody." "State security structures exerting pressure on business." "Government official strikes pedestrian and escapes justice." These headlines evoke justified rage from the reader and that rage is directed against the government.

It's easy to understand their frustration. The plot is the same in every news report. On one side, those with power and authority. On the other, the people whose tax dollars support them. The longer the government remains ineffective and corrupt, the lower its support.

But here's the thing—in this scenario, it is actually the state that is weak and failing.

All those corrupt, bribe-taking, lawless officials hide their own personal gains behind the shield of the state. Which they then rob for their own benefit. Which they weaken with their mocking of the very concept of the "common good."

We have generally thought that the people at the Ministry of Internal Affairs, the prosecutor's office and the courts were representing the state. In reality, they're only representing their own caste. Their only honor is thieves' honor. They are only interested in self-preservation and expanding their own power. In short, they don't work for the state—they work for themselves.

This became obvious in occupied Crimea when security and government officials immediately swore new oaths of office to the occupiers. They didn't defend the state, they just maintained their own comfort zone. For them, the only purpose of the system to ensure the comfortable existence of their own caste. They feel no sense of obligation to it.

In Crimea, the few exceptions simply proved the rule. For most people, their oath of loyalty was just a formal initiation rite in accepting their official powers—powers they would then use to further their own interests and the interests of others in their caste.

None of that has anything to do with the state.

Maybe our fundamental error has been that we used the word "state" to refer to a Ukrainian reality that has no right to the name. And then we realize that actual "state building" actually began quite recently in Ukraine.

It began when the aggression of hostile institutions forced us to form our own institutions. But the turnover was incomplete. Today every Ukrainian institution is split between the agents of the new forms and adherents of the old ones. The ratio varies from department to department. In some places, like the army, where successful reform is essential for the very survival of the country, there are more agents of change. Other departments, particularly civilian industries with high levels of corruption, actively reject new people and new rules.

News articles describing corruption and lawlessness are not actually about the state, but about its lack. About our caste system. The lack of fair ground rules. Imbalances in the system. The weakness of state mediation. About people who benefit from the lack of effective institutions and actively work to prevent their creation.

The absence of the state is profitable to the people who earn money from its imbalance. Its profitable for big business who violate the rules of fair competition; for cops who charge "protection money" to street vendors; for judges who accept bribes; for state security organs that threaten private businesses. They are all parasites living off the privatization of the common good.

Every news item on this topic offers additional evidence that the Ukrainian state is not strong, but weak. Unlike the caste system, which has grown powerful over the last quarter century. They really want us to believe that *they* are the state.

But it's not true.

Survivorship Bias

According to the idea of survivorship bias, it's impossible to draw conclusions based solely on the experience of the victors. If you want to know the truth, ask the losers.

For instance, we talk about the kindness of dolphins based on the stories of people who have been saved from drowning by dolphins who pushed them to shore. We don't take into account the experiences of people who were pushed in the other direction.

This theory also applies to Ukrainians' relationship with the state.

For instance, in the Russian collective unconscious, the government and the state are inseparable. They are flesh of each other's flesh, like a snake biting its own tail. And so, Russians perceive a change in government as an attack on the state.

In Russia, a vote for the incumbent is a vote for the status quo. A vote for the current borders and steady interest rates, the flag and infrastructure. Any proposal for change frightens the average Russian. In their collective imagination, a discussion that starts with addressing corruption could end with reexamining Russia's nuclear posture.

The trauma of 1991 is so massive that the very concept of "change" has been discredited. And Vladimir Putin turns out to be the embodiment of the "stability" that allows the average Russian to escape responsibility. You don't need to change anything. The people at the top always know best.

And Ukraine is the complete opposite. In our subconscious, government and state exist on opposite ends of the spectrum. And don't tell the average Ukrainian not to "rock the boat."

It was our very determination to go all the way that made the Maidan possible. Calls from the government to "stop" had no effect on the course of events. In the average person's mind, the idea of overthrowing the current government carried no threat to our statehood. The street won out. But, to be fair, we also have to recognize that Ukrainian institutions survived, for all their weakness and amorphousness.

As a result, both Maidans, in 2004 and 2013-14, have given us a survivorship bias. We believe that internal political struggles will never lead to the collapse of statehood. We believe we can endure upheavals without risk of collapse. Our experience of losing our statehood one hundred years ago is too far in the past — we don't even try to draw conclusions from it. And so, we don't sense any limits to what is acceptable in the fight for a "bright future."

The Ukrainian public is convinced that all means are fair in the fight against the authorities. Including actions that threaten the very body of Ukrainian statehood. That's why the fight against a particular president devolved into a blow against the institution of the presidency itself. A fight against the sitting parliament is a blow against the institution of the parliament. And so on down the list.

Ukraine loves to contrast itself to Russia. Particularly in our willingness to change reality, regardless of the cost. If Russia descends into total stagnation, we fall into total chaos. We are too enchanted with the extremes and forget that just because something is opposite to Russia, that doesn't mean it is automatically the best model.

The countries that Ukraine wants to emulate recognized long ago that the government and the state are two separate entities. A change of the one, doesn't threaten the other. At the same time, unlike us, they are not prepared to strike a blow against the very institutions of state power in their struggle for control. If only because they don't have an alternative to those institutions, despite their obvious imperfections.

We imagine that in our battle for the future we only risk some minor drawbacks. That our modern comforts are now a constant, are irreversible. We imagine the water will continue to flow from the tap, the trains will continue to run, goods won't disappear from the shelves. We forget that all of this is only possible because Ukraine's institutions continue to exist.

Memoirs from a century ago should sober us up. A country without a state descends into chaos. Weapons determine the path to social advancement and the only remaining institution is the institution of violence.

There's a sci-fi novel in which the pilots aren't allowed to practice on flight simulators, because the simulators give the impression that any mistake can be replayed. You can just go back to the last moment before your error. Sometimes it seems as though we believe in our ability to hit "replay" whenever we make a mistake.

We're like people who make extra cash dismantling unexploded ordnance for the metal. "We've been doing this for thirty years and nothing's gone wrong yet." The problem with that logic is that the person who does make a mistake won't live to tell the tale.

Growing Pains

Sometimes, it's tempting just to run away from social media. It's too emotional. Every disagreement gets fanned into a fight. Opinions are overly categorical.

At those times, it can be helpful to read the news from other post-Soviet states. For instance, the capital and major streets in Kazakhstan have been renamed Nur-Sultan in honor of the previous president. You will also discover laws against "discrediting the government." Limitations on the right to gather peacefully. Bans on collecting firewood. Isolation of the local internet from the world wide web.

Of course, people will tell me I should be comparing Ukraine with the news from Europe instead. The problem with that idea is that much of the country was separated from Europe for too long. We were cut off from Europe by the Iron Curtain and centuries of history. If you take 1991 as the starting point, we've been slowly moving from east to west the whole time. By reading news articles from our former compatriots in the USSR, we can clearly see the outlines of the path we've chosen vs. the paths our neighbors have taken.

Yes, Ukraine is a young and fragile democracy rife with internal strife, phobias and illusions. Yes, we'll fight until our knuckles are bruised and argue until we're blue in the face. Yes, our present is confusing and our future unclear, but our past is certainly no use to us. Our past has nothing we'd like to bring along in our luggage.

We have no idea who will win the next election. We can only guess which parties will take over the parliament. We're ready to vote with youthful enthusiasm for neophytes as we grope around for some new future. We want nothing to do with the "old" names that got us here.

We argue about priorities. About which is more frightening: corruption or war. About which is more important: sovereignty or prosperity. But whatever our disagreements, we're the ones who create the demand and the politicians respond to our political demand. That's what makes us different from our former compatriots.

Our country could be described any number of ways. You could call it fractured. You could describe it as rich in complexity. In any case, it looks better than what we left behind. Better than what we see in those countries where the media answers to the politicians and not the other way around. In countries where the power vertical is like a column ringing with tension.

Yes, our country is awash in corruption. We score high on the corruption perceptions index. But that high index just shows that we can discuss it. We're able to assess the scale and destructiveness of it. Many of our former neighbors in the Soviet communal apartment have no such opportunity.

Our diversity of voices is better than singing in unison. Our jagged rhythms are better than a unanimous hum. All of our growing pains are more appealing than a concrete wasteland.

We're far from those countries we look to as role models. But we're just as far from those with whom we once lived under a shared roof. Their stability is built on hydrocarbons, their unanimity on propaganda, their predictability on total control of power.

All of our defects are directly related to our virtues. It's better to be neurotic than comatose. Fighting is better than silence. Our instability entails risks, but absolute peace only reigns at the cemetery.

I don't know how this all turns out. The war isn't over and there's no guarantee that we'll win. We argue and debate and stumble—but maybe this is what growing up looks like. Adolescence is always difficult, but no one's managed to skip this stage entirely.

I don't know our future. We are feeling our way in real time, one day at a time, one year after the next. Sometimes process is more important than product—mistakes are inevitable. Even if our present-day reality has too much politics, it's better than one with no politics at all.

After the Credits Roll

Let's be honest: any success we achieve is riddled with risks.

Progress on reforms will lessen our dependence on Europe. Economic growth will encourage bending the law. Success will lead to a fit of national complacency and then the "Orbanization" of Ukrainian politics. Elected and appointed officials will declare that Europe "can't boss us around."

As we get richer, there will be more and more politicians and bureaucrats of that type. They may not all be pro-Russian, but they will all be anti-Brussels, anti-EU. They will start defending our sovereign right to stupidity and to live above criticism. They'll start talking about our "national bonds" and "unique path."

The Ukrainian church could come down with a bad case of egoism and begin placing its own interests above ethics. It could fall into the embrace of the state and start granting awards to highly ranked officials. It could start blaming its failures on other people's mistakes.

We aren't immune to the issue of the wrong people in cassocks. Our priests will wreck their cars and build themselves palaces. They'll show indifference to the needs of their flock and deference to power. They'll provoke scandals and debates about who is above the law.

We will still be hostages of geography and history. Ukraine is a country in Eastern Europe with all the accompanying traditions. Xenophobia, homophobia, traditionalism—these are inescapable features of the political process in our neighborhood and we're unlikely to become the shining exception to the rule.

The examples of Poland and Hungary suggest that satiety/ a full belly can give rise to the most unexpected slogans. Our country is not immune to a conservative U-turn. No more than our neighbors to the west were.

Our idols could become anti-heroes. Our frontline veterans will have a range of outcomes. Some of their names will appear in the crime blotters. Some will be associated with questionable political projects or act as corporate raiders. We'll have to get used to the idea that prior combat experience can't prevent future mistakes.

It's still going to take us a long time to recover from our post-Soviet hangover. To break the habit of viewing the state as our nanny and guardian. We will retain our hostility to the rich and public apathy will be replaced by calls to arms and street rebellions/riots. We will demand "the law" for our neighbors and "justice" for ourselves.

We were a colony for too long. We've become too accustomed to seeing the government as an occupying force. We'll dream of Robin Hoods, fail to value our institutions or respect the laws. We'll raid common property for private benefit. Anyone who takes responsibility for managing collective resources will immediately be seen an enemy, because we're grown used to seeing them as the emissaries of distant imperial capitals.

Even if all of our dreams come true tomorrow, disillusionment will follow close behind. The other shoe will drop. The threads on our flags will fray. Everything we respect and honor will occasionally let us down.

And that's alright.

Happy endings only happen in movies. The characters only clasp hands and walk off into the sunset in romcoms. Life after the credits roll is filled with ordinary problems.

There's no point dreaming of utopia. "The City of the Sun" only looks perfect from the outside. Any successful country is loaded with internal conflicts.

We are children of our time. Of our historic memory. Of our geography. We will inevitably make mistakes, skin our knees and choose the wrong path.

And that's okay.

Some historic wrong turns can be measured by the alternatives, by looking at what happens if we fail. We can't predict what our future holds after our victory, but we certainly know what happens if we lose. The twentieth century was a cruel teacher.

The opposite of our past isn't some paradise on earth. A normal country isn't a monastery with holy elders. Normal life is a constant debate about the future and the present.

If we win, we don't become Germany or the US. We become Ukraine. The Ukraine we are building right now. A Ukraine that will continue to have scandals and scoundrels and shifting demands. It will have room for populists, fools, patriotic charlatans, and crime blotters. The same range of what you'd see in any of the countries we view as our role models.

Sometimes life gets easier when you realize that it doesn't get any easier.

The Burdens of Parenthood

Nine months of morning sickness. Mood swings. Labor pains. The first sleepless months. Major expenses. Sleep deprivation. Weight gain. Vaccinations. Adjustment issues.

A career pause. Lack of social interaction. And then it's teeth. They're breaking through: the neighbors can hear it and the mother can feel it. Childhood illnesses. Crying. Advice from all sides: some helpful, some not.

More expenses. Preschool. Kindergarten. School. A completely rearranged schedule. New family traditions and giving up old ones. And no matter how much you love the child, adolescence will arrive. He will start to separate from his family, pierce his ears, try everything that was forbidden. And with any luck he won't do anything so stupid it can't be fixed.

And none of that takes away from the main thing: the joys of parenthood.

We take family life as a given. We accept the consequences in advance. We understand that we can't trick biology and sociology. Good parents can distinguish between what can be corrected and what just has to be endured. It's the same for all newborns. Including new-born nations.

Most Ukrainians are older than their state. This state is the fruit of the Maidan, that pulled the country out of its state of suspended animation. And of the war which destroyed the illusion that the private and the collective are separate. It turned out that the only thing that can oppose a "foreign" institution is institutions of your own. And we're fumbling our way forward.

There are certain pitfalls in relationships. For example, the attempt to barter for love or set preconditions for our loyalty. "If he behaves, then we'll love him." Occasionally, we look over at the neighbor's kids. Not only do they grow faster than ours, but they also seem better behaved. But behind every model child you'll find parents her poured all their efforts into raising her.

Growing up is the same for everyone. You can't buy your own nation ready-made at the store, with an ideal set of laws and taxes, good bureaucrats, and guarantees of fair play. You have to do the work of raising a good nation, losing sleep, accepting advice from the people who've been successful and rejecting the recommendations of those who've failed.

None of this is a call to just accept our defects. Consider it a reminder that raising a newborn is a community effort. Some people will take action to make it happen, and some people won't. It's also a reminder that some processes are as inevitable as rain.

War creates a demand for easy answers. A lack of justice creates demand for kangaroo courts. Poverty creates a demand for populists. None of this is surprising—you would expect all of it in a recipe book for how to form a nation. If someone decided to write one.

You would never ask a 1-year-old to describe where it hurts. You wouldn't expect a five-year-old to reason like an adult. In the process of growing up, a country is likely to act infantile—our main task is to learn from our own mistakes. Some things just have to be endured, like chickenpox. And there are plenty of illnesses that are better experienced in childhood: measles is much more dangerous for adults.

It's natural to want your child to look like the ones in the catalog. Well-behaved, without scraped knees or bad habits. Never sick, capricious, or bored. Preferably an athletic, straight-A student who respects her elders, helps the weak and gives up her spot on the tram. But you have to admit: that's not why we love her.

Sometimes love is unconditional. Just a fact. And that's why you go to defend the child against the neighborhood bullies. And you don't just snap, "Well, you deserved it…"

Because you may not get a second chance.

6 The Future

Ours to Lose

We're lucky in a way.

Just look at our geography. What would have become of us if we didn't live at a crossroads of civilizations? Would the more successful nations have even noticed us if we weren't essential to their self-interest? Would they bother to help us if they didn't see our failure as a threat to their own borders and stability?

We also got lucky in terms of our enemy. For plenty of people, our relevance is directly related to the fact that Russia is the one invading us. Plenty of people would be perfectly happy to forget that we even exist, but an increasingly aggressive Russia won't let them. This Russia that loves to play-act at being the Soviet Union keeps reminding Europe and the US of the not-so-distant past. We've become part of Europe if only because Russia has so clearly separated itself from Europe. If the country invading us were less significant in international relations, or were less problematic, our allies might have turned away already.

We've obviously been lucky with the patience of our partners. It's difficult to explain their persistence in dealing with the Ukrainian elites. We're going on three decades now that they've been trying to convince our presidents to wash their hands before eating, stop eating off the floor and brush their teeth before bed. Raising a nation is exhausting.

We definitely got lucky with timing. A few centuries ago our disunity, distrust and indifference would have resulted in a blitzkrieg from Russia. You can't compare the scale of the current war with the intensity of the battles of the twentieth century. Who knows if we could have held back an invasion comparable in scale to what the Finns experienced 80 years ago?

For the third time in the last hundred years we're fighting for independence. We've never had such favorable conditions. Our predecessors could only have dreamed of such support. Yet even now we don't want to deny ourselves the opportunity to waste our chance. Who knows where Ukraine would be now if Kyiv had been able to continue borrowing from Moscow? If every tranche of support from the West didn't come with a set of demands? If Western donors weren't willing to explain the same basic truths to Ukrainian politicians with infinite patience? They continually explain free competition, the fight against monopolies, transparent public spending and fair hiring practices.

You have to give the West credit for their stubbornness. It wasn't so long ago that Europe was trying to convince a Ukrainian president to release the opposition leader from prison. They offered the EU Association Agreement in exchange. It was practically yesterday that Europe proposed anti-corruption legislation. And offered visa-free travel for Ukrainians in return. Now they are offering financial assistance in exchange for judicial reforms. Sometimes they seem to care more about our future than we do.

Of course, our allies also benefit from these changes. Our stability protects their borders. Our resilience protects them from floods of refugees. Our evolution protects them from out-of-control smuggling and the export of criminality. Their goals are entirely pragmatic. The thing is, we also benefit from their rationalism.

Unfortunately, you could hardly call us dedicated students. We relapse at every opportunity. We substitute our personal interests for community interests. We think about ratings, not our place in future textbooks. Our planning horizons scarcely extend beyond the election cycle. We readily exchange our birthright for a bowl of stew.

History has been kind to us. Mannerheim could tell us about wedge formations in tank warfare. Golda Meir could teach us about a war of annihilation. Edvard Beneš could tell us all about the worth of allied agreements. Just thirty kilometers from the front line, we don't even feel the impact of the current war. The people screaming about how awful the current moment is have forgotten to take a look at the past..

We have every opportunity to not lose. Every resource to prevail in this fight. Plenty of time to concentrate. We have no right to blame the era or the circumstances. In fact, both have been exceedingly dedicated to our cause. By 20th century standards, we've hit the jackpot in the lottery of opportunities.

If our dreams for the future don't come true, we'll have only ourselves to blame.

Not Everything is Moscow's Fault

Ukraine learned the name of evil in 2014.

Crimea was the turning point. At that point the crackpots and the sober-minded traded places. It turned out that "Russian tanks" wasn't just a figure of speech and "occupation" wasn't just a historical term. It turned out that war can be experienced here and now. Ukraine discovered a new reality and was plunged into it headfirst.

The war eliminated any gray—everything became black and white. It created passwords and countersigns. It also introduced a direct threat. Evil acquired a name and a location. Ukraine began an audit of our jointly acquired cultural property, trying to separate out what was actually ours and what wasn't.

But there were still temptations along the way. For instance, the temptation to ascribe everything we didn't like to the aggressor. A temptation to blame Russia for everything that was hidebound and backwards. To attribute to Russia all of our innate flaws, even those to which they have only the most tangential connection.

People saw the Kremlin's fingerprints in all of our corruption. In the bribe-takers. The populists. It's certainly true that the Kremlin's impact can't be discounted in all of these events. After all, anything that weakens Ukraine benefits Russia. Everything that weakens our institutions, sows distrust and slows progress is an advantage for Russia. But "the Kremlin" can't serve as a universal indulgence for our sins that allows us to reclassify our general chaos as evidence of external interference and attribute our own basic incompetence to Russian conspiracies.

Of course we could try to claim infallibility and declare that everything we don't like is caused by outside influence. But that wouldn't have much in common with reality.

"Hanlon's Razor" tells us never to attribute to malice that which can be explained by stupidity. And we have to admit that "the Kremlin's fingerprints" serves as an awfully convenient explanation. Not least of all because it serves not only as an explanation, but as an excuse. "We're not like that." It's all Russia's fault.

No one is denying the existence of our enemy or that this hybrid war is less a fight for reality and more a fight to control how we perceive it. But we're not ready to don the white robes of virtue. That's what we're doing when we blame everything we don't like on orchestration from Moscow.

Any society is prone to contradictions. No country is free of stupidity. People make mistakes and cling to self-deception. Remnants of the Middle Ages can be seen everywhere and they don't always correlate to measures of social well-being. Even if Russia suddenly lost interest in us, that wouldn't solve all of our problems. Our problems have roots that extend well beyond the politics of our aggressive neighbor.

The war continues. The confrontation is raging. We were plunged into this reality in 2014 and we don't have a clue when we'll be able to swim away from it. But it would be a mistake to use the war as an all-encompassing self-justification. After all, we've been fighting for our own freedom all these years. And there will be room for error too in that freedom.

Something for Everyone

You know what's special about Romanian roads? The drivers flash their headlights to warn you about police ahead. They'll also honk if you dare drive the speed limit or follow other traffic laws. The laws that *they've* set up in their own country.

We've been told since childhood not to expect every household to have the same rules. But in some countries, the people who make the rules are also upset when people follow them. And that's what differentiates more successful states from less successful ones.

Travel can inoculate us against illusions. Each country is a reflection of its inhabitants. The quality of the highways, the cleanliness of the roadsides, the tidiness of the streets—we take it all into account as we form our opinions of new places and people. Public spaces speak volumes about a people's ability to reach shared agreements. Build institutions. Establish rules. Follow those rules.

The tourist's gaze is unbiased. No discounts. No excuses. Whatever exists within a nation's borders is the creation of the people living within those borders. And if they show more solidarity with unknown drivers than with their own police—they've got problems.

It shows that they have failed to create a trusted institution of "night watchmen." Guards they trust. Who will protect and serve. Which means they're paying a salary to people who don't deserve it. Otherwise, they wouldn't be flashing their lights at me.

The laws of the polis are established by the citizenry of the polis. They choose their representatives, vote for the politicians, pay taxes from their salaries to maintain the state. If they fail to follow their own rules, then something's out of joint.

An adult keeps his word, honors his agreements, and bravely acknowledges his mistakes. But here's the thing: societies are like people, and they can be very infantile. An infantile society believes that the common people are superior to the elites. The problem with that belief is that it allows you to transfer responsibility.

If you're unwilling to pay your elected representatives a decent salary, that suggests that you don't believe they actually represent you. If you remove their immunity from prosecution, that also suggests they don't represent you. If you don't trust the courts, the prosecutors or the investigators, that means you've failed to create an actual system of justice.

It's all about collective responsibility.

That same collective responsibility that leads us to generalize about the other countries we visit. We add up the pluses and minuses and attribute the result to the local citizenry, holding each of them responsible for the state of affairs in their homeland.

Even usurpation of power can only occur where people agree to it. Or at least where their willingness to fight for fair rules of the game is less intense than someone else's will to impose their own rules.

Ukraine is no exception.

Unlike Israel, Ukraine did not come into existence because the people wanted independence. Ukraine came into existence because people wanted to be comfortable. In 1991, it was the demand for comfort that led the residents of Crimea to vote for independence. For them, independence meant that the country's resources wouldn't get spent on feeding the other, dependent, republics of the Soviet Union.

Unfortunately, in the mass consciousness, this desire for comfort did not entail any willingness to accept responsibility. If you want to understand who is responsible for what's happening outside: take a look in the mirror.

No one forced politicians from Venus on us: we elected them ourselves. No one forces me to pass on the wrong side of the road: I press the gas pedal myself. The only people stealing from the government are the people I gave the power to do so.

Look around. Whatever we don't like is our own doing. Bad courts, an oligarchic economy, crooked politicians—we did it. We think it all belongs to "them." But there is no "them." There's only "us." "They" are just a part of us.

We can keep telling ourselves that everyone's different. That there are activists and regular people. That there are always more regular people than active citizens. But those explanations will only work inside the country. The outside observer doesn't see any difference. He relies on his own perceptions.

A successful country doesn't win their country in a lottery. They build it. A failed country doesn't lose their country in a poker game. They create their own hell.

Collective responsibility's a heartless bitch.

Land of the Helpless

We've managed to create a decent number of myths about ourselves over the last 30 years. Most of them serve to explain why nothing is our fault.

"*A Government of Usurpers.*" That argument makes sense when you're occupied by a foreign power and they build your structures. When locals don't determine the present or the future of their country. But Ukraine has held competitive elections every year since 1991. Each new president has won by criticizing the previous one. The people's desire for change has won out every time. That doesn't happen where the state has been usurped.

"*The Oligarchs Decide Everything.*" The oligarchs appeared after we gained our independence. That means we Ukrainians created them ourselves, with our actions and our inaction; our naivete, inertia and failure to understand the basic rules of the game. All of our problems, the weak institutions, political corruption, backroom dealing, only came about because of the way our country was privatized and we allowed it. That's it.

"*The People are Better than the Elites.*" Take a look at opinion polls. If the elites are so bad, why do people keep voting for them? Someone will always say that some people just don't see their candidate among the list of options. Well then, why don't the surveys result in new options? If no one is willing to go into politics, then the Parliament will consist of crooks. If Ukrainians vote with their hearts, then populists will rise from the electoral ashes. After all, who is responsible for the fact that genuine reform can't garner more than 10 percent of the vote? Who is responsible for the fact that for the average person, "reforms" just means nationalization, lower prices, and higher pensions?

"*I'm not the problem.*" It's always convenient to blame someone else. Then you get to wear the white hat. It also creates the illusion that simple solutions are effective. If we're not the problem, if they're the problem, then all you have to do is change "them." I mean, that's much easier than changing yourself. But why would we assume that under the current conditions of consumer demand we would have a fundamentally different political offering?

"*The government didn't ask my opinion* when they..." Honestly, do you suppose that every step the government takes is going to be decided by a nationwide referendum? The entire system of representative democracy is based on delegating authority through the use of elections—not on the idea of making every specific decision through direct consensus. No, it doesn't mean that everyone will be satisfied all the time. This is the point of the electoral cycle: the people can extend the mandate of the current ruling group or transfer their authority to someone else if the previous group didn't manage well.

"*I'm not going to accept responsibility for other people.*" Yes, of course, everyone has to determine their own realm of responsibility. One person takes responsibility only for his own apartment, while another takes on the staircase, as well. Yet another person actively volunteers and takes on additional civic roles, becomes an activist. There are any number of intermediate steps between these extremes. Everyone chooses for themselves. But we're still all in the same boat. And the consequences of action or inaction are shared out in equal proportions.

"*I'm not interested in politics.*" Politics is everywhere. If you choose not to vote, that just means that you've delegated your rights to the person who does vote. You aren't "outside the system," you've just handed over your right to determine the future to someone else. But you don't get to abdicate your responsibility for the outcome. You've just agreed in advance to someone else's decisions about your future.

"*The government is bad.*" A country is a geographical territory. A government is a system of mutual interactions between people living in that territory. If their mutual interactions are bad, who's fault is that?

And so, some people make the world go round. And some people run alongside shouting, "Where the hell do you think you're going?!" To each his own.

Subconscious Ukraine

An adult is made up of childhood traumas; a nation is made up of historical experiences. Our past influences our habitual behaviors and our reactions. Our votes and our actions are like therapy sessions. These last 30 years are just a confession on the therapist's couch. The whole country on the couch.

Ukraine is changing, but some things remain the same. Our emotional baggage includes our lack of previous statehood. This results in the habit of viewing any representative of the government as an outsider sent from the imperial center. Ukrainians are highly skilled at surviving under external control. Unfortunately, that skill turns into a millstone around our necks when it comes time to build our own government.

Ukrainians hold the most extreme anti-elite opinions. We frequently talk about this as a worldwide trend, but it has a long historical tradition in Ukraine. Our lands have been controlled by a variety of different empires in the course of its history, so words such as "rights" and "law" are typically heard as something imposed from outside to serve the interests of the imperial center. Anyone who holds office or is granted any form of authority is perceived as representing the interests of the "masters."

This absence of a tradition of statehood made itself felt the moment independent Ukraine appeared on the map. The tradition of resisting governance hasn't gone anywhere — in fact, it's grown stronger over the last 30 years. Anyone who decides to cross over from "one of us," who agrees to manage our collective resources, immediately becomes both a member of the "elite" and a social outcast.

This colonial mindset only values one type of service. We accept that the services of a mechanic, doctor, or tutor are expensive because they provide personal services from which we immediately benefit. But we absolutely refuse to value services that benefit society as a whole. A colony doesn't think in those terms, so we remain fragmented and divided. The "commons" is no one's. The "commons" is someone else's. The "commons" is never ours.

Individuals with colonial status are denied agency. Therefore, they refuse to recognize the value of governance. Administrative services are not on their list of daily needs. Personal needs take priority over collective ones and there is no development of a shared "we." There is only "I" and an intimate circle of family and friends. Reliance on personal connections is a survival skill.

These processes result in "negative selection." If you don't believe that civil servants are meeting a need, you won't be willing to pay them market rate wages. As a result, there is not even the remotest possibility that genuine professionals will enter government service. Instead we get those who are willing to plunder state resources to meet their needs.

Distrust of the government and power structures is only a part of the picture. The biggest issue is that Ukrainians distrust almost everyone. In northern Europe, the index of interpersonal trust stands at about 60%. In Central Europe, about 40%. In Ukraine, that number hovers around 25%, similar to levels in Bangladesh and Pakistan.

All of this was essential for survival when Ukrainians were controlled by external powers enforcing their own rules. Each person's sphere of responsibility was limited to their own home and loved ones. But when the situation changed, the old habits remained.

In a colony, the individual has no control over public space. It doesn't belong to him. What point is there in beautifying your local park if a company of soldiers could show up for maneuvers the next day? According to the ethics of colonial survival, the only thing worth beautifying is what lies within your own individual perimeter. That which you have some hope of defending, some hope of protecting from external interference. Whatever lies beyond that perimeter isn't yours—it's someone else's. There's no point in investing in it. On the contrary, it makes perfect sense to appropriate whatever you can from that "other" to add it to your own individual benefit.

One example was the widespread practice of theft from Soviet factories, in which workers took anything that wasn't nailed down. The condition of roadsides and streets is another example to measure social solidarity. Collective responsibility is only possible when you believe in the future. A colony doesn't think in terms of the future or opportunity, because the colony has no control over either.

In a democracy, government workers are employed by the society. Society agrees to pay people to solve social challenges. And everyone can take credit for the results. Of course, there's always the temptation to hold back on your own contributions. After all, the commons lie beyond the fence. Whereas whatever's inside the fence—that's yours.

Soviet ethics didn't disappear with the stroke of a pen. We continue to live in a society that was trained for decades to value equality in poverty. Sociologists have yet to explore the actual underpinnings of demands for anti-corruption measures. Do people actually want a level playing field or is this just another form of the old "class struggle?"

Ukrainian society celebrates prison time for corrupt officials. It threatens to hang the greedy from lamp posts. And yet, it also fiercely resists any attempts to raise government salaries — even though that is the best way to encourage honest people to enter government service. And so we're back to our question — what does the common man want? No honest men? Or no rich men?

Ukrainian society is accustomed to living without a government. Ukrainians have learned to survive in circumstances where the state institutions are not theirs. We have hoisted the banners of freedom-loving rebels and insurgents. But, when it came time to build our own power structures rather than just tearing down the enemy ones, our historical experience betrayed us.

The 1990s saw the "parceling out" of the Soviet inheritance. Only the scale of appropriation varied from one person to the next. While one person "squeezed" a factory out of the state, someone else just built himself a garage on the community playground. No one saw anything shameful about converting "common goods" into personal ones. The top priority was to maximize one's own square meters. Collective property had value only insofar as it could be privatized.

Things changed in 2014. The Revolution of Dignity and the Russian invasion snapped society out of its torpor. It turned out that the only way to fight the "other" with its institutional backing was to develop institutions of our own. As a result, we saw the emergence of a volunteer army, a massive volunteer effort to support the army, and civic activism on a broad scale. Large numbers of people chose to invest their personal resources in the common good. And yet, the attitudes of the passive majority were unchanged and they continued to view government officials as "enslavers and abusers" with "bags of money" stolen from the people.

Centuries of colonial status have created a degree of learned helplessness in Ukrainians. In 1967, psychologist Martin Seligman described learned helplessness as a state in which an individual gives up trying to improve his situation. He is passive, refuses to take action, loses his sense of freedom and agency and ceases to believe that he has any power at all.

A great deal depends on the individual's willingness to take responsibility for his actions. In psychology, this is called the "locus of control." People with an external locus of control attribute their successes and failures to external factors and conditions. Those with an internal locus of control take personal responsibility for the circumstances of their lives. This difference doesn't operate solely on the individual level. To a significant degree, the difference between more and less successful countries can be recognized by the style of thinking that characterizes its citizens.

We Ukrainians take pride in our successful transfers of power. But the transition of political leaders here is different from more developed countries. In stable democracies, there is a certain legitimacy based on continuity, which links the current group in power with their predecessors and their successors. They may have varying political platforms, but the essential message is consistent: "we govern because our right to do so is no different than our predecessors." Ukrainian politicians have a different message: "we govern because we have a greater right to do so than our predecessors."

All of which leads to the fact that each change in government sets off a crisis scenario. Each new government denies the legitimacy of the previous one. Each new president rejects his predecessor and the version of statehood he developed. To be fair, this endemic illness isn't unique to us. Many countries in Latin America fall into the same trap, but that doesn't make the approach less toxic. In fact, it only confirms the problem.

Each new opposition leader proposes to reshape the country. Moreover, voters only recognize a party as a genuine opposition if they propose to "tear down the old system to the foundations." Anyone who doesn't propose to destroy everything that was done previously is viewed as a pseudo-opposition.

Until recently, this seesaw was part of Ukraine's civilizational vacillations. Those who held a pro-Russian vision of the future could not reach agreement with their pro-European opponents and vice versa. Now even those groups that agree on the question of Ukraine's European choice continue to use revolutionary rhetoric. If you imagine that this problem is limited to politicians, you would be mistaken. The politicians are only responding to the demands of the voter.

Survival values don't simply contradict the idea of a comfortable state. They contradict the very possibility of the state. They deny the idea of a shared fate. Why pay taxes if they'll just benefit someone else? Why follow the rules if they'll make you lose money? Why contribute to the commons when you can limit yourself to your own personal success?

The problem is that this matrix complicates the task before us. Our turn away from Russia requires that Ukraine become part of Europe, but the values that have taken root in our country have nothing in common with Western values.

In the framework of Western values, compromise doesn't mean defeat, but mutual benefit. Compromise is the foundation of cooperation and cooperation is based on trust. If you want to successfully develop, you have to trust the person next to you — even if you didn't baptize each other's children, perform on the same stage, or serve in the same unit. Trust is more economical. You can save money on the height of your fences and the thickness of your doors, on security guards and court cases. In the long run, distrust is too expensive.

Another Western value is freedom. Of course, that freedom comes with responsibility. State coercion appears when you choose to avoid that responsibility, but not a moment before. Man isn't wolf to man, but rather an object of care. Solidarity is the ability to work toward a common goal.

The lack of a history of nationhood is our true childhood trauma. It has had extreme consequences as we approach adulthood.

The value of a mistake lies in our ability to learn from it; if you don't acknowledge your errors, you don't learn the lessons.

But Ukrainian society elevates itself to an unattainable pedestal: "We're good and the rest of them are bastards."

And so skepticism is the most wide-spread attitude. It's understandable from a psychological perspective: what's more satisfying than wearing the white hat? But it is this very attitude that leads us to do nothing. We're already at the top of the moral pyramid looking down on everyone else.

Ukrainians are convinced that they're better than their politicians — even though they elected those politicians. They condemn people who are too successful, but everyone wants to get rich. They dream of justice, but lack respect for the "law." They demand the eradication of corruption, but enjoy its benefits.

All this results in a society capable of the "revolutionary sprint." Ukrainians are great at uniting "against someone" and are incredibly effective in the short run. However, when it comes to longer distances and extended reforms, we face mass desertion.

It's understandable. Reforms require long, slow work and gradual evolutions. You have to work on yourself, invest in yourself, reinvest capital in yourself and the country. That only works if you're realistic about your initial valuation. If you overvalue yourself, you'll start to expect that everyone else just needs to catch up and you'll stand still.

Our greatest deficit is still responsibility. Taking responsibility means letting go of the comforts of non-involvement. It means acknowledging mistakes and drawing the appropriate conclusions. Taking responsibility means no more hiding behind "that's just how it is."

The Problem of "the Little Man"

Do you know what all of our political satire has in common? Mockery of politicians.

Every comedy sketch, stand-up routine, and youtube video is the same. The object of satire is someone who wants to gain power. We're encouraged to laugh at the greed, stupidity and hypocrisy of politicians.

People say it's normal. That satire is based on mockery and it defends the "little man" from those who are bigger and stronger.

That we have to desacralize power so it doesn't put itself on a pedestal.

Okay, fine. But here's the thing: the little man put them in power in the first place.

Mocking politicians is like blaming the mold rather than the damp. Confusing outcomes with causes. Every representative was put there by the electors. Every mayor received the support of his citizens. Every president has taken office thanks to the voters.

"They" are us: our mirror and our choice—a sampling of Ukrainian society. When we laugh at them, we're laughing at our own reflection while refusing to acknowledge that we're standing in front of a mirror.

We've created a myth. The myth of "the little man," whose value lies in his simplicity. Who is repeatedly swindled by others. Like Caesar's wife, always above suspicion. And thereby, we absolve him of all responsibility for his own fate or the fate of the country.

Anyone who decides not to act according to public opinion is an immediate outcast. It is customary to love the common man, call him the "salt of the earth," and forgive his excesses. In fact, we must never hold him responsible for those excesses. And so, we blame the losing candidates for the success of their opponents. Well, they must not have run a good campaign. They didn't say what the electors needed to hear. They didn't construct the right message.

At the same time, we're much harsher when it comes to other countries. We talk about the shortsightedness of the voters who chose Brexit. We puzzle over the motives of Trump voters. And we blame Russian voters for Kremlin politics.

We take the opposite perspective when it comes to our own politics. We coddle our own infantilism and irresponsibility. It's entirely unacceptable to think that the ordinary man made an error, that he lacks education and competence. Anyone who suggests that the Ukrainian voter is responsible for Ukrainian problems will face harsh judgment.

But here's the thing: just because you choose not to accept responsibility, that doesn't change the facts. The nation's political elite is a reflection of the population's health. They are flesh of our flesh. And if we think that there's a problem with Ukraine's politicians, that's not a question for the politicians. That's a question for us.

Treatment begins with a correct diagnosis, but we desperately resist the idea that the cause of our illness is our own lifestyle and immune system. It's much more convenient to blame everything on other people and to nurture conspiracy theories. Those explanations don't require us to make any changes: everything is someone else's fault.

That's why we never satirize the voter. We've managed to absolve ourselves of our sins. Shortsightedness is a trait of the politicians. Stupidity is the birthmark of the government. The voter is never guilty. Since the voter doesn't make mistakes, there's no need to work on them.

There's nothing sacred about simplicity. Naivety doesn't have to elicit sympathy. Most often the "little man's" problem is the little man himself.

The Dangers of Stupidity

Even worse than a politician who is too far from the common people, is a politician who is no different from them.

In any society, there are people who only pursue their own interests, priorities, egoism and emotion. Those people are easily manipulated, because they're always willing to believe empty promises.

They're willing to exchange strategic planning for immediate satisfaction, principles for expedience. They're not interested in the common good or anything beyond their immediate environment.

In any society, you will also find people who understand that an effective course of treatment can require unpleasant decisions, that it is necessary to live within your means, and that parties are followed by hangovers.

The main difference between these two camps is that the latter group is able to recognize that actions have consequences. It is the difference between a child and an adult.

There's nothing demeaning about this differentiation. It would be absurd and naive to demand the same insight and foresight from everyone. That's why in any country, the political, social, and intellectual elites provide the safety net. While our instincts may prompt us to jerk away from an injection, our reason must do the work of accepting the necessity of injecting the medicine into the social vein.

We often say that politicians in a given country are more or less relevant to their society and that demand determines supply. While that's true, there still has to be some distance between the common man and the person responsible for managing collective resources. If that gap disappears, chaos ensues.

The world is complicated. Governance requires knowledge and skills. No matter how much we may love the common man, he lacks the preparation to run the government.

A good politician isn't the one who can gather the biggest crowd. Or give the most fiery speeches. Or find a common language with the crowd. A good politician is the one who understands that part of his job is to build guardrails against bad decisions.

If you want to make a political career, the easiest way is to merge with the common man until you are indistinguishable and consume any resources that have been put away for the future. The hardest way to succeed in politics is to sell people on the necessity of making difficult decisions, when all they want is simple answers.

We live in a state of deep contradiction. On the one hand, we live in a world of increasing complexity. New solutions are inevitably more complicated than what preceded them. If we're going to manage, it will take increased educational and mental effort.

On the other hand, we live in a world where the electorate demands simple solutions. Where the ability to "find a common language" with the voter is enough to guarantee success at the polls. Where the average person wants explanations that are shiny, new and simple.

Ukraine isn't alone in this. In many places, the average person has become frustrated with an increasingly complex reality and has started voting for the peddlers of simplicity. And wherever that tendency triumphs, the nation begins to consume its accumulated resources.

But here's the thing: it doesn't work. The world is complicated. The works of thinkers such as Hernando de Soto, Eric Berne, Martin van Creveld, Benedict Arnold, Brian Greene and Dick Swaab describe that complexity.

The consequences of dabbling with political dilettantes only differ in terms of the price to be paid. Sometimes the price is money. Sometimes it's time. And sometimes it's the loss of a historic opportunity.

That's all.

Fighting Against the Present

The Ukrainian opposition is divided into two groups: those who are fighting against the present for the sake of the past, and those who are fighting against the present for the sake of the future.

There's plenty not to like about the present day. You may dislike the president for his politics. The Verkhovna Rada for its populism. The government for its corporatism. All of them for corruption.

You may be angry at the Transportation Department for the state of the roads. Social services for their sluggishness. The courts because there's no justice. After all, it wouldn't make sense to like all those things that fray our nerves while stealing our time and money.

So then the question is which side you'll take in the fight against the present day. Are you on the side of the past or the future?

The supporters of the past can call themselves the "opposition." They can criticize the status quo with harsh and accurate invective. That doesn't change the fact that all those "ex's" want to return us to the past.

We lived in that past for the first 25 years of independence. As a colony in every sphere from culture to economics. As a buffer state deprived of the right to protest our status. Nostalgia replaced our dreams for the future. Our inherited resources were parceled out to a select few who benefited, and seemed to operate on a belief that "God has given us Ukraine, let us enjoy it."

We only started making our way out of that swamp after the Maidan and the start of the war.

Of course, our present day reality isn't all that attractive. It has to be changed and reshaped, improved and optimized. But that only makes sense you're fighting against the present on the side of the future.

If someone proposes peace at the price of capitulation—that's the past. If someone offers pain relievers instead of treatment—that's the past. If someone proposes that you accept dissolution and relinquish sovereignty—that's the past.

The past tries to eliminate the ontological difference between past and future. That way it can claim to be the future. In reality, it aims to move the country back to yesterday rather than into tomorrow. That's what makes it the past. It lacks any ethical basis.

After all, everything that happened in 2014 was a direct continuation of the past. The annexation of Crimea, the invasion of the Donbas, inflation and crises weren't the start of a new epoch. They were direct consequences of the previous era. The logical conclusion. They were the consequences of having been governed by the people who then either fled with Yanukovych to Moscow or to Vienna.

The past goes by a variety of names. We can think of the past in terms of "ex-" officials and all the people who dependent on them. Or we can think of the oligarchs. The civil service lobby. The judicial caste. The "regular guy" who misses Stalin. The "regular guy" dreaming of the "purity" of the nation. Each of them can accurately diagnose the problems of the present. Where they differ is on the proposed treatment.

It's easy to complain about the present. There are plenty of reasons. But we need to understand what reality it is the person complaining prefers. In Russia, people criticize Vladimir Putin for being both "too Putin" and "not Putin enough." There is an abyss between those two positions.

Context matters. In the battle between the past and the present, I'll be on the side of the present. Otherwise the future will never come.

The Specter of Counter-revolution

The specter of counter-revolution haunts Europe.

The motives are identical: Euroscepticism and a drive to return to our separate national apartments. And it's not limited to the continent either. Russia adopted this ideology at the start of the last century and now joyfully applauds as a wave of change fatigue engulfs Europe. Only one country goes against the flow: Ukraine. Of course, Ukraine would love to run back to her own "golden age," but we don't have one.

Earlier revolutions shared two essential elements: transformative potential and a call to the future. Around the middle of the 20th century, something changed. The drive for revolution was replaced by the drive for counter-revolution. The image of the future started to hearken back to the past. Rather than moving ahead, this wave of counter-revolution aims to go backwards into some idealized past.

Maybe it's because by the end of the 20th century, the future became too hard to imagine. The concept of "tomorrow" became hard to comprehend and people started to substitute the past for the future. The idea that "today is just an imperfect tomorrow" started being replaced with the idea that "today is just a spoiled yesterday." The banners of the new trend are conservative, antidemocratic and antiestablishment.

Why not just storm this fortress of prejudices? It's certainly not difficult to demonstrate the dangers of believing in "the glorious past." You could bring in statistics about increasing life expectancy, illnesses that have been eradicated, and epidemics prevented. You could explain that life in the past was difficult and miserable for all but the top five percent.

You could say it. But it won't help.

The main appeal of the myth of "spiritual bonds" and "the past" is the retreat from change. And that change has continued to gather momentum over the last century.

For centuries, the realities of daily life changed very little. For a huge swath of human history, the tools, daily routines, and understanding of the world and norms remained relatively consistent. Now the world is changing so rapidly that people are struggling to adapt.

The promoter of "spiritual bonds" offers certain benefits to his followers: accept his perspective and you can view yourself as the norm. Your unwillingness to accept new realities and your attachment to an outdated image of the world are normalized. The truth is that intelligence is the ability to adapt to change, while "spiritual bonds" are just an excuse to justify stupidity and inaction.

The promoter of spiritual bonds sells his audience a myth in which they are the heirs and standard bearers of truth. He deals in simplicity, convincing his followers that their problems are caused by change rather than their inability to change. He lulls his flock with the narcotic assuring them of their own innocence combined with a persistent sense of grievance.

There are no recipes to be found in the past. If you want to find them there, you'll have to reconstruct the Middle Ages. Efforts to escape into "yesterday" are doomed from the start. You can break all the looms you want—the Industrial Revolution is still coming. You can refuse to vaccinate your child—but you're just putting her in danger when the next epidemic arrives.

The tragedy is that it's impossible to defeat myths with facts. A myth is self-sufficient and encloses its adherents in a powerful armor of biases and self-justifications. To abandon the myth would mean leaving your comfort zone. It would mean giving up your monopoly on truth.

The current popularity of counter-revolution is driven by the average person's fear of change. The future is unpredictable, rapid transformations are underway, and in the new reality, you have to run as fast as you can just to stay in place. The people who try to ride this wave of fear offer simple answers to complicated questions. They intensify the effect by leveraging anti-elite sentiments.they claim they will return the country to its citizens, protect national manufacturing from the world market, and abandon the global in favor of the local.

It's an aphorism by now: the world is changing faster than people. In the second half of the twentieth century, liberals battled against the old elites. The liberals fought for the future, while the old elites dreamed of preserving the past. Slogans for a world of equal opportunity and positive discrimination pushed tradition to the side. 1968 won.

But then, the Woodstock generation grew up and became the establishment. So they set themselves up as the new norm: yesterday's rabble-rousers and rebels went mainstream.

And so, the players swapped roles. Now the conservatives have taken on the role of the minority fighting the dominant majority. Anti-political correctness is popular now for the same reason its opposite was for decades. It's a battle between what we consider "normal" vs "new." And if the "old" views now look new, should we really be surprised?

In this reality, Russia has turned out to be a trendsetter. Vladimir Putin made the conservative turn part of his platform well before the West had any idea of the political future that lay ahead. Since then, Russia has found an ally in every politician willing to spout slogans against anti-globalism.

What Russia doesn't seem to grasp in this search for allies, is that for many Eurosceptics and anti-globalization activists, their connection with Russia is purely a friendship of convenience based on their own agendas. It's just a public stake in the sand: if our political opponents are against Russia, we'll be for Russia. However, after they win at the polls, one European "conservative" after another discards Moscow's interests. A victorious politician will pursue his own national agenda and interests—not necessarily those of Moscow.

However, there is cause for cautious optimism. Ukraine will never follow this particular trend. Unlike our neighbors to the east and west, we don't have an image of the past we'd like to return to. Unlike Warsaw, Budapest, or Moscow, there's no basis for nostalgia.

We have been a colony for almost our entire history. The short period of independence in the early 20th century was too short, and too tragic, to rely on. Bohdan Khmelnytsky's 17th century wars of independence were too long ago. That past is too different from today: we can turn to it for rhetorical myths, but certainly not as a guide for state-building.

So Ukraine is forced to believe in a unified Europe — sometimes more than Europe believes in itself. Ukraine has no choice but to forge ahead, even when its European neighbors are ready to take several steps back. Some people will say this Euro-optimism is dictated by necessity. Maybe. But that doesn't change the fact that it is Euro-optimism.

The Rainbow Bright Future

Humans are naturally afraid of the future. Especially when it disrupts everything they're used to. Anti-LGBT protestors are just another proof of this reality.

Time flows at varying speeds. One decade of the 20th century introduced more change than a couple of centuries of the early Middle Ages. We still think in terms of "generations" of 20 years, but that's an illusion. Between the "us" who saw the Revolution on the Granite in 1990 and the "us" who saw the Revolution of Dignity in 2014 lie kilotons of maturation and kilotons of cynicism, wired phones and videotapes.

Changes are coming so fast that the new revolutionaries are no longer selling images of the future, they're offering images of the past. And this is the case for all of Ukraine's neighbors. In the ontological sense, Orban and Kaczynski, Lukashenko and Putin are quite similar: they're selling nostalgia and historical embalming fluid.

Homophobia is one consistent element in the package deal.

No surprise there. The new reality has eliminated whole industries and professions. It scraps familiar social structures and traditions. Before too long progress will eliminate truck drivers, lawyers, and accountants. Artificial intelligence will cease to be an abstract concept. The institution of marriage will go into crisis as it ceases to be economically justifiable. Population growth coupled with increasing automation will lead to mass unemployment.

Humanity's consistent habits and traditions have provided the walls to support us in the winds of history. But now the future is even destroying those. In their desperate attempts to survive, people are grasping at the straws of their own gender.

A person clings to his own gender like a life preserver. One of the few absolutes granted by nature becomes the whole basis of his identity. And he starts to view defending this identity as the final bunker shielding his own sense of self.

"Gays don't give birth." "LGBT ideology leads to extinction." "They need conversion therapy." "Why do they need to publicize it?" These aren't just slogans—they're complaints. Lamentations over the last absolutes the average person still has: childbearing and reproductive function.

This is where things get a bit uncomfortable. Absolute honesty isn't going to sound comforting here.

We have to tell them that sex and procreation will most likely be decoupled in the future.

Thirty years from now, we'll be debating whether to implant a child with an internet-capable chip at birth or wait until they turn 12.

In fifty years, the new traditionalists will be preaching that marriage is a sacred union between a man and a man, a woman and a woman, or a man and a woman, but under no circumstances between a person and an android.

The people out protesting LGBT marches today will be looking back at them with nostalgia in another fifty years. As the warm, cozy reality of their childhoods. As an absurd atavism from a time when the rights of an adult person to do as they please with their own body was still a matter of debate.

We just don't read enough.

Otherwise, we would know that homosexuality was removed from the ICD-10 back in 1992.

We would be aware that scientists have traced the establishment of sexual identity to the second semester of pregnancy. That sexual preference can be influenced by hormones and chemistry. That high testosterone levels during pregnancy increase the likelihood that the infant girls will be gay or bisexual.

It's funny. When Dutch neuroscientist Dick Swaab first published the results of his research he was called a Nazi. He argued that sexual preferences have nothing to do with a person's upbringing. They can't be "corrected" because they develop during gestation. Swaab wrote that the functional circuits of the brain work differently in people with different sexual orientations. As a result, he fended off accusations of eugenics for a long time.

This all goes to show that the entire second half of the 20th century was characterized by the debunking of myths. It turns out that homosexual behavior has been identified in 1500 animal species, from insects to mammals.

It turns out that being raised in a gay family doesn't determine a child's sexual orientation.

It also turns out that attempts to treat homosexuality medically are pointless. In the best case, people learn to hide their feelings. And this often leads to depression and suicide. A 2009 report from the American Psychological Association established this clearly.

The most painful truth of all for homophobes is that history has already made the decision. It is just a matter of time before the LGBT community enjoys the same civil rights as everyone else.

100 years ago, these very questions were being debated about civil rights for women. Women couldn't vote in Denmark until 1915, Britain until 1928, and Greece until 1952. Women in Spain only gained the right to vote in 1977. Women's rights groups led the struggle for equality, demanding that they have the same rights as men.

100 years ago, the advocates for the "traditional way of life" used the same arguments we hear today. The sphere of women was Kinder, Küche, Kirche. Outside the spheres of the children,

kitchen and church, men needed to make the decisions. The argument was that "age-old traditions" must not be eroded or the world would tumble into the abyss, its foundations drowning in oblivion.

Somehow the world held on.

Not only that — any questioning of the idea that women can vote, and run, in elections sounds like heresy. Anyone who questions it looks like a fossil, hiding his insecurity in some desire to brag about his sex traits. In most countries, gender equality is no longer even on the political agenda.

The same will soon be true for LGBT rights.

In general, by the time an issue of equal rights reaches the national agenda, liberalization follows close behind. Feminists couldn't have appeared in the 18th century; they appeared in the second half of the 19th. Within a few decades, all of their demands had been met. The same was true for Black Americans: only 46 years passed between Martin Luther King Jr's "I Have a Dream" (1963) and the inauguration of Barack Obama (2009). Scarcely more than two generations.

Denial, anger, bargaining, depression, acceptance. With each new change, society passes through these classic stages of adaptation to new realities. That's how it went with equal rights for women, other social issues, and race. Now the world is going through those stages for gay rights.

Different countries are at different stages. The United States is currently on the final stage: "acceptance." Ukraine is still working through "anger." And some have gotten stuck at the first stage — denying the inevitable, aka reality. But society will inevitably move from one stage to the next until finally the question of whether adult people have the right to live their personal lives as they wish no longer concerns anyone.

Arguments about LGBT rights are not a matter of "European values." It's an argument between the past and the future, between prejudice and knowledge, between backwardness and the logic of human development. On one side of the barricades: the "party of the past." On the other: the "party of the future."

And we already know which of these two camps is destined to win.

A Trap for the Far Right

The first thing I noticed when I moved to Kyiv was its lack of diversity. Growing up in Crimea, I was accustomed to a range of eye shapes, cheekbones and phenotypes. A variety of last names. You went to school with Dilaver. Studied in college with Emine and Server. Worked with Osman and Mustafa.

Kyiv felt homogenous in comparison. Sure, you could go to the Troieshchyna Market and find some Vietnamese vendors. Or take a look down Tatarka Street and spot a mosque. But you had to seek out diversity—it wasn't part of the daily fabric of the streets.

This homogeneity was actually a consequence of our poverty. The reason Ukraine hasn't had labor migrants is that the countries around us offered higher wages and more opportunities. As a result, Ukrainian reality remained homogenous.

When Ukraine becomes more wealthy, that will change.

As soon as there is demand for more workers, labor migration will begin. When wages start improving, people will start coming. And they'll be coming from different traditions, have different ways of life, and look different from us.

They'll move in next door. Limit their expenses. Save up money to send home. They'll stand out from the social-ethnic landscape we're used to.

They'll pray to other gods. Celebrate other holidays. They won't be like us and we won't be like them.

There will inevitably be some criminals. Some alcoholics. Some drug addicts. And every news editor will face the temptation to list nationality when printing the police reports.

The richer the country becomes, the broader a range of people there will be in Ukrainian cities. That is just the basic logic of labor migration. It's the same logic that sends Ukrainians out looking for jobs in Poland and Czechia. Our neighbors from poorer countries will come to take their places.

Does the far right understand this reality?

Do they understand that our lack of diversity is a result of our poverty? That economic growth will inevitably lead to labor migration? That the richer we grow, the more different accents we'll hear on the streets?

The dream of a Slavic sea from Donetsk in the east to Uzhhorod in the west is a dream of poverty. The poverty which right now means that the only migration is out of the country. Economic growth will result in migrant diasporas in Ukraine.

If you want uniformity, plan to stay poor. If you want monoculturalism, don't demand prosperity. If you dream of homogeneity, understand that it comes with a side of misery.

The New Paganism

An obsession with conspiracy theories is an excellent litmus test for archaic thinking.

The pre-scientific worldview explained everything through divine providence. In one part of the globe, thunder was caused by Elijah riding his fiery chariot through the skies. Elsewhere, lightning was in the hands of the supreme deity, who did as he wished with it.

Religious perception denies the possibility of coincidence. Every natural phenomenon is the work of a higher power. Every event is attributed to an act of will. Humans invented signs and talismans to survive. They imagined external powers who had responsibility for the elements and then brought them sacrifices to gain favor. Recent centuries have seen a battle between scientific thinking and mythological.

As time passed, science began to explain reality. Lightning was no longer a message from the heavens, but simply a discharge of electricity. Medicine conquered epidemics, biology extended human life, botany battled poor crop yields. Physics and chemistry provided answers to most of the questions that had previously been the monopoly of religion. But the general demand for "gods" didn't go anywhere. It was just transferred from heaven to earth.

THE FUTURE 231

So it's no coincidence that we live in an age of conspiracy theories.

According to conspiracy theorists, the world is still controlled by those same all-powerful beings. Those beings which deny individuals the right to free will. Everything that happens is the result of a secret world behind the scenes, where the puppet master pulls the strings of ordinary people.

The "Rockefellers," the "Rothschilds," the "Washington Obkom." People give various name to these new gods, but the essence is the same. Conspiracy theorists endow these various characters with endless power and capacity to control the world. Free will doesn't exist. Neither does the natural course of events. Seeming coincidences are actually part of a master plan without deviations.

Gods were needed to explain the natural world. When science took over explaining the natural world, gods were needed to explain the social world. The explanations offered by sociology, political science, economics and history are too complicated and boring. It's much more appealing to invent an omnipotent force, bring it from heaven down to earth, endow it with free will and give it the ability to pass judgment on random crowds of people.

It would have been pointless to explain the science of earthquakes to a medieval peasant—he couldn't have comprehended it. It is just as pointless to explain the complexity of the Catalan referendum or Islamic fundamentalism to a conspiracy theorist. He will always find someone to identify as the mastermind. Someone he will endow with unimaginable, deliberate and ultimate power. In whom he will fervently believe.

It's convenient to believe in conspiracy theories. If you're surrounded by all-powerful gods, what can you do? You're just a cog in the machine, so you might as well just live your life, enjoy the simple things and not worry about the big picture, because nothing depends on you anyway. "Social gods" have replaced the heavenly ones because nature abhors a vacuum. And there is always infinite demand for a lack of responsibility.

People don't change. Talking heads have become the new religious fanatics. They are incompetent people who've appropriated a monopoly on the right to explain reality. There are no unknowns in their explanations. And if reality doesn't fit in their schemas — too bad for reality.

We Ukrainians have inherited this worldview at least in part from our own 20th century. We spent seventy years of the century as subjects of a mass social experiment. Seventy years of total powerlessness, decades of conversations about what was happening "behind the scenes," three generation believing in enemies who were "viciously oppressing" others. All that took its toll. We fall easily into mystical beliefs because we spent decades denied the right to rational thought.

Of course there will always be major players. We live in a world where the weak must take into account the priorities of the strong. A world in which agents of influence do exist and compromises are at the expense of the less powerful.

But it is also a world of complexity. Sometimes economics dictate politics. But sometimes it goes the other way around and politics overrules economics. And sometimes both politics and economics are taken hostage to a single person's ambition. Or emotions. Or phantom pains of empire. Or historical tradition.

Conspiracy theorists are like shamans reading signs and portents. They simplify the world through ignorance. Appropriate the right to explain reality. Depict everything as black and white. They substitute faith for knowledge, doubt for certainty, and ignorance for rationality.

Welcome to the new paganism.

Serf Logic

The pandemic became a perfect laboratory for the study of conspiracy theories.

This should come as no surprise. Any extreme event creates a flock in need of a preacher. What the new apostles don't realize, is that their new leaders are confessing not proselytizing.

The pandemic gave the conspiracists new platforms. They moved to centerstage to tell us all about the global plan. What was happening behind the scenes. The world government and the new world order. They think they're ripping the covers off, but they're actually only revealing themselves. We are watching the confessions of serfs.

A serf sees only the master and the master is entirely responsible for this world. The serf is not free and everything that happens is attributed to malicious intent from the more powerful. Feeling his own *lack* of freedom, he suspects that there must be an excess of freedom somewhere else.

Whenever the conspiracist sets out to make accusations, he just points back to his "overlord." To the person he has identified as the alpha and omega. The person to whom he assigns responsibility for his own fate. For some, that person is Soros. For others, it's the Freemasons. Some point to "the Jews." In each case, he is akin to primitive man complaining about how the gods control his fate: only the names change.

And now these voluntary serfs are peddling their revelations. Billionaires invented the coronavirus. Or ecologists. Or the vaccine companies. Every new preacher triumphantly says "follow the money" and then pulls his invented demon out of this air.

Conspiracists always live in the middle of a conspiracy. Of course, a secret conspiracy is always important. If the conspiracy is revealed, he won't believe the explanation. Higher powers don't make mistakes. Therefore, if they are unmasked, then either they're not the actual higher-ups or they're in a power struggle with someone equally strong. The Rothschilds vs the Rockefellers, the Illuminati vs the Freemasons, the Elders of Zion vs the Bilderberg Meeting.

Conspiracists take pride in their version. It is entirely free of coincidences or errors. The adept in conspiracy theory has already eliminated free will, transforming the world into a plaything in someone's hands. And then, like Pygmalion, he enjoys the beauty of his invented Galatea, protecting her from anyone who finds her ridiculous.

Conspiracists generally aren't very smart and don't understand the world they live in, so they come up with explanations. There are no accidents. Nothing happens without a reason. Proximity in time indicates a causal relationship. It couldn't be a coincidence that there's a population control conference one month before something bad happens. If someone bought shares in a company one week before an event, there's your motive.

They're really just scared. A world without a script feels dangerous and unpredictable. No script means that each person must take responsible for his own life. That your actions and your inaction determine your outcomes. It's much easier to transfer responsibility to a new deity and then wink proudly at everyone else to show that you've figured out the secret plan.

"They" needed the coronavirus in order to implement "total control." "To lower the birth rate." To "reset" the global economy. Conspiracists offer a dozen versions and can find proof for each of them. They tie together a whole range of motivations and connect what is unconnected. He has a deep fear of chaos, so tries to name it, reading the signs like a priest. Divine will excuses a lack of personal responsibility. Who are we to resist it?

Of course, faith in the new social gods is entirely compatible with faith in the traditional ones. For example, some anti-vaxxer motivations exist in the realm of the religious and mystical. For a person with that mindset, the pandemic is part of God's plan. He finds himself at a fork in the road. He can accept his fate and get sick. Or he can get the vaccine and risk angering the heavens with his rebellion.

And the person who feels himself a toy in the hands of fate, is more afraid of the second scenario than he is of the intensive care unit. Mandatory vaccination is akin to spitting on an icon. It is a revolt against the gods and it won't go unpunished. Their worldview is reduced to "whatever will be, will be."

Is there any point in explaining the complexity of reality to a conspiracy theorist? He'll see it all as heresy. Psychological projection will lead him to accuse you of naivety and stupidity. He'll decide you're part of the conspiracy and assign you your rightful place in the bestiary. You can't reach a cult member.

We don't have a simple task: the conspiracists use intelligent words and are pretty savvy. On the other hand, it is pretty simple: at least they no longer have actual power. The new volunteer serfs compete for the role of unknown prophet, denying the world's freedom and systematizing people's fears. Fortunately, their total monopoly on "truth" is long gone. Priests of the new cults are more like village idiots.

Even their own gods aren't interested in them.

Facts and Cults

An epidemic is like a war. Until it starts, you can believe whatever you want. But when the catastrophe arrives, everything gets sorted into proper places.

Before the war started, the army seemed like an unnecessary relic. People in uniform were just parasites on society. People who talked about the threat of occupation were doomsayers. We reassured ourselves about the peaceful modern age. We believed in the inviolability of borders and had confidence in treaties and agreements.

So we could brush off NATO. Trade Sevastopol for cheap gas. Accept pro-Russian political parties as a normal part of the domestic political landscape. But then came 2014, and the invasion and the winds of history blew away our houses like so much straw in the wind.

Seven years later it happened all over again.

Before Covid arrived, we could believe in homeopathy. Consider vaccinations unnecessary. Prefer psychics to doctors. Healers talked about medicine and fortune-tellers about the future. We had hundreds of reasonably honest ways to reassure ourselves. Then came the pandemic, and our house of sticks blew away as well.

We lived for too long in a post-truth world. We believed that everyone is entitled to their perspective. We would say that "the truth is somewhere in the middle." In reality, the truth is where it is and alternative suggestions don't change its coordinates whatsoever.

The problem is that people are emotional and they get tired. Also, facts have weak marketing—ordinary truths lost their shiny newness long ago. At some point, the crowd gets tired of dull logic and wants some emotion. That's the moment when the false prophets enter the arena and start peddling their commandments.

But this whole carnival of idiocy has an expiration date. Wars and epidemics activate cause and effect mode. And everyone will have to pay for their illusions.

Why you believed them isn't important. Naivety and stupidity aren't much different. Alternative facts don't exist. There's a price to be paid for willful ignorance.

Facts are boring, but they do allow us to evaluate risk, take appropriate measures and weigh consequences. They prevent us from losing touch with reality and take an audit of the alternatives. They help us determine the relative weight of a bird in the hand vs two in the bush. At some points in history, that can be extremely important. Because sometimes, natural selection returns to the stage.

The relationship between cause and effect permeates our reality in all directions. If you don't believe in vaccines, don't expect immunity. If you don't seek treatment, you'll get sicker. And if you prefer psychics—don't complain about the outcome.

A wooden idol can survive a catastrophe. But his flock may not.

God in a Test Tube

In 2015, Yuval Noah Hariri wrote that humanity could overcome famine, plague, and war.

When Covid-19 arrived, people mocked the Israeli author's words. What victory are you talking about when a pandemic is ruling the world?

Skeptics suddenly had a platform. Each of them was free to denounce technical progress. After all, it was technology that had released viral mutations to spread across the earth. According to the new Luddites, all our beloved technology was helpless against the virus. How was this not punishment for excessive pride? Was it not a reminder of the weakness of man and the absurdity of his claims to be the crown of creation?

But here's the thing, these prophets of the apocalypse who pop up after every disaster, they have very short memories. In reality, humanity has always lived with epidemics: the only difference now is the price we pay.

The current pandemic does look severe. They say that the most recent similar event was a hundred years ago during World War I when the Spanish flu infected a third of the planet and killed between 50 and 100 million people, which represented about 5% of the world's population at the time. And yet, for all their tragic scale, 20th century pandemics fell far short of their predecessors in terms of death rate. The illnesses themselves have moved from the realm of "divine punishment" to the category of medical/social challenges. You don't need to go far to find examples.

In the 14th century, the bacterium Yersinia pestis, which is carried by fleas, began to infect people who were bitten. The plague started in Asia and gradually made its way west. In total, it killed a quarter of the population of Eurasia, in the range of 75 to 200 million people.

In the 16th century, smallpox arrived in Mexico via the Spanish fleet. Within nine months, it had killed 8 million people from an initial population of 22 million. Other infectious diseases brought by the conquistadors wrought havoc, leaving only two million of the original inhabitants alive.

Two years later, the same took place in Hawaii, where James Cook introduced a whole range of infectious diseases. Within 75 years, only 70,000 native Hawaiians remained from an initial population of half a million.

Against this backdrop, the epidemics of the last century look relatively mild. We are frightened by the number of zeros in figures counting deaths from cholera, typhus, and tuberculosis. But in comparison with the total population of the earth, they no longer look like Biblical punishments. The increase in population and advances in the transportation network were expected to have helped new illnesses match the records of the medieval pandemics. That didn't happen.

In reality, humanity has defeated the diseases which have caused the greatest mortality throughout history. Smallpox was defeated in 1979 thanks to vaccination. There are occasional outbreaks of plague in various parts of the earth, but the numbers of dead are counted in the dozens and mortality doesn't exceed 5-10%. Humanity has armed itself with medicines, antibiotics and disinfectants. We won.

Modern medicine can solve our problems. It wasn't available to the Mayans, who believed that smallpox was spread by evil gods who flew from village to village. Or the Aztecs, who tried to fight the disease with a treatment protocol that consisted of smearing the afflicted with tar and applying poultices of crushed beetles.

The people who talk about man's defenselessness generally don't know history. Or they are more comfortable with magical thinking than scientific reasoning. That doesn't change the fact that magical thinking is most often a sign of undeveloped thought, schizophrenia or an adjustment disorder.

Covid-19 wasn't the first significant outbreak in this century. In 2002, we were tracking SARS. In 2005, it was bird flu. In 2009, we saw swine flu and in 2013, Ebola. Compared to its predecessors, Covid-19 looks poised to become the most serious of the challenges. (Before this, the most deadly was Ebola which took 11,000 lives.) But still, we need to take one fact into account. Modern epidemics are much more about infrastructure and economy than about medicine.

It takes humanity up to two years to bring a new illness "under control." New viruses can generally be identified and understood in that time frame. They can't always be eliminated — we still live with the flu (which kills 300-600,000 people annually) and AIDS. But, flu vaccines do allow us to manage outbreaks and medical therapies have changed AIDS from a death sentence to a chronic illness.

Medicine will find a solution to the current coronavirus outbreak, too. And so, rather than a harbinger of apocalypse, the pandemic will become a test of our healthcare infrastructure. It will reveal which systems succeed and which fail. It will differentiate between effective treatments and ineffective ones. Once it is over, we will evaluate the competence of politicians and international organizations. We'll be able to see which medical systems work and which are empty shams. In the end, it will be a stress test for every country, testing every single one of them for strength and effectiveness.

It will also be a stress test for economic systems. That doesn't just mean the size of an economy and the strength of its reserves. The pandemic also tests the adequacy of public response. Similar to the way in which terrorism becomes a similar test of competence.

Contrary to popular belief, terrorism does not represent a clear and present danger. The arithmetic can seem cynical: in 2012, terrorism claimed the lives of 15,500 people. Meanwhile, well over a million people die annually in traffic accidents. This shows why terrorism's destructive effects aren't found in the moment of the attack, but in the reaction. Disproportionate responses risk far greater destruction. We saw this in the September 11 attacks, when the war in Iraq destabilized the Middle East and led to the rise of the Islamic State.

In recent decades, we've seen how politicians regularly peddle in fear of terrorism. They receive increased powers, start wars, tighten the screws and limit freedoms. As novelist Max Brooks wrote "Fear is the most basic emotion we have. Fear is primal. Fear sells." The people who sell us on the fear of fanatics, convince us to grant them total political control and we hand over our most basic freedoms.

The current pandemic carries the same risk. It frightens us with its suddenness and its ubiquity, its novelty and its relentlessness. There is a risk that we will be offered methods to battle it that have little to do with common sense. People are inclined to imagine that a pandemic, like war, could erase everything. And so the politicians will trade in fear and panic until they get what they want from us.

The pandemic could become a harsh test for every country, testing it for basic competence and corruption, social trust and cooperation, steadiness and solidarity. Maybe it will shake people's faith in false gods. Then there will be fewer anti-vaxxers in the world — for a couple of different reasons.

Who Caused the Pandemic?

There didn't have to be a pandemic. Progress caused it.

If it weren't for civilization, we would never have encountered viruses and other infectious diseases. We wouldn't have flu or smallpox, we wouldn't die of tuberculosis and coronavirus.

There were no epidemics in the earliest human societies. It took one square kilometer to feed a single person, so hunters and gatherers rarely formed large groups. Low population density made pandemics impossible.

Not only that — infectious diseases came about as a result of the agricultural revolution. When humanity domesticated livestock, we got diseases as a bonus. Animals are the primary vectors of most infectious diseases. Mutations allow pathogens to jump from animal hosts to humans. If we had never domesticated cows, goats and sheep, we'd have no problem.

If people gave up progress, we wouldn't live in cities. We wouldn't be crowded together anymore. We wouldn't encounter strangers. We wouldn't need to vaccinate against illnesses, because they would have no way to reach us. It's all because of revolutions. Especially the Neolithic one.

The critics of the current system are absolutely right. Progress really did ruin everything. If we hadn't domesticated barley, wheat and rice 10,000 years ago, we wouldn't have so many illnesses to worry about. If we hadn't tied ourselves to farming, our vulnerability to natural disasters would be an order of magnitude lower.

We would be strong, tenacious, tough and observant. We would eat a greater variety of foods and wouldn't overindulge in carbs. We wouldn't have to fight one another because, statistically speaking, one tribe was unlikely to encounter another.

This is what the sacred books tell us. Even the expulsion of Adam and Eve from the Garden of Eden echoes the transition from foraging to farming. The consequences of the Fall are clear:

food was more scarce, illnesses were more common, and work became harder. And now there's the coronavirus.

I think about this every time I meet the proponents of some golden age in the past. They're easy to recognize. They complain about modern civilization and try to figure out who's at fault.

I have an answer for them. It's the Neolithic Revolution. The one that gave us agriculture and metalworking, permanent settlements and cities, social stratification and theism.

If it weren't for them, we wouldn't have ceramics or axes, fishing nets, intertribal barter, writing, painting, overcrowding or viruses. We wouldn't be dying of modern-day diagnoses for the simple reason that we wouldn't live long enough.

They're absolutely right. Progress destined us to live in a world with private property and war. Progress created social and material inequality, which then led to violence and hierarchies. And it also allowed humans to dominate the planet and waste our time on social media.

It is, in fact, progress that created a world in which obesity kills three times as many people as malnutrition. A world in which violence accounts for one percent of all deaths. In which diabetes claims more lives than wars or crime.

We live in the best of all worlds, but we convince ourselves of the opposite. All this grumbling is due to our short memories. We don't want to remember that our grandmother's prescription to treat a cold, warm milk and honey, is a throwback to periods of malnutrition, in which a sick person was given the highest calorie food available in the household.

There isn't some carefree life hiding in an earlier time. Folk medicine was relevant only until the discovery of penicillin. The people who peddle in our fears don't care to remember that.

Let's be honest. Our reality is comfortable and safe. And if you're still unhappy, it's not reality's fault.

Here's the thing. The only things that can make us happy are oxytocin, dopamine and serotonin. Our degree of happiness comes from biochemicals, not life circumstances. At different times in history, different elements have encouraged the release of those chemicals into our bloodstream. Three hundred years ago, eating your fill was enough to ensure happiness. Today, we want to win a million dollars in the lottery.

Progress has allowed us to satisfy the lower levels of Maslow's pyramid, the ones focused on safety, and now our quest for happiness leads us to storm the upper levels — the ones focused on self-actualization. We forget that it was never an easy task.

It's true that progress hasn't made us any happier. But it has removed the greatest sources of unhappiness. And it gives us the time to think about why we're unhappy.

These words aren't going to stop the new prophets. They'll continue to fight vaccines and technology, progress and scientific knowledge. The world is too complex for them and they'll keep trying to simplify it.

Despite the fact that our reality allowed each of them to reach adulthood.

Thanks to Quarantine

When I was young, time had no value. A day lasted for a week. The weekend lasted a month. The summer holidays were an eternity.

We had the universe at our disposal and we traded it for candy wrappers. Nothing belonged to us, so everything did. There was plenty of time, so time was cheap. I thought about all this when the lockdown forced us into isolation. The world decided to slow down a bit and suddenly you could stroll rather than running at top speed just to stay in place. Hello, Alice. Would you like me to tell you how deep the rabbit hole is?

As you get older, time gets more precious. Sooner or later, you come to understand that there are only two currencies in life: time and money. And your life is just a quest to find the most favorable exchange rate. People rush from the countryside to the city to exchange their abundance of time for the capital's abundance of cash. And then they go back, when they realize that their time is worth more than the capital is willing to pay.

That understanding comes later — right around the time we each find ourselves like the bottom of a ship, covered in barnacles of obligations and seashells of habit. When our days are parceled out by the hour and our weekends to other people. When we begin to measure a proposal by its consequences and an idea by its costs. When other people's priorities control our time. In the best case, it's our loved ones. In the worst, our bosses.

We've become sociophobes. We have everything at home that we need to make friends: drinks, food, space. The only thing we don't have is time.

We treat our own lives an afterthought — along with our children, our parents, freetime... Yes, we place ourselves onto the scales: we are only valuable insofar as we contribute increased value in transferring X to Y. We expect our families and loved ones to be grateful. In reality, most of them want something entirely different from us.

We've put ourselves into the account books. We measure our self-worth by numbers on a balance sheet. Our complaints about business trips are a form of bragging. Our Instagram accounts are the marketplace of vanity. We try to make up for the minimal amount of time together with the maximum drink prices. Our self-esteem is like a bloodthirsty god. We sacrifice our families, friends and ourselves to it.

We imagine that all this burning of incense will eventually achieve the desired results. That the smoke from the life we burn will return a hundredfold and we will earn the right to be reborn. That this life is a rough draft and we'll get another chance. hey've been lying to us.

Lockdown didn't rob me of travel. It didn't deprive me of my job or income. It took away my sense of time. The world around me hit pause and there I was looking around in confusion, not understanding why work days look like weekends.

I had never stood on an empty avenue in the middle of the work day. I'd never seen the city center empty during rush hour. I'd never heard ringing silence in Kyiv's streets.

It took me back to my childhood. I couldn't change my circumstances: they were the same for everyone. I couldn't change the situation: it wasn't under my control. All I could do was accept the new rules of the game and hope that they'd change eventually

. At that same moment, I received the right to be a spendthrift. I could spend my days exactly as I pleased. The exchange kiosk that let me trade my time for money had closed.

I was reset to factory defaults. I could sit on a park bench and chat about trivia. Go for a bike ride with sandwiches in my backpack. Invite a friend to meet at the park because there wasn't anywhere else to go.

And I wasn't playing hooky. I shook that feeling I always used to have when I would give myself a day off on Wednesday instead of Saturday. The world was filled with colors instead of traffic jams and it was hard to get used to. The universal moment of downtime was a shared respite. For once, I didn't have the feeling that while I was taking a quick breather someone else was breathing down my neck to take my spot.

It was a strange feeling. I was twelve years old again and time didn't cost anything. My time was filled with books, movies, and walks. All the things I hadn't given myself in the preceding years. All the things I hadn't allowed myself for the previous decade. You're on summer holiday again and the world has hit pause: you're no longer orbiting it, it's now orbiting you. Everything became extremely honest, unadorned with the trappings of business, status, or the ability to pick the best restaurant.

Because at that moment, there were no restaurants, movie theaters, or trips. Your passport meant nothing. The most your car could do was take you to the park. And so, the only question that made sense after a date, a question you might previously have delayed for months, came to sound very simple:

"Your place or mine?"

Trump, Vaccines, and the Antichrist

The essential precondition for any meaningful discussion is intellectual honesty. It presupposes that you're ready to hear the arguments of the other side and change your perspective based on what you've heard. Moreover, if your opponent's arguments are convincing enough, you're willing to acknowledge their superiority over your own.

THE FUTURE 245

However, discussion is frequently replaced by debate. In a debate, facts, logic, and evidence are secondary. Participants are free to make use of the whole arsenal of unconventional weapons, including emotion and disrespect. The main goal in a debate is to win.

Few people are willing to pay the price of losing.

Journalist Stanislav Aseev writes that in the Donetsk torture camp "Isolation," about half the prisoners were separatists. They were "infantry" and "generals" who had run afoul of their compatriots and then been "sent to the basement." Even there, many of them refused to acknowledge that they'd chosen the wrong path in 2014. They would say their arrest "must have been a mistake," but it would still serve as "an example for others."

And of course, these weren't isolated instances of madness. On the contrary, it's perfectly rational behavior for the human psyche. Each of those fighters found himself at a fork in the road. On one side of the scales, your personal fate. On the other side, the fate of your beliefs.

You can admit that you've been killing people all this time just for the sake of some obscene imitation of a lumpen dictatorship that has no right to exist. Or you can affirm the values of the pseudo republic and explain your own misfortunes with the old "you can't make an omelet without breaking some eggs." Which choice you make says a lot about you. But if you think this is only relevant about supporters of the so-called "Luhansk People's Republic," you're mistaken.

We live in a world that can't always bring us to reason. People are always ready to protect their beliefs from hard facts. Donald Trump's supporters continue to believe that the election was stolen. Antivaxxers dismiss evidence-based medicine. Adherents of traditional values cling to the idea of a "golden age."

On the surface, these groups have nothing in common. In reality, each of them lives according to the exact same rules. Each of them sees themselves as the archetype of all that is good and their opponents as the source of all chaos and destruction. One person fights satanist pedophiles in pizza parlors, one rebels against plans to microchip all of humanity and a third battles against the liberal world order that threatens to destroy tradition and the foundations of society.

The scale of these goals make these groups untouchable. Each participant is fighting not for himself, but for everyone. Not for his own benefit, but a common goal. Every real cult grants its adepts added value. A task of cosmic import breaks into the space of private life. And offers happiness.

When it comes right down to it, we delude ourselves imagining that happiness consists of minimizing unpleasantness and maximizing pleasure. In reality, happiness has a powerful cognitive and ethical component. The person who knows the answer to "why" can cope with any "how." And this is why it is almost impossible to change their minds. If they accept our counterarguments, they will be faced with losing their happiness, losing the Goal. Not many people are ready to agree to such a thing.

That's the strange thing about our reality. The phrase "time will tell" only applies to very large time scales. It only works when the person evaluating events has no stake in that evaluation. When the acknowledgment of someone else's contributions or failures won't mean the collapse of one's own values.

None of that is relevant when it comes to judgments against the present. People aren't computers. Their calculations include lots of personal and situational factors. We are often held captive by what we've said in the past, when the situation was different. Our surroundings and our social network hold us captive. Any reevaluation of our values will be met by accusations of betrayal. A revision of our beliefs will boomerang back as a personal crisis.

We discuss how social media has ostracized Donald Trump, but we also have to recognize that social media created him. Not the physical, actual 45th President of the United States, but the "donaldtrump" phenomenon.

It was social media that brought the cranks together. Flat Earthers, QAnon, and anti-vaxxers became powerful thanks to the internet. Social media allowed people with bizarre ideas to find each other and demand a specific type of politics. Donald Trump is the "supply" to meet that "demand." And now the whole world is arguing whether there are limits to freedom of speech and, if so, what they are.

The people who argue that there are no limits, need to answer the question of whether Donald Trump's supporters can be convinced of reality. Are there any arguments that could return them from the arena of debate to the arena of honest argument? Would any amount of evidence change their perspective?

The people who argue that there are limits, have to determine where they are. Where does the boundary beyond which the acceptable blends into the socially harmful? Who decides the limits of what is acceptable and who watches the Watchmen?

Just twenty years ago, a small group of gatekeepers controlled the mass media. Then came the era of media without intermediaries. Now, at the start of the 2020s, we find ourselves amidst a new transformation. It's entirely possible that discussions of freedom and responsibility will again shape our discussions of the future.

Let's just hope it doesn't slide into debate.

Eastern Europe's Wild West

You know, I'd really like to see some boring politicians.

Politicians without hyperbole or hysterics. Without showmanship or shock value. I'd like to watch bureaucrats in suits talking about figures and percentages.

I want to watch boring political talk shows. Shows that no one will watch because the talking heads are going into nitty-gritty details. There won't be a stand-up routine. No one will come with pitchforks. Nothing will devolve into a fistfight. The shows will have terrible ratings, because they won't be entertainment. Our conversations about the future won't resemble a circus.

I want an actual political platform instead of personalities. We confuse the two now. We argue about names instead of plans. We consider novelty a measure of quality and youth as innately progressive.

I really want to see an emphasis on reputation and longer memories. I want those long memories applied to political reputations. I want investigations to matter beyond social media. And for the law to never be used as a tool for settling accounts with political adversaries. I want to see boundaries and limits which can't be crossed.

I want to live to see trust, solidarity, synergy, and cooperation. All of our nepotism is a remnant of our suspiciousness. It costs us dearly and I'm tired of overpaying.

I've never lived in a boring country. I've only visited them as a tourist. We tend to poke fun at their sense of order and daily habits but, in the best cases, it's not hard to see the jealousy under our patriotic bravado. In the worst cases, it's just our provincialism.

We call ourselves Eastern Europe's Wild West. The land of social mobility. It's true. Our windows of opportunity are so wide open that anyone can climb in. Our celebrities are famous just for being famous.

We're a land of unpredictable biographies. Our heroes and villains regularly switch roles. Our resumés are packed with mutually exclusive entries. We have company directors driving cabs. We put cab drivers in charge.

We're emotional. We go to the polling station like we're going to the wedding chapel. We fill out the ballot with elevated dopamine and norepinephrine and reduced serotonin. Neurophysiologists tell us that this cocktail of hormones is called love. It doesn't leave any space for cold hard logic.

In our arguments, we don't fight for truth, but for the right to wear a halo. We readily unite against something, but almost never in support of something. We manage quite well in bypassing the state, because we don't see it as belonging to us. But our entire history demonstrates what a meat grinder our lack of a state is.

We invent new thousand-year-old traditions on a daily basis. We trust in charlatans and magic. Our Holy Grail is a happiness switch. Every five years we go to the polls, looking for the person who can get it for us.

Magical thinking has taken root. We see ourselves as little people in the crosswinds of history. We live among gods and worry about falling under their chariots. One person refuses the vaccine so the social gods won't be able to control him. Others do the same so as not to anger the heavens and fate.

We habitually blame other people for our problems. Our biographies are like pure-driven snow. The little man has been canonized. Another person's success isn't cause for celebration, but for condemnation. Our dream of equality is just the old class struggle poured into new bottles.

We overestimate ourselves. We figure history owes us something. We believe someone else lives well at our expense. We're waiting for them to start paying us back.

Our dream of joining the West is built on believing in miracles. We want their comfortable lives and social safety nets. Their standard of living and well-functioning cities. But no one knows for sure whether we're willing to pay—in the form of taxes and personal responsibility. Whether we're ready to become law-abiding citizens and show solidarity.

All of our forward motion is like rolling a square wheel. With massive effort we rotate it forward from one side to the next. We could grind down the corners, but we're convinced that they're our national treasures. As a result, we stand idle while others pick up speed.

Our luck is enviable. We're like a Charlie Chaplin hero. We step over open manholes without noticing and bend to tie our shoes as a beam passes over. History doesn't generally forgive such carelessness. So far, we've gotten lucky.

It almost seems as though our brazenness is amusing to fate. Our fickleness, naivety and willingness to bet on zero. We act as though we could recover from any mistakes, so we undertake the most extreme experiments. Only the favor of providence could explain our luck.

I'd really like to live in a boring country. Of course, that's not likely to happen in my lifetime. The only thing that depends on our generation comes down to a very simple binary. Will all of the above become the cause of our failure? Or the prerequisites of our victory?

Neither the first option, nor the second, are beyond the realm of possibility.

Epilogue

I was born in 1983 and our nation was born in 1991. Ukraine gained its independence the year I started school.

Some stages can't be skipped and many processes can't be rushed. There are costs associated with growing up. Most Ukrainians are older than their country. What we see around us is our own doing. "Don't even both trying to raise your country right: it will just turn out like you anyway."

It's very tempting to look at how other people live. Of course, they always show us their best side, hiding the family scandals and mutual resentments. Looks can be deceiving: from the outside it can seem as though other families don't have any disagreements or problems. It's never the case.

It's tempting to add a thousand years to Ukraine's age, but that's only partially true. Our past is too fragmented. Our family tree is splintered. Unlike most of our neighbors, we don't have our own "golden age" to escape to. That's especially clear today, when politicians all over have taken to peddling nostalgia.

Our attempts at statehood a hundred years ago were too short-lived to have an impact. Their dramatic finale only tells us what not to do. Earlier periods of independence are too far back in time to offer us a roadmap for the present, much less for us to dream of returning to them.

Many of our neighbors began maturing earlier than us. I'm talking about the ones who managed to break free of the empire a hundred years ago and held onto their independence for at least a generation. Even though the empire swallowed them up again, the experience of independence served as an inoculation. They had learned what it meant to live without the empire and they held onto that knowledge throughout the decades of occupation. In 1991, it came in handy again.

But we had to start from scratch. We argued about what should have been obvious. We had to negotiate the starting point. We hadn't even begun the important conversations in advance and so we had to work through everything day-by-day. You might say we wasted a lot of time. But, it was probably inevitable. Sometimes you just have to suffer through the common childhood illnesses.

It does seem that we successfully acquired immunity. Otherwise, we would never have made it through 2014. The empire may not believe in Ukraine, but Ukrainians believe in Ukraine. Our flag came to mean something, our words gained meaning, our symbols gained power. Value is gained through sacrifice and our nation survived the stress test.

In other countries, you read about history in textbooks. For us, history is being created here and now. It is our fate to be living through Ukraine's moment of greatest agency—there has never been a more crucial moment in our country's history. All of our previous attempts ended in failure, but now we are living in the deciding moment. Our generation will determine what future encyclopedias will say about Ukraine.

When it's all over and done, the outcome will seem inevitable. If we win, they'll explain our victory according to the logic of history, the evolution of processes and states of mind. If we lose, they'll blame our failure on those same factors. Either way, they'll smooth out the corners, straighten the zigzags and level out the roads. In one of those scenarios, they're describing our "happy ending." In the other, they're not.

We can rage about the last three decades all we want. We can talk about stagnation and how we were just marking time. In reality, these last three decades were our "save point" in terms of history. Even if the worst happens now, future generations will see it as our "assembly point." Just like the Baltic States never forgot their own period of independence between the two World Wars.

It fell to us to live in the middle of history. Someday the faces of our contemporaries will adorn the currency and streets will bear their names. Names that are familiar to us now will be engraved on monuments and plaques. We'll tell our grandchildren about the things that are happening now, because they'll be learning about it in school. And it falls to us to determine where those textbooks will be published.

We're creating our own future. Twenty-four hours a day, seven days a week. We are all the authors of the text; no one gets to declare themselves "uninvolved."

Fate made me older than my country. I will do all I can to ensure that my grandchildren are younger than it.

Postscript

I have a dream. I want this book to become outdated.

All of our disputes are growing pains. The moment Ukraine actually becomes Ukraine, they will lose their relevance. At that moment, we will find a new equilibrium and explain ourselves to ourselves.

When that happens, my generation of writers will become irrelevant. All the disputes over which we break our rhetorical spears will fade into oblivion. After all, who cares about texts that argue for the Baltic states' rights to freedom when they've already acquired it?

We will become obsolete. Just like the German writers who fought for the fall of the Berlin wall. Their works are now the domain of archivists, Cold War historians, and PhD students writing dissertations about the fight for German reunification.

In an ideal Ukrainian future, the same fate will befall this book. In that version of the future, there will be no room for disputes about sovereignty or independence. The theme of imperial revanche will provoke bewilderment rather than anger because it will have lost all relevance.

Today our public debates center around where "they" end and where "we" begin. Where to draw the line between Europe and the Russian World. About why Ukraine is not Russia. As long as we're still arguing, that means the question hasn't been resolved. If my texts are still relevant twenty years from now, that will mean that we are still at war.

And so, this book needs to sink into oblivion. Lose its topicality. Fall out of tune with the times. All the words I've written here should become truisms that are obvious and broadly accepted.

Sometimes obsolescence equals victory.

UKRAINIAN VOICES

Collected by Andreas Umland

1. *Mychailo Wynnyckyj*
   Ukraine's Maidan, Russia's War
   A Chronicle and Analysis of the Revolution of Dignity
   With a foreword by Serhii Plokhy
   ISBN 978-3-8382-1327-9

2. *Olexander Hryb*
   Understanding Contemporary Ukrainian and Russian Nationalism
   The Post-Soviet Cossack Revival and Ukraine's National Security
   With a foreword by Vitali Vitaliev
   ISBN 978-3-8382-1377-4

3. *Marko Bojcun*
   Towards a Political Economy of Ukraine
   Selected Essays 1990–2015
   With a foreword by John-Paul Himka
   ISBN 978-3-8382-1368-2

4. *Volodymyr Yermolenko (ed.)*
   Ukraine in Histories and Stories
   Essays by Ukrainian Intellectuals
   With a preface by Peter Pomerantsev
   ISBN 978-3-8382-1456-6

5. *Mykola Riabchuk*
   At the Fence of Metternich's Garden
   Essays on Europe, Ukraine, and Europeanization
   ISBN 978-3-8382-1484-9

6. *Marta Dyczok*
   Ukraine Calling
   A Kaleidoscope from Hromadske Radio 2016–2019
   With a foreword by Andriy Kulykov
   ISBN 978-3-8382-1472-6

7. *Olexander Scherba*
   Ukraine vs. Darkness
   Undiplomatic Thoughts
   With a foreword by Adrian Karatnycky
   ISBN 978-3-8382-1501-3

8. *Olesya Yaremchuk*
   Our Others
   Stories of Ukrainian Diversity
   With a foreword by Ostap Slyvynsky
   Translated from the Ukrainian by Zenia Tompkins and Hanna Leliv
   ISBN 978-3-8382-1475-7

9. *Nataliya Gumenyuk*
   Die verlorene Insel
   Geschichten von der besetzten Krim
   Mit einem Vorwort von Alice Bota
   Aus dem Ukrainischen übersetzt von Johann Zajaczkowski
   ISBN 978-3-8382-1499-3

10. *Olena Stiazhkina*
    Zero Point Ukraine
    Four Essays on World War II
    Translated from the Ukrainian by Svitlana Kulinska
    ISBN 978-3-8382-1550-1

11 Oleksii Sinchenko, Dmytro Stus, Leonid Finberg (compilers)
    Ukrainian Dissidents
    An Anthology of Texts
    ISBN 978-3-8382-1551-8

12 John-Paul Himka
    Ukrainian Nationalists and the Holocaust
    OUN and UPA's Participation in the Destruction of Ukrainian Jewry, 1941–1944
    ISBN 978-3-8382-1548-8

13 Andrey Demartino
    False Mirrors
    The Weaponization of Social Media in Russia's Operation to Annex Crimea
    With a foreword by Oleksiy Danilov
    ISBN 978-3-8382-1533-4

14 Svitlana Biedarieva (ed.)
    Contemporary Ukrainian and Baltic Art
    Political and Social Perspectives, 1991–2021
    ISBN 978-3-8382-1526-6

15 Olesya Khromeychuk
    A Loss
    The Story of a Dead Soldier Told by His Sister
    With a foreword by Andrey Kurkov
    ISBN 978-3-8382-1570-9

16 Marieluise Beck (Hg.)
    Ukraine verstehen
    Auf den Spuren von Terror und Gewalt
    Mit einem Vorwort von Dmytro Kuleba
    ISBN 978-3-8382-1653-9

17 Stanislav Aseyev
    Heller Weg
    Geschichte eines Konzentrationslagers im Donbass 2017–2019
    Aus dem Russischen übersetzt von Martina Steis und Charis Haska
    ISBN 978-3-8382-1620-1

18 Mykola Davydiuk
    Wie funktioniert Putins Propaganda?
    Anmerkungen zum Informationskrieg des Kremls
    Aus dem Ukrainischen übersetzt von Christian Weise
    ISBN 978-3-8382-1628-7

19 Olesya Yaremchuk
    Unsere Anderen
    Geschichten ukrainischer Vielfalt
    Aus dem Ukrainischen übersetzt von Christian Weise
    ISBN 978-3-8382-1635-5

20 Oleksandr Mykhed
    „Dein Blut wird die Kohle tränken"
    Über die Ostukraine
    Aus dem Ukrainischen übersetzt von Simon Muschick und Dario Planert
    ISBN 978-3-8382-1648-5

21 Vakhtang Kipiani (Hg.)
    Der Zweite Weltkrieg in der Ukraine
    Geschichte und Lebensgeschichten
    Aus dem Ukrainischen übersetzt von Margarita Grinko
    ISBN 978-3-8382-1622-5

22 Vakhtang Kipiani (ed.)
    World War II, Uncontrived and Unredacted
    Testimonies from Ukraine
    Translated from the Ukrainian by Zenia Tompkins and Daisy Gibbons
    ISBN 978-3-8382-1621-8

23 *Dmytro Stus*
Vasyl Stus
Life in Creativity
Translated from the Ukrainian by
Ludmila Bachurina
ISBN 978-3-8382-1631-7

24 *Vitalii Ogiienko (ed.)*
The Holodomor and the
Origins of the Soviet Man
Reading the Testimony of
Anastasia Lysyvets
With forewords by Natalka
Bilotserkivets and Serhy
Yekelchyk
Translated from the Ukrainian by
Alla Parkhomenko and
Alexander J. Motyl
ISBN 978-3-8382-1616-4

25 *Vladislav Davidzon*
Jewish-Ukrainian Relations
and the Birth of a Political
Nation
Selected Writings 2013-2021
With a foreword by Bernard-
Henri Lévy
ISBN 978-3-8382-1509-9

26 *Serhy Yekelchyk*
Writing the Nation
The Ukrainian Historical
Profession in Independent
Ukraine and the Diaspora
ISBN 978-3-8382-1695-9

27 *Ildi Eperjesi, Oleksandr Kachura*
Shreds of War
Fates from the Donbas Frontline
2014-2019
With a foreword by Olexiy
Haran
ISBN 978-3-8382-1680-5

28 *Oleksandr Melnyk*
World War II as an Identity
Project
Historicism, Legitimacy
Contests, and the (Re-)Con-
struction of Political Commu-
nities in Ukraine, 1939–1946
With a foreword by David R.
Marples
ISBN 978-3-8382-1704-8

29 *Olesya Khromeychuk*
Ein Verlust
Die Geschichte eines gefallenen
ukrainischen Soldaten, erzählt
von seiner Schwester
Mit einem Vorwort von Andrej
Kurkow
Aus dem Englischen übersetzt
von Lily Sophie
ISBN 978-3-8382-1770-3

30 *Tamara Martsenyuk, Tetiana Kostiuchenko (eds.)*
Russia's War in Ukraine
During 2022
Personal Experiences of
Ukrainian Scholars
ISBN 978-3-8382-1757-4

31 *Ildikó Eperjesi, Oleksandr Kachura*
Shreds of War. Vol. 2
Fates from Crimea 2015–2022
With an interview of Oleh
Sentsov
ISBN 978-3-8382-1780-2

32 *Yuriy Lukanov*
The Press
How Russia Destroyed Media
Freedom in Crimea
With a foreword by Taras Kuzio
ISBN 978-3-8382-1784-0

33 *Megan Buskey*
Ukraine Is Not Dead Yet
A Family Story of Exile and
Return
ISBN 978-3-8382-1691-1

34 *Vira Ageyeva*
   Behind the Scenes of the
   Empire
   Essays on Cultural
   Relationships between Ukraine
   and Russia
   With a foreword by Oksana
   Zabuzhko
   ISBN 978-3-8382-1748-2

35 *Marieluise Beck (ed.)*
   Understanding Ukraine
   Tracing the Roots of Terror and
   Violence
   With a foreword by Dmytro
   Kuleba
   ISBN 978-3-8382-1773-4

36 *Olesya Khromeychuk*
   A Loss
   The Story of a Dead Soldier Told
   by His Sister, 2nd edn.
   With a foreword by Philippe
   Sands
   With a preface by Andrii Kurkov
   ISBN 978-3-8382-1870-0

37 *Taras Kuzio, Stefan
   Jajecznyk-Kelman*
   Fascism and Genocide
   Russia's War Against
   Ukrainians
   ISBN 978-3-8382-1791-8

38 *Alina Nychyk*
   Ukraine Vis-à-Vis Russia
   and the EU
   Misperceptions of Foreign
   Challenges in Times of War,
   2014–2015
   With a foreword by Paul
   D'Anieri
   ISBN 978-3-8382-1767-3

39 *Sasha Dovzhyk (ed.)*
   Ukraine Lab
   Global Security, Environment,
   and Disinformation Through the
   Prism of Ukraine
   With a foreword by Rory Finnin
   ISBN 978-3-8382-1805-2

40 *Serhiy Kvit*
   Media, History, and
   Education
   Three Ways to Ukrainian
   Independence
   With a preface by Diane Francis
   ISBN 978-3-8382-1807-6

41 *Anna Romandash*
   Women of Ukraine
   Reportages from the War and
   Beyond
   ISBN 978-3-8382-1819-9

42 *Dominika Rank*
   Matzewe in meinem Garten
   Abenteuer eines jüdischen
   Heritage-Touristen in der
   Ukraine
   ISBN 978-3-8382-1810-6

43 *Myroslaw Marynowytsch*
   Das Universum hinter dem
   Stacheldraht
   Memoiren eines sowjet-
   ukrainischen Dissidenten
   Mit einem Vorwort von Timothy
   Snyder und einem Nachwort
   von Max Hartmann
   ISBN 978-3-8382-1806-9

44 *Konstantin Sigow*
   Für Deine und meine
   Freiheit
   Europäische Revolutions- und
   Kriegserfahrungen im heutigen
   Kyjiw
   Mit einem Vorwort von Karl
   Schlögel
   Herausgegeben von Regula M.
   Zwahlen
   ISBN 978-3-8382-1755-0

45 *Kateryna Pylypchuk*
   The War that Changed Us
   Ukrainian Novellas, Poems, and
   Essays from 2022
   With a foreword by Victor
   Yushchenko
   Paperback
   ISBN 978-3-8382-1859-5
   Hardcover
   ISBN 978-3-8382-1860-1

46 *Kyrylo Tkachenko*
Rechte Tür Links
Radikale Linke in Deutschland,
die Revolution und der Krieg in
der Ukraine, 2013-2018
ISBN 978-3-8382-1711-6

47 *Alexander Strashny*
The Ukrainian Mentality
An Ethno-Psychological,
Historical and Comparative
Exploration
With a foreword by Antonina
Lovochkina
Translated from the Ukrainian
by Michael M. Naydan and
Olha Tytarenko
ISBN 978-3-8382-1886-1

48 *Alona Shestopalova*
From Screens to Battlefields
Tracing the Construction of
Enemies on Russian Television
With a foreword by Nina
Jankowicz
ISBN 978-3-8382-1884-7

49 *Iaroslav Petik*
Politics and Society in the
Ukrainian People's Republic
(1917–1921) and
Contemporary Ukraine
(2013–2022)
A Comparative Analysis
With a foreword by Mykola
Doroshko
ISBN 978-3-8382-1817-5

50 *Serhii Plokhy*
Der Mann mit der
Giftpistole
Eine Spionagegeschichte aus dem
Kalten Krieg
ISBN 978-3-8382-1789-5

51 *Vakhtang Kipiani*
Ukrainische Dissidenten
unter der Sowjetmacht
Im Kampf um Wahrheit und
Freiheit
Aus dem Ukrainischen übersetzt
von Christian Weise
ISBN 978-3-8382-1890-8

52 *Dmytro Shestakov*
When Businesses Test
Hypotheses
A Four-Step Approach to Risk
Management for Innovative
Startups
With a foreword by Anthony J.
Tether
ISBN 978-3-8382-1883-0

53 *Larissa Babij*
A Kind of Refugee
The Story of an American Who
Refused to Leave Ukraine
With a foreword by Vladislav
Davidzon
ISBN 978-3-8382-1898-4

54 *Julia Davis*
In Their Own Words
How Russian Propagandists
Reveal Putin's Intentions
With a foreword by Timothy
Snyder
ISBN 978-3-8382-1909-7

55 *Sonya Atlantova, Oleksandr Klymenko*
Icons on Ammo Boxes
Painting Life on the Remnants of
Russia's War in Donbas, 2014-21
Translated from the Ukrainian by
Anastasya Knyazhytska
ISBN 978-3-8382-1892-2

56 *Leonid Ushkalov*
Catching an Elusive Bird
The Life of Hryhorii Skovoroda
Translated from the Ukrainian
by Natalia Komarova
ISBN 978-3-8382-1894-6

57 *Vakhtang Kipiani*
Ein Land weiblichen
Geschlechts
Ukrainische Frauenschicksale
im 20. und 21. Jahrhundert
Aus dem Ukrainischen übersetzt
von Christian Weise
ISBN 978-3-8382-1891-5

58 Petro Rychlo
„Zerrissne Saiten einer
überlauten Harfe …"
Deutschjüdische Dichter der
Bukowina
ISBN 978-3-8382-1893-9

59 Volodymyr Paniotto
Sociology in Jokes
An Entertaining Introduction
ISBN 978-3-8382-1857-1

60 Josef Wallmannsberger
(ed.)
Executing Renaissances
The Poetological Nation of
Ukraine
ISBN 978-3-8382-1741-3

61 Pavlo Kazarin
The Wild West of Eastern
Europe
A Ukrainian Guide on Breaking
Free from Empire
Translated from the Ukrainian
by Dominique Hoffman
ISBN 978-3-8382-1842-7

62 Ernest Gyidel
Ukrainian Public
Nationalism in the General
Government
The Case of Krakivski Visti,
1940–1944
With a foreword by David R.
Marples
ISBN 978-3-8382-1865-6

63 Olexander Hryb
Understanding
Contemporary Russian
Militarism
From Revolutionary to New
Generation Warfare
With a foreword by Mark Laity
ISBN 978-3-8382-1927-1

64 Orysia Hrudka, Bohdan Ben
Dark Days, Determined
People
Stories from Ukraine under Siege
With a foreword by Myroslav
Marynovych
ISBN 978-3-8382-1958-5

65 Oleksandr Pankieiev (ed.)
Narratives of the Russo-
Ukrainian War
A Look Within and Without
With a foreword by Natalia
Khanenko-Friesen
ISBN 978-3-8382-1964-6

66 Roman Sohn, Ariana Gic
(eds.)
Unrecognized War
The Fight for Truth about
Russia's War on Ukraine
With a foreword by Viktor
Yushchenko
ISBN 978-3-8382-1947-9

67 Paul Robert Magocsi
Ukraina Redux
Schon wieder die Ukraine …
ISBN 978-3-8382-1942-4

68 Paul Robert Magocsi
L'Ucraina Ritrovata
Sullo Stato e l'Identità Nazionale
ISBN 978-3-8382-1982-0

69 Max Hartmann
Ein Schrei der Verzweiflung
Aquarelle zum Krieg von Danylo
Movchan
Paperback
ISBN 978-3-8382-2011-6
Hardcover
ISBN 978-3-8382-2012-3

70 Vakhtang Kebuladze (Hg.)
Die Zukunft, die wir uns
wünschen
Essays aus der Ukraine
ISBN 978-3-8382-1531-0

71 Marieluise Beck, Jan Claas
   Behrends, Gelinada
   Grinchenko und Oksana
   Mikheieva (Hg.)
   **Deutsch-ukrainische
   Geschichten**
   Bruchstücke aus einer
   gemeinsamen Vergangenheit
   ISBN 978-3-8382-2053-6

72 Pavlo Kazarin
   **Der Wilde Westen Ost-
   Europas**
   Aus dem Ukrainischen übersetzt
   von Christian Weise
   ISBN 978-3-8382-1843-4

73 Radomyr Mokryk
   Ukrainian Sixtiers
   Against the Empire
   ISBN 978-3-8382-1873-1

74 Leonid Finberg
   **My Ukraine—Rethinking the
   Past, Building the Present**
   ISBN 978-3-8382-1974-5

75 Joseph Zissels
   **Consider My Inmost
   Thoughts**
   Texts and Interviews on
   Ukrainian Matters at the Turn
   of the Century
   ISBN 978-3-8382-1975-2

76 Margarita Yehorchenko,
   Iryna Berlyand, Ihor
   Vinokurov (Eds.)
   Jewish Addresses in Ukraine
   A Guide-Book
   With a foreword by Leonid
   Finberg
   ISB 978-3-8382-1976-9

77 Viktoriia Grivina
   Kharkiv—A War City
   A Collection of Essays from
   2022–23
   ISBN 978-3-8382-1988-2

78 Hjørdis Clemmensen,
   Viktoriia Grivina, Vasylysa
   Shchogoleva
   Kharkiv Is a Dream
   Public Art and Activism 2013–
   2023
   With a foreword by Bohdan
   Volynskyi
   ISBN 978-3-8382-2005-5

79 Olga Khomenko
   The Faraway Sky of Kyiv
   Ukrainians in the War
   With a foreword by Hiroaki
   Kuromiya
   ISBN 978-3-8382-2006-2

80 Daria Mattingly, Jonathon
   Vsetecka (eds.)
   **The Holodomor in Global
   Perspective**
   How the Famine in Ukraine
   Shaped the World
   ISBN 978-3-8382-1953-0

81 Olga Khomenko
   Ukrainians beyond Borders
   Nine Life Journeys Through the
   History of Eastern Europe
   With a foreword by Zbigniew
   Wojnowski
   ISBN 978-3-8382-2007-9

82 Mykhailo Minakov
   From Servant to Leader
   Chronicles of Ukraine under the
   Zelensky presidency, 2019–
   2024
   ISBN 978-3-8382-2002-4

83 Wolodymyr Hromov (ed.)
   A Ruined Home
   Sketches of War, 2022–2023
   ISBN 978-3-8382-2008-6

84 Olha Tatokhina (ed.)
   Why do they kill our people?
   Russia's war against Ukraine as
   told by Ukrainians
   ISBN 978-3-8382-2056-7

Book series "Ukrainian Voices"

Coordinator
Andreas Umland, National University of Kyiv-Mohyla Academy

Editorial Board
Lesia Bidochko, National University of Kyiv-Mohyla Academy
Svitlana Biedarieva, George Washington University, DC, USA
Ivan Gomza, Kyiv School of Economics, Ukraine
Natalie Jaresko, Aspen Institute, Kyiv/Washington
Olena Lennon, University of New Haven, West Haven, USA
Kateryna Yushchenko, First Lady of Ukraine 2005-2010, Kyiv
Oleksandr Zabirko, University of Regensburg, Germany

Advisory Board
Iuliia Bentia, National Academy of Arts of Ukraine, Kyiv
Natalya Belitser, Pylyp Orlyk Institute for Democracy, Kyiv
Oleksandra Bienert, Humboldt University of Berlin, Germany
Sergiy Bilenky, Canadian Institute of Ukrainian Studies, Toronto
Tymofii Brik, Kyiv School of Economics, Ukraine
Olga Brusylovska, Mechnikov National University, Odesa
Mariana Budjeryn, Harvard University, Cambridge, USA
Volodymyr Bugrov, Shevchenko National University, Kyiv
Olga Burlyuk, University of Amsterdam, The Netherlands
Yevhen Bystrytsky, NAS Institute of Philosophy, Kyiv
Andrii Danylenko, Pace University, New York, USA
Vladislav Davidzon, Atlantic Council, Washington/Paris
Mykola Davydiuk, Think Tank "Polityka," Kyiv
Andrii Demartino, National Security and Defense Council, Kyiv
Vadym Denisenko, Ukrainian Institute for the Future, Kyiv
Oleksandr Donii, Center for Political Values Studies, Kyiv
Volodymyr Dubovyk, Mechnikov National University, Odesa
Volodymyr Dubrovskiy, CASE Ukraine, Kyiv
Diana Dutsyk, National University of Kyiv-Mohyla Academy
Marta Dyczok, Western University, Ontario, Canada
Yevhen Fedchenko, National University of Kyiv-Mohyla Academy
Sofiya Filonenko, State Pedagogical University of Berdyansk
Oleksandr Fisun, Karazin National University, Kharkiv
Oksana Forostyna, Webjournal "Ukraina Moderna," Kyiv
Roman Goncharenko, Broadcaster "Deutsche Welle," Bonn
George Grabowicz, Harvard University, Cambridge, USA
Gelinada Grinchenko, Karazin National University, Kharkiv
Kateryna Härtel, Federal Union of European Nationalities, Brussels
Nataliia Hendel, University of Geneva, Switzerland
Anton Herashchenko, Kyiv School of Public Administration
John-Paul Himka, University of Alberta, Edmonton
Ola Hnatiuk, National University of Kyiv-Mohyla Academy
Oleksandr Holubov, Broadcaster "Deutsche Welle," Bonn
Yaroslav Hrytsak, Ukrainian Catholic University, Lviv
Oleksandra Humenna, National University of Kyiv-Mohyla Academy
Tamara Hundorova, NAS Institute of Literature, Kyiv
Oksana Huss, University of Bologna, Italy
Oleksandr Iwaniuk, University of Warsaw, Poland
Mykola Kapitonenko, Shevchenko National University, Kyiv
Georgiy Kasianov, Marie Curie-Skłodowska University, Lublin
Vakhtang Kebuladze, Shevchenko National University, Kyiv
Natalia Khanenko-Friesen, University of Alberta, Edmonton
Victoria Khiterer, Millersville University of Pennsylvania, USA
Oksana Kis, NAS Institute of Ethnology, Lviv
Pavlo Klimkin, Center for National Resilience and Development, Kyiv
Oleksandra Kolomiiets, Center for Economic Strategy, Kyiv

Sergiy Korsunsky, Kobe Gakuin University, Japan
Nadiia Koval, Kyiv School of Economics, Ukraine
Volodymyr Kravchenko, University of Alberta, Edmonton
Oleksiy Kresin, NAS Koretskiy Institute of State and Law, Kyiv
Anatoliy Kruglashov, Fedkovych National University, Chernivtsi
Andrey Kurkov, PEN Ukraine, Kyiv
Ostap Kushnir, Lazarski University, Warsaw
Taras Kuzio, National University of Kyiv-Mohyla Academy
Serhii Kvit, National University of Kyiv-Mohyla Academy
Yuliya Ladygina, The Pennsylvania State University, USA
Yevhen Mahda, Institute of World Policy, Kyiv
Victoria Malko, California State University, Fresno, USA
Yulia Marushevska, Security and Defense Center (SAND), Kyiv
Myroslav Marynovych, Ukrainian Catholic University, Lviv
Oleksandra Matviichuk, Center for Civil Liberties, Kyiv
Mykhailo Minakov, Kennan Institute, Washington, USA
Anton Moiseienko, The Australian National University, Canberra
Alexander Motyl, Rutgers University-Newark, USA
Vlad Mykhnenko, University of Oxford, United Kingdom
Vitalii Ogiienko, Ukrainian Institute of National Remembrance, Kyiv
Olga Onuch, University of Manchester, United Kingdom
Olesya Ostrovska, Museum "Mystetskyi Arsenal," Kyiv
Anna Osypchuk, National University of Kyiv-Mohyla Academy
Oleksandr Pankieiev, University of Alberta, Edmonton
Oleksiy Panych, Publishing House "Dukh i Litera," Kyiv
Valerii Pekar, Kyiv-Mohyla Business School, Ukraine
Yohanan Petrovsky-Shtern, Northwestern University, Chicago
Serhii Plokhy, Harvard University, Cambridge, USA
Andrii Portnov, Viadrina University, Frankfurt-Oder, Germany
Maryna Rabinovych, Kyiv School of Economics, Ukraine
Valentyna Romanova, Institute of Developing Economies, Tokyo
Natalya Ryabinska, Collegium Civitas, Warsaw, Poland

Darya Tsymbalyk, University of Oxford, United Kingdom
Vsevolod Samokhvalov, University of Liege, Belgium
Orest Semotiuk, Franko National University, Lviv
Viktoriya Sereda, NAS Institute of Ethnology, Lviv
Anton Shekhovtsov, University of Vienna, Austria
Andriy Shevchenko, Media Center Ukraine, Kyiv
Oxana Shevel, Tufts University, Medford, USA
Pavlo Shopin, National Pedagogical Dragomanov University, Kyiv
Karina Shyrokykh, Stockholm University, Sweden
Nadja Simon, freelance interpreter, Cologne, Germany
Olena Snigova, NAS Institute for Economics and Forecasting, Kyiv
Ilona Solohub, Analytical Platform "VoxUkraine," Kyiv
Iryna Solonenko, LibMod - Center for Liberal Modernity, Berlin
Galyna Solovei, National University of Kyiv-Mohyla Academy
Sergiy Stelmakh, NAS Institute of World History, Kyiv
Olena Stiazhkina, NAS Institute of the History of Ukraine, Kyiv
Dmitri Stratievski, Osteuropa Zentrum (OEZB), Berlin
Dmytro Stus, National Taras Shevchenko Museum, Kyiv
Frank Sysyn, University of Toronto, Canada
Olha Tokariuk, Center for European Policy Analysis, Washington
Olena Tregub, Independent Anti-Corruption Commission, Kyiv
Hlib Vyshlinsky, Centre for Economic Strategy, Kyiv
Mychailo Wynnyckyj, National University of Kyiv-Mohyla Academy
Yelyzaveta Yasko, NGO "Yellow Blue Strategy," Kyiv
Serhy Yekelchyk, University of Victoria, Canada
Victor Yushchenko, President of Ukraine 2005-2010, Kyiv
Oleksandr Zaitsev, Ukrainian Catholic University, Lviv
Kateryna Zarembo, National University of Kyiv-Mohyla Academy
Yaroslav Zhalilo, National Institute for Strategic Studies, Kyiv
Sergei Zhuk, Ball State University at Muncie, USA
Alina Zubkovych, Nordic Ukraine Forum, Stockholm
Liudmyla Zubrytska, National University of Kyiv-Mohyla Academy

Friends of the Series

Ana Maria Abulescu, University of Bucharest, Romania
Łukasz Adamski, Centrum Mieroszewskiego, Warsaw
Marieluise Beck, LibMod—Center for Liberal Modernity, Berlin
Marc Berensen, King's College London, United Kingdom
Johannes Bohnen, BOHNEN Public Affairs, Berlin
Karsten Brüggemann, University of Tallinn, Estonia
Ulf Brunnbauer, Leibniz Institute (IOS), Regensburg
Martin Dietze, German-Ukrainian Culture Society, Hamburg
Gergana Dimova, Florida State University, Tallahassee/London
Caroline von Gall, Goethe University, Frankfurt-Main
Zaur Gasimov, Rhenish Friedrich Wilhelm University, Bonn
Armand Gosu, University of Bucharest, Romania
Thomas Grant, University of Cambridge, United Kingdom
Gustav Gressel, European Council on Foreign Relations, Berlin
Rebecca Harms, European Centre for Press & Media Freedom, Leipzig
André Härtel, Stiftung Wissenschaft und Politik, Berlin/Brussels
Marcel Van Herpen, The Cicero Foundation, Maastricht
Richard Herzinger, freelance analyst, Berlin
Mieste Hotopp-Riecke, ICATAT, Magdeburg
Nico Lange, Munich Security Conference, Berlin
Martin Malek, freelance analyst, Vienna
Ingo Mannteufel, Broadcaster "Deutsche Welle," Bonn
Carlo Masala, Bundeswehr University, Munich
Wolfgang Mueller, University of Vienna, Austria
Dietmar Neutatz, Albert Ludwigs University, Freiburg
Torsten Oppelland, Friedrich Schiller University, Jena
Niccolò Pianciola, University of Padua, Italy
Gerald Praschl, German-Ukrainian Forum (DUF), Berlin
Felix Riefer, Think Tank Ideenagentur-Ost, Düsseldorf
Stefan Rohdewald, University of Leipzig, Germany
Sebastian Schäffer, Institute for the Danube Region (IDM), Vienna
Felix Schimansky-Geier, Friedrich Schiller University, Jena
Ulrich Schneckener, University of Osnabrück, Germany
Winfried Schneider-Deters, freelance analyst, Heidelberg/Kyiv
Gerhard Simon, University of Cologne, Germany
Kai Struve, Martin Luther University, Halle/Wittenberg
David Stulik, European Values Center for Security Policy, Prague
Andrzej Szeptycki, University of Warsaw, Poland
Philipp Ther, University of Vienna, Austria
Stefan Troebst, University of Leipzig, Germany

[Please send requests for changes in, corrections of, and additions to, this list to andreas.umland@stanforalumni.org.]

ibidem.eu